After Work

After Work

*A History of the Home and
the Fight for Free Time*

Helen Hester and
Nick Srnicek

VERSO

London • New York

First published by Verso 2023
© Helen Hester and Nick Srnicek 2023

1 3 5 7 9 10 8 6 4 2

Verso
UK: 6 Meard Street, London W1F 0EG
US: 388 Atlantic Avenue, Brooklyn, NY 11217
versobooks.com

Verso is the imprint of New Left Books

ISBN-13: 978-1-78663-307-1
ISBN-13: 978-1-78663-309-5 (US EBK)
ISBN-13: 978-1-78663-310-1 (UK EBK)

British Library Cataloguing in Publication Data
A catalogue record for this book is available from the British Library

Library of Congress Cataloging-in-Publication Data
A catalog record for this book is available from the Library of Congress

Typeset in Fournier by MJ & N Gavan, Truro, Cornwall
Printed in the UK by CPI Group (UK) Ltd, Croydon CR0 4YY

Contents

1

Introduction

The End of the End of History

After the fall of the Soviet Union, up until the global financial crisis of 2008, capitalism appeared to have 'won'. The end of history had been reached and some inflection of liberal democratic capitalism was now deemed the insurmountable apex of social organisation. Even the anticapitalist left largely contented itself with pointing out capitalism's flaws, leaving postcapitalist speculation to the side.[1] The crash of 2008 upset this settled consensus. Suddenly, capitalist realism didn't seem so unimpeachable.[2] In its wake there has been growing austerity, misery, inequality, and suffering – but also new spaces of hope, optimism, and determination. There has been a flourishing of imagination and reflection upon what a postcapitalist future might look like. Ecosocialist projects – aimed at sustainability, the end of the GDP fetish, and a rethinking of luxury – have all developed considerably in recent years.[3] Ideas of digital socialism and platform co-operatives have proliferated as alternatives to our world of platform capitalism.[4] There has been a resurgence of debates over the possibilities and limits of economic planning.[5] And there has been a return to first communist principles, with work reflecting on the failures of the twentieth century and the potentials of communism in practice.[6]

One of the most prominent strands of this general future-oriented turn has been the rise of projects based around the end of work – that is, projects which see work as something to be reduced to a minimum. There is little doubt that contemporary work, even in the relatively privileged regions of the Global North, is increasingly intense, unrewarding, and precarious.[7] While some believe the goal should therefore be to improve the conditions of work and create decent jobs,[8] for post-work thinkers this remains insufficient. The problems of work lie not only in its contemporary incarnation, but also in its general capitalist form. Work, understood as wage labour, is doubly unfree. We see this most obviously in the daily forms of subjection workers experience during their time on the job (and increasingly outside of it). Wage labour means that we sell a considerable portion of our time to people or organisations, who then have significant control over us.[9] In December 2021, for instance, six Amazon workers died when the warehouse they were working in collapsed during a tornado – after management had forced them to continue working until the last moments.[10] It's no surprise, then, that the labour republicans of the nineteenth century labelled the new capitalist forms of market dependence 'wage slavery' – deliberately invoking and expanding the notions of slavery that were prominent social features of the time.[11] Beyond the personal domination exhibited by managers and bosses, wage labour is also unfree by virtue of the impersonal domination of capitalism's imperatives.[12] For the vast majority of humanity this translates to the fact that subjecting ourselves to wage labour is necessary for survival.[13] We are coerced into work on pain of homelessness, starvation, and destitution. Post-work begins from these premises – that wage labour is doubly unfree, regardless of working conditions – and proposes alternative visions of the world that aim to abolish this social form.[14]

The recent saliency of this project is due in no small part to media-fuelled popular anxiety around the future of work. Many have forecast that an inevitable wave of automation, based around new technologies like machine learning, is set to swamp the labour market and dramatically reduce the number of jobs available for humans.[15] Whatever the veracity of these predictions, they have both grasped and generated a real anxiety about a lack of good jobs.[16] While more orthodox approaches have responded through efforts around reskilling and education, and through endeavours to create 'decent work', the more radical post-work approach has been to reject the centrality of work entirely. Post-work's advocates take this perceived crisis – of too few good jobs – and argue that it should form the basis of a new political and economic order where everyone sees their work reduced and dependency on the market lessened. Work, these thinkers suggest, should be framed as a problem rather than a solution, and we must seek to be emancipated from (rather than through) our labour. Contemporary post-work positions, then, represent a proactive response to the imagined end of job-based cultures; they eschew a celebration of work, emphasising instead the possibilities that are opened up when we no longer centre our lives and societies around wage labour.

But What Is Work?

The recent renaissance of post-work perspectives has, however, tended to miss the full spectrum of work. In particular, post-work thinking has almost entirely focused on wage labour – and primarily on industries and jobs that are dominated by men.

As a result, the work of *social reproduction* – the work which nurtures future workers, regenerates the current workforce, and maintains those who cannot work, while also reproducing and sustaining societies – has largely been neglected in speculations about the 'end of work'.[17] When post-work imagines the end of work, it typically envisions robots taking over factories, warehouses, and offices – but not hospitals, care homes, or nurseries.

Why has this work been overlooked? In some cases, reproductive labour has simply been ignored – deemed to be not really work at all. This is particularly the case when the activities involved are unpaid or take place within the family. Andre Gorz, for example, says the goal of post-work should not 'be that of liberating women from housework but of extending the non-economic rationality of these activities beyond the home'.[18] Such ideas often underpin the approach to waged work as well: feminised caring jobs such as teaching, nannying, and nursing are framed as a vocation, the rewards of which should be viewed as separate from or in excess of any financial benefit. Immense efforts have been made to naturalise this work as an expression of innate feminine qualities, such as being houseproud or maternal. This encourages the idea that reproductive work is somehow special and beyond the scope of post-work's ambitions. It is seen as autonomous affection, a labour of love, and even postcapitalist resistance.[19] The family, likewise, is popularly understood as a space of respite from the stresses and burdens of the outside world, and the intimacies that it contains are often deemed to be a model for a better world. (It is not a coincidence that businesses often want employees to feel like they're all part of 'one big family'.)

Other thinkers, however, recognise reproductive labour *as* work and yet argue that post-work ambitions are simply incompatible with this sphere of activity. In recent decades, attempts to refuse or reduce reproductive labour have been deemed hubristic, ill-conceived, and even unethical. For instance, the idea of reducing working time via automation seems relatively straightforward when it comes to imagining robots in factories, farms, warehouses, and offices. One would simply replace humans with machines, thereby freeing up time for human flourishing. Yet what happens when, as is the case with a lot of reproductive work, it isn't possible – or desirable – to automate this work? In fact, a defining feature of much of this labour is that it is resistant to productivity increases. Wouldn't a reduction of work-time simply mean a reduction in care – less time spent looking after others, leading to the perpetuation and deepening of neglect already felt by many recipients of care?[20] There are no simple answers to these sorts of questions, which has led many to believe that the only hope for reproductive work is to valorise and celebrate it – or at best, to share it more equitably across the population.[21] Earlier radical proposals *against* domestic work have been forgotten and we appear at an impasse: post-work has nothing to say about the organisation of reproductive labour.

Working Is Caring, Caring Is Working

And yet, time spent on reproductive labour is an immense and growing part of advanced capitalist countries. In the formal economy, social reproduction is a major source of jobs. The UK's National Health Service (NHS), for example, is among the largest employers in the world, and as of 2017 employed (directly and indirectly) around 1.9 million people.[22] In Sweden, three of the top five employing jobs are linked to care work and education.[23] Across the last five decades, there has been a

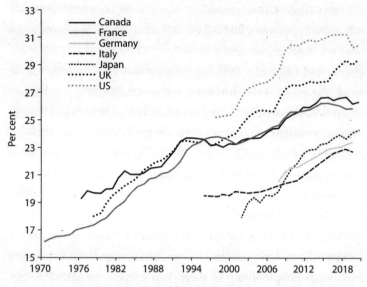

Figure 1.1: Social reproduction jobs as a percentage
of all wage labour, 1970–2021[26]

growing proportion of jobs devoted to the sectors of healthcare, education, food service, accommodation, and social work (see Figure 1.1). In the US, for example, care work has taken up an increasing proportion of low-wage job growth for decades now – accounting for 74 per cent by the 2000s.[24] In the G7 countries, social reproduction jobs employ around a quarter or more of the labour force. For comparison, at its peak in the 1960s, America employed 30 per cent in manufacturing. If we once spoke of the US as a manufacturing powerhouse, today we must speak of economies centred around the reproduction of their workforces.[25]

This will only continue, as the future of work is not coding but caring – more high-touch than high-tech. Nearly all the fastest growing jobs in America revolve around the tasks of cooking, cleaning, and caring (see Figure 1.2), with almost half of all new jobs coming from these areas. Similar trends hold for the United Kingdom, where again well over half of all net job growth between 2017 and 2027 is set to be in sectors like healthcare, cleaning, and education.[27] While many of the most visible and culturally influential narratives about the future of work assume that the dominant job sectors will be highly specialised, dependent on digital skills, and command high salaries, the reality is that most future jobs are likely neither to require a great deal of advanced formal education nor to pay very well. For instance, of the eleven occupations listed in Figure 1.2, only *one* tends to pay above the national median wage. Most of the new jobs being created are not for doctors or registered nurses making decent wages; instead they are for home health aides, food workers, and janitors. A domiciliary carer, who supports and assists people living in their own homes, for instance, can expect to earn roughly the same amount as a fast-food worker.[28] As things stand, this is likely to be the future of work.

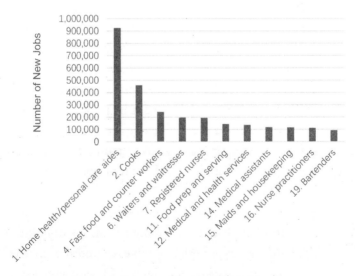

Figure 1.2: Selection of the top 20 fastest growing occupations, US 2021–2031[29]

And this only takes into account the paid aspect of social reproduction. There is, in addition, a vast amount of *unpaid* work done in the home that remains largely invisible to the statistical agencies of the state.[30] This opaqueness leads to some perverse consequences: as Nancy Folbre notes, 'If you marry your housekeeper, you lower GDP. If you put your mother in a nursing home, you increase GDP.'[31] It is only recently that we have begun to systematically collect information that can shine a light on the size of this unpaid sector.[32] It turns out that the amount of unwaged reproductive work being done in the home is immense. In the UK, 8.1 billion hours were spent doing unpaid long-term care work in 2014.[33] Americans spent 18 billion unpaid hours just taking care of family members with Alzheimer's.[34] And the International Labour Organization estimates that, for the sixty-four countries on which it has data, 16.4 billion hours are given over to unpaid work every single day.[35] Overall, most countries spend 45–55 per cent of their total

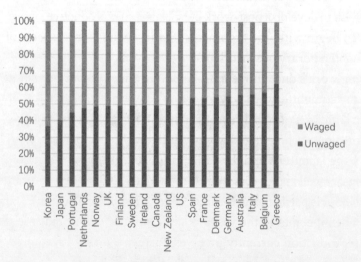

Figure 1.3: Proportion of labour hours devoted to waged and unwaged work[36]

labour time on unwaged reproductive work (see Figure 1.3). By any measure, social reproduction therefore occupies a large and rapidly growing share of our economies. To ignore this work is to ignore a significant proportion of the concrete labour that advanced capitalist societies are performing.

After Work

So are post-work ideas irrelevant for understanding how we should organise this work? The simple proposition of this book is that the supposed stalemate between reproductive labour and post-work ambitions isn't the end of the story; instead, the post-work project, suitably modified, has significant contributions to make to our understanding of how we might better organise the labour of reproduction. And conversely, the post-work project can only be fully realised when it takes into account this immense sphere of activity.

There are considerable efforts to be made, however, if we wish to develop a post-work perspective on reproductive labour. To begin with, the arguments that motivate many aspects of contemporary post-work perspectives – namely, those regarding work's dual unfreedom – hold for waged labour but not in any straightforward way for the unwaged labour that makes up a large part of social reproduction. To be sure, a growing proportion of contemporary reproductive labour *is* performed by wage labourers, and the earlier arguments for post-work hold just as well in those cases (perhaps with the added point that care labour is particularly ill-suited to capitalist rationalisation). But when it comes to the vast amount of unpaid labour that social reproduction currently involves, further thinking is required. Why should we want to reduce the time spent on unwaged social reproduction in the first place?

We might begin with the point made by socialist feminists, that this work remains *work*, much of which can be boring, monotonous, and isolating. To be sure, there can be pleasurable and fulfilling aspects of reproductive labour: playing with a child, cooking for friends, helping an elderly neighbour, and so on. Yet much of reproductive labour is also drudgery and can be particularly exhausting when there is little respite – a state of affairs that can lead to depletion (including worsening mental health) for over-taxed carers.[37] Much of this work is, as the saying goes, 'never done'. As the inventor of a self-cleaning home once put it, housework is 'a nerve-twangling bore. Who wants it? Nobody!'[38] Angela Davis likewise criticised proposals that focused solely on the gendered redistribution of this work, noting that 'the desexualisation of domestic labour would not really alter the oppressive nature of the work itself. In the final analysis, neither women nor men should waste precious hours of their lives on work that is neither stimulating, creative nor productive.'[39] All of this provides motivation to keep some parts of reproductive labour to a minimum.

The dominant argument for reducing unpaid work, however, is that it enables women to enter into *waged* work. This proposal has a long history and many proponents, ranging from revolutionaries like Friedrich Engels and Alexandra Kollontai to middle-class second-wave feminists like Betty Friedan, to arch-capitalists such as Sheryl Sandberg, and has been widely accepted and adopted by contemporary welfare states.[40] For many, it is an established fact that the emancipation of women comes through the labour market. While waged work has undoubtedly granted women a measure of financial independence and social recognition, the generalised expectation that everybody must earn a wage is hardly something to be celebrated. As we have seen, waged labour is itself a form of domination, oppression, and exploitation that should be abolished. Far from being an emancipatory project, efforts to reduce unpaid reproductive work in order to enable waged labour are simply trading one form of unfreedom for another. Moreover, these efforts nearly always entail passing this work on to a poorly paid workforce – a redistribution of labour, not a collective reduction.

Against this approach, we must insist that the reduction of unwaged work is necessary, not because it lets people take on more waged labour, nor simply because much of it is drudgery. Rather, this reduction is essential because it expands the availability of free time that is a prerequisite for any meaningful conception of freedom. *The struggle against work – in all its forms – is the fight for free time.* It is only on the basis of this free time that we can be allowed to determine what to do with our finite lives – to commit ourselves to life paths, projects, identities, and norms. This is not simply a matter of making 'more time for families',[41] nor is it a question of more time for waged labour, nor does it concern some mythical idea of work-life balance. The fight for free time is ultimately a matter of opening up the realm of freedom itself and maximising the extent of autonomously chosen activity.

The normative project of this book is therefore to develop an approach to social reproduction that values freedom for all – that *recognises* reproductive labour as work, that *reduces* this work as much as possible, and that *redistributes* any remaining work in an equitable manner. By aiming to reduce the amount of time necessary for some elements of social reproduction, we can respond to the depletion affecting providers of care and the neglect all too commonly experienced by receivers of care. Moreover, insofar as this is a universal project of reducing work, it requires that the obligations of this work, its pains and pleasures, be shared equally and not be disproportionately borne by any one group of people. The current system – which so often pushes work onto immigrant women and leaves intact the gendered division of labour in the home – is not a viable approach to a universal project of post-work social reproduction. It is a series of displacements, not solutions.[42]

To try to lay out the parameters for this project, we will give a contemporary account of how social reproduction has changed over the past century, with a particular focus on the unwaged work performed in the home and the efforts made to reduce housework. The home is significant because of the relative disinterest from capitalists, the growing reliance on it by advanced welfare states, and the obstinance of the household division of labour. Our focus in this book will be on high-income countries, predominantly in the West, though the scope inevitably expands globally as chains of care and other international influences are taken into account. The countries we focus on typically display sufficient socioeconomic similarities for their trajectories to be meaningfully grouped together. They are also globally significant insofar as ideas such as those around gender roles, proper familial organisation, appropriate forms of cleanliness, ideal housing, or the correct approach to healthcare (among many other things) have been exported from these countries to elsewhere through colonial means and through being embedded in a very wide range of systems that have both intensified and extended them: product design, research and development, marketing and advertising, journalism, academia, education, other state agencies, and so on.[43] A much-needed global and comparative history of social reproduction, however, remains to be written.

With those caveats in mind, the next chapter begins by looking at the historical promise of technology for reducing the burdens of socially reproductive work and at how this promise largely failed to be realised. It considers how contemporary innovations in domestic technology have mostly given up any labour-saving ambitions, as well as how the automation of housework and care work has become something of a dead end, despite its unrealised potentials. Chapter 3 turns to one of the key drivers of technology's failure to reduce domestic labour – rising standards. As new domestic technologies were introduced in the early twentieth century, domestic expectations, including those around standards of cleanliness and hygiene, were simultaneously ratcheting up and erasing any prospect of substantial labour saving. Today we see similar patterns of expectation setting and work imperatives being established across the domestic sphere, leading to a continued encroachment on free time. In Chapter 4 we move the discussion to the social relations of the household – specifically, to the nuclear family as a means of managing social reproduction under capitalism. The family, we suggest, is not a natural or immutable formation, but in part an adaptative response to the economic system in which it is situated. Work and the family are fundamentally connected and attempts to resist one must inevitably reckon with the other. Lastly, Chapter 5 looks towards the house itself – the container of domestic technologies – to see what the spatial organisation of domestic labour can teach us about the possibilities of extending our post-work ambitions to social reproduction. It considers the extent to which the challenges of unwaged intrafamilial housework and care work stem from the architectural forms within which they are typically pursued and looks to historical experiments in and with living space to see where illuminating counter-imaginaries might be found. Chapter 6 concludes the book by advancing a series of proposals, drawn from the analysis pursued across the previous chapters. We attempt to formulate demands according to three overarching themes: communal care, public luxury, and temporal sovereignty. Our argument here is that these three concepts can help shape the fight for free time, extending it beyond the kinds of wage labour that have traditionally been the focus of post-work demand making.

2
Technologies

In any discussion of post-work ideas, technology looms large. It is easy to see why: technology promises to retain existing standards of living while simultaneously reducing the amount of work collectively required. So why not just use technology to reduce the work of social reproduction? After all, such technologies are often desired by those who perform the work: women, for instance, appear particularly keen to introduce service robots into the home, especially in countries where women do significantly more domestic work than men.[1] The early years of the smart home in the 1990s likewise saw new cleaning technologies as the most desired aspect of home automation. And more recently, a 2019 survey found self-cleaning homes to be the speculative technology that people would most like to see become a reality.[2] Those who currently do the work appear quite happy to see the back of (some of) it. Recipients of care are often similarly supportive of the idea of more technology. Surveys, for instance, find that pensioners are significantly more open to the use of robots in eldercare than are other groups.[3]

Yet in contemporary discussions about reproductive labour, the issue of technology is often passed over in silence – or invoked only in the context of rejection.[4] These debates typically position social reproduction as the constitutive limit of automation, with nanny- and nurse-bots featuring heavily in dystopian visions of cold and loveless techno-futures.[5] Silvia Federici, for example, responds to the idea of household robots and carebots with the rhetorical question, 'Is this the society we want?'[6]

Against the blanket rejection of technology's application to social reproduction, we should insist on some key qualifications. First, the concept of 'social reproduction' is often so large as to blind us to important variations in the types of tasks that fall under that category. While some types of reproductive labour may indeed be deemed ethically inviolable by machines, and the automation of other activities may simply be technically unfeasible at the moment, this does not mean that all the work of reproduction is as resistant. After all, 'automation can do very, very good things like remove the kind of ... simple basic caring functions that so many carers have to undertake and frees them to be in other kinds of emotional relations'.[7] Anecdotally, we have found in the course of our own discussions with waged care workers that a similar sentiment seems to hold; many freely point to elements of their jobs that could usefully be automated away – often precisely to allow them more time to perform the more explicitly human-centred aspects of their jobs.

There is also a typically unstated assumption on the part of many critics of automation that care work is something which humans are peculiarly good at and that automation risks stripping those in receipt of care of human interaction. Yet this overlooks the fact that such interaction is frequently hostile and abusive, both within and beyond the family home, and it ignores the myriad physical and psychological burdens associated with certain forms of caregiving. Caring takes work. It is often exhausting and frustrating. And for unpaid carers, the situation is even more difficult, with a majority reporting that they find the work emotionally stressful, financially straining, and devastating to work-life balance.[8] For these and other reasons, we should investigate whether the judicious application of technology could play a role in alleviating the burdens associated with reproductive work.

The Industrial Revolution of the Home

We start our exploration of the impact of domestic technologies in the opening decades of the twentieth century, when there was an 'industrial revolution in the home'.[9] This period of unprecedented change saw the means of social reproduction utterly transformed, from the deep infrastructural underpinnings of this work right up to the specific tools and technologies used by individuals.

Prior to this transformation, housework was exhaustingly laborious. The raw materials necessary for sustaining life and the home were brought in from outside the domestic residence. Lighting for instance, was provided through kerosene lamps and fireplaces, but required significant effort to maintain: chopping wood, collecting coal, tending lamps, and so on. Likewise with heating, stoves required large amounts of wood to be chopped and carried inside. Water had to be pumped and brought in for cooking, cleaning, and bathing (a job that still takes up a significant portion of women's work around the world[10] – and as late as the 1960s, took up hours of most women's daily time in rural Ireland[11]). And just as resources were required to be imported *into* the home, so were waste products required to be exported *from* it. Laundry suds, chamber pots, ashes, and so on were all constantly flowing out of domestic residences, frequently carried in the hands and on the backs of family members. In the 1890s, 'the average household lugged around the home 7 tons of coal and 9000 gallons of water per year'.[12]

For the most part, the essentials of life – food and clothing – were still produced in the home. Women, for instance, often spent the majority of their 'free time' sewing, knitting, and doing embroidery.[13] The transition to market-based purchases was beginning at this time but still largely remained the preserve of wealthier households. Laundry was among the most difficult tasks, typically relegated to a single washday every week that would take up many hours. According to one source, the 'washday was as exhausting as swimming five miles of energetic breast stroke'. Water had to be brought in, clothes run on a washboard, hung out to dry, and then eventually ironed with a cumbersome flatiron that required a hot stove to be running all year round.[14]

Technology was minimal within the home, with one socialist feminist of the time lamenting that 'industrially, [women's work and men's work] are three centuries apart'.[15] Childcare and eldercare as we know them, however, were far less of a concern during this period. The notion of the majority of children spending their time in education, and of the family actively supporting and contributing to the learning process from home, was yet to gain widespread acceptance. More often than not, younger members of the family were instead recruited into the domestic workforce, effectively reducing rather than generating labour. Retirement as we know it was virtually non-existent as well, due to both shorter lifespans and the absence of pensions. Working until death was standard and the requirements of eldercare minimal.

Yet as the twentieth century dawned, much of this work began to undergo significant transformation. Many of the most important changes were infrastructural: the introduction of running water, electricity, and gas. Cities (and, later, rural areas) were increasingly building municipal systems that could supply water and take away refuse. By the early 1900s, most European cities had widespread sewer and water systems in place.[16] The physically and temporally demanding tasks of moving water in and out of the home were becoming a thing of the past. It has been estimated that the emergence of running water saved households around one and a half to two hours a day of work spent pumping, carrying, and heating water.[17] Many European cities at this time were also rolling out gas infrastructure, enabling shifts away from coal-powered stoves.[18] This transformation saved around thirty minutes per day that had previously been spent on cleaning up and removing coal dust.[19] And whereas waste removal once involved lugging refuse to an open fire, burning it, and then removing the ashes, by the 1930s it simply meant dragging a rubbish bin out to the street so that a publicly funded service could collect and dispense with it.[20] More than individual devices, it was these sorts of infrastructural transformations which had the most significant impact on the nature and extent of work being done in the home.[21]

This is not to deny the significance of individual domestic technologies, however; part of infrastructure's importance was that it laid the foundation for a series of new technical devices to emerge. Turning spits over open fires, for example, had once been so laborious that contraptions were built for use with specially bred working dogs (the appropriately named – and now extinct – turnspit dog).[22] The animals had been largely replaced by automatic roasting jacks by the mid-nineteenth century, and coal and wood stoves further reduced the need for physical labour (be it human or canine). These were replaced with gas, oil, and electric stoves in the 1920s, leading to significant labour-saving gains.[23] This meant a major reduction in the work

of cooking and cleaning. The elimination of 'such chores as
loading the fuel and removing the ashes', made the household
stove 'much easier to light, maintain, and regulate', and kitchens
became 'much easier to clean when they did not have coal dust
regularly tracked through them'.[24]

Freezers, meanwhile, enabled economies of scale in food
production – rather than cook a meal from scratch every night,
food could be prepared in batches days ahead of time. The
idea of 'leftovers' was popularised, and recipe books appeared
devoted to their preparation.[25] The work of laundering clothes
saw a similar revolution. Initially, much laundry work shifted
from the unwaged sector to the waged one, with commercial
laundries becoming popular in the 1920s – even the poorest
families would use them for at least some of their clothing.[26]
The household washing machine emerged shortly afterwards,
spreading quickly during the course of the decade and returning much of this work to the domestic residence in a new, less
intensive form.[27] The invention of detergents made washing
machines significantly more effective, reducing the amount of
physical labour required to get clothes clean. Synthetic fabrics
also served to make machine laundering more viable; the clothes
of the nineteenth century would barely have survived a vigorous
cycle in one of today's washer-dryers. Wash-and-wear clothing,
meanwhile, enabled a major reduction in time spent ironing.
Both the infrastructure and the devices of the home were rapidly
changing. Throughout this industrial revolution, groups like the
Electrical Association for Women worked to inform consumers
of new developments in household appliances while simultaneously advocating for a women's perspective in the (typically
male-dominated) design of these machines.[28]

Aside from these major technological transformations,
however – and equally important for the nature of domestic

work – was the ever more decisive shift away from the household mode of production in favour of market-purchased goods. The production of flour had been one of the first tasks to be industrialised, moving from being milled at home to being produced in increasingly large and automated flour mills.[29] Other foods soon followed; refrigeration enabled perishable goods to be stored for longer, mass production techniques lowered prices, and shops began stocking more items. Campbell's iconic soup can, for instance, emerged in the 1890s and was joined by an expanding plethora of tinned goods and convenience foods (such as breakfast cereals) in the decades after.[30] By the turn of the century, 20 per cent of US manufacturing was devoted to food processing, with mass production and new large-scale chain stores making such food accessible even to working-class families.[31] By 1944, 600 million pounds of frozen food was being sold in America.[32] The unwaged work of producing food – and preparing it for storage[33] – was transferred from the home to the market, with these tasks increasingly structured by the demands of capital accumulation.

Like food production, the work of making clothes also shifted away from the home. The rise of mail-order catalogues, along with the emergence of department stores in the late nineteenth century, made the purchase of clothing increasingly simple and cheap. Lastly, in addition to food and clothing production moving into the waged sector, healthcare also moved out of the domestic residence. It was increasingly professionalised (sometimes to the detriment of patients, not to mention female healthcare practitioners) and eventually made subject to public provision in many countries.[34] The discovery of the germ theory of disease led to a new emphasis on sterilisation – a process which was better handled at hospitals designated as hygienic spaces. By the turn of the century there were around 4,000 hospitals in America,[35] and by the 1930s they had moved from being a place in which to die to also being a place in which to be cured. With this shift of healthcare into the waged sphere, women's traditional work as unpaid nurses in the home was reduced – meaning not simply the elimination of a burden (one particularly hard to bare for time-poor working women), but also – and less positively – the outsourcing of a challenging, skilful and potentially rewarding sphere of activity. As many white, middle-class commentators of the period complained, the home was becoming an ever more limited site of routinised drudgery in the late nineteenth and early twentieth century.

So, with the industrialisation of the home, a number of processes occurred: the infrastructure of the home was radically changed, with water, heat, and electricity now flowing in and out of the domestic residence with more ease than ever before; a whole series of new technologies arose to take advantage of these changes and significantly reduced the burdens of much reproductive labour; and at the same time, food production, clothing production, and healthcare all changed from unwaged labour done in the home to waged labour often carried out under direct market pressures. These were revolutionary changes, but what was their impact on workloads?

The Cowan Paradox

Over the course of the 1940s and 1950s, these technologies became standardised throughout Western households. Yet in spite of all the new technologies, a surprising fact emerged in the 1970s: time spent on housework was *not* decreasing. This unexpected stubbornness of domestic labour was first pointed out by Joann Vanek in a 1974 article, in which she marvelled at discovering full-time housewives spent fifty-two hours a week on housework in 1924, and fifty-five hours a week in the 1960s.[36] Ruth Schwartz Cowan, outlining the paradox that now bears her name,[37] went on to demonstrate that despite all the new labour-saving devices, labour did not appear to have been saved in the home. In particular, her research showed that the time spent on domestic work did not decrease between the 1870s and the 1970s.[38] A later study of twelve countries at varying stages of economic development similarly demonstrated that technology made little difference to the amount of housework done,[39] and others have gone on to confirm this broad trend across a number of countries.[40] Exploring why this occurred can help to illustrate the intricate ways in which technology and the work of social reproduction are connected.

In the first place, the industrial revolution of the home was accompanied by a dramatic shift in the social organisation of this work as it was increasingly individualised and concentrated into the figure of the 'housewife'. Previously, work tended to be shared among unwaged workers (e.g., children, relatives, neighbours) and a large domestic servant industry. In Britain, for instance, around 14 per cent of the working population were employed as domestic servants at the turn of the century. This meant that the work was carried out collectively (though by no means equitably); while it may have taken a large number of total hours to complete, the workload was at least spread across several people. Yet new technologies often facilitated (and responded to) the increasing individualisation of this workload throughout the nineteenth century – placing it in the hands of the lone housewife. Children were increasingly being recruited into education and were no longer as available to help out in the home; men were being positioned as family bread-winners; and well-off families who had relied upon domestic servants were increasingly seeing their 'help' dwindle away. The under-supply of domestic servants became more pronounced as the years progressed. As new jobs emerged for poor women, and their experiences of alternative work in World War I altered their horizons, the domestic servant industry went into further decline. Changing social relations therefore encouraged the adoption of domestic technologies, while domestic technologies facilitated the individualisation of this work. The ultimate result was that, while fewer workers were available to help out with social reproduction, activities which once required coordinated collective efforts could now be undertaken by a single unwaged worker. As Mariarosa Dalla Costa and Selma James put it, the housewife's 'workday is unending not because she has no machines, but because she is isolated'.[41]

This individualisation also had a significant impact on the design and development of domestic technologies. New technologies were conceived of and marketed as replacements for servants — with piecemeal tasks being shunted off to machinery — instead of being part of a wholesale rethinking of how this work was done.[42] Laundry is a particularly good example of this, with washing machines imagined as a replacement for the work of individual servants. Prior to this, laundry was often done by laundresses (market-provided workers — in America, often Black women) or by commercial laundries.[43] It could have been the case that commercial laundries were improved and the work of washing clothes collectivised. Indeed, as early as 1869, women were arguing for the socialisation of laundry work, with Catherine Beecher suggesting that one commercial laundry be made available for every dozen families.[44] But the washing machine turned what could have been a collective industrial process into the work of a lone housewife, and the economies of scale (or government support) which could have made collective laundering a reality were never achieved. Moreover, the manufacturers of these devices saw more profit potential in mass market production than in production for collective use.[45] A mixture of factors contributed to the eventual downfall of launderettes – technological improvements to home washer/dryers, the power of large appliance manufacturers with substantial advertising budgets (versus smaller, typically locally owned launderettes), rising wages for launderette workers, and often classist and racist anxieties about one's washing mixing with that of other households all played a role.[46]

A second reason for Cowan's paradox is that just as new domestic technologies were being introduced, standards of cleanliness and hygiene were ratcheting up. This is a topic that will be more thoroughly examined in the next chapter, but for now we can point to some of the key elements that increased work in the first half of the twentieth century. Particularly significant were the circulation of new knowledge around hygiene, the solidification of the germ theory of disease, and the emergence of nutritional science. As members of the general public learned about the health virtues of cleanliness and proper nutrition – and as more responsibilities were placed onto individual households – increased efforts were made to maintain exacting (that is to say, highly labour intensive) standards of hygiene and to plan and prepare more complex, nutritionally balanced meals. The extra work generated served to offset some of the potential time-saving benefits afforded by many emerging technologies.[47] Each of the new devices became 'the material embodiment of a task, a silent imperative to work'.[48]

Lastly, the industrial revolution of the home may have meant the reduction or elimination of some tasks, but it also meant the creation of a series of new ones. For instance, as mass-market clothing spread, people bought more clothes, increasing the amount of laundry that had to be done. Likewise, running water created new work, insofar as the creation of bathrooms meant they had to be cleaned (and more frequently so than other areas of the household). The expansion of lawns and the introduction of gardening technologies channelled an immense amount of work and energy into the upkeep of outside spaces. There was also a gender bias to many of these technologies. For instance, early inventions such as the stove, manufactured cloth, and industrialised flour enabled the reduction of men's work (e.g., cutting and hauling wood, producing leather goods, milling flour) while simultaneously increasing women's work (e.g., cooking a wider variety of food, laundering cotton clothing, and lengthier preparation for baking with the new white flour).[49] This is a bias that held throughout the expansion of appliances, with one study noting that in cases where 'domestic technologies do encourage less household work, it tends to be men who are the beneficiaries'.[50]

The general shift from the household as a space of production to one of consumption entailed both the expansion of some existing responsibilities and the addition of new ones: shopping, managing finances, travelling to purchase goods, and so on. Some aspects of food preparation, for example, may have been reduced by the emergence of convenience food, but now shopping for these goods became more frequent and laborious.[51] Women were the primary shoppers for these new consumer goods, informing themselves about them, managing the household budget and expenditures, and purchasing most products for the family.[52] During the first decades of the twentieth century, goods and services were largely delivered to the house: food, linens, medicines, repair work, healthcare, and so on, were borne by people travelling to the home.[53] When people stopped into a store, clerks would provide information about the products, collect them for the customers, check out the goods, bundle them together, and then deliver them. The rise of mail-order catalogues in the late nineteenth century made the labour of transport even less burdensome for the home.

Yet this era of full-service retail rapidly changed with the rise of the automobile in the early decades of the twentieth century. As larger chain and department stores started stocking more goods, travelling for shopping started taking up more and more time. (In recent years, shopping has typically taken up around three hours of an individual's week.)[54] With the spread of consumer products and rise of mass consumption, profit pressures compelled a reorganisation of retail as well. During the Great Depression, stores started experimenting with self-service instead of the more traditional method of having clerks pick out the items and bring them to the customer. Demonstrating the impact of shifting this work to the market, the belief was that productivity could be increased by reducing the downtime of clerks that previously had to wait around for customers. Now these workers could instead be made to focus on stocking shelves and doing other retail work. World War II accelerated this shift by inflicting labour shortages and bringing about new efforts to cut costs, spurring more stores to adopt the self-service approach. By the 1950s, with the introduction of technologies designed to present products to customers, facilitate checking out, and monitor potential theft, most shops had reorganised their labour process.[55]

In the end, Cowan's paradox raises a series of important points. Technology alone is insufficient to reduce work; individual devices exist within a broader sociotechnical system, and their impacts are mediated by this context. Changes in social norms and expectations, the nature of the gendered division of labour, the shape of the household (e.g., multigenerational, collective, nuclear) all help determine whether or not labour-saving devices are in fact capable of saving labour. Any project using technology to facilitate a reduction of socially reproductive work would do well to remember these factors.

Stagnation in the Home

A second key phase for social reproduction and technology took place between the seventies and noughties. In this period, despite the rapid changes seen in previous years, technological development slowed to a crawl. In every sphere and for nearly every task, the technologies seen at the end of the previous period remained virtually the same by the first decade of the new millennium. A housewife from the 1870s would find a house in the 1940s virtually unrecognisable, whereas a housewife from the 1940s would find the home of the 2020s almost entirely the same.[56] Since the 1950s, the only major new domestic appliance has been the microwave.[57] It was invented in the 1940s, but cost and safety concerns meant it wasn't widely adopted until the 1980s.[58] Technologies such as fridges, dishwashers, vacuum cleaners, and ovens have all seen minor improvements (some new features, more energy efficiency, and so on), but very little that is substantially new has been added.[59] The world of kitchen appliances has seen a series of fashionable trends come and go – the bread maker, sous vide cookers, and the Instant Pot all proved to be minor hits in the kitchen – but none had any real labour-saving potential. Washing machines have been subject to new developments, but in several cases, these tweaks were designed to make the manufacturing process simpler rather than to make housework easier. Top-loading machines, for instance, are less demanding on a user's back but more difficult to produce – hence the rise of front-loading machines instead.[60] Roombas were invented and released to the public in 2002, but their initially high prices (often three to four times that of a better performing manual vacuum cleaner) meant they have only recently become more widely adopted.

A more significant development (and one not often viewed in the context of domestic labour-saving technologies) has been the spread of birth control, which helped to bring down the fertility rate during this time and arguably reduced the labour of looking after many children. As Federici notes, contraceptives may be 'the only true labour saving device women' used in the period.[61] In relation to childcare, disposable nappies have also been a major innovation (though one with significant impacts on municipal landfills). Created in the 1940s, they have gone on to become the dominant approach to diapering babies.[62] In terms of reducing childcare work, disposable nappies have been particularly significant not just in the reduction of laundry work but also in the fact that babies in disposables tend to be changed less often than those in cloth nappies.[63] Breast pumps are another relatively new technology, moving from being an expensive piece of hospital equipment to an affordable and portable tool in the 1990s.[64] Their potential as a labour-saving device is relatively marginal, but they do allow 'time-shifting': the capacity to move a task to a different, more ideal moment. Under current circumstances, particularly in America, this capacity is often used to plaster over fundamental contradictions in the social system. While official guidance encourages breastfeeding, America's practically non-existent maternity support means most gestational parents have to engage in wage work that takes them away from their babies. Instead of extending maternity and parental leave, the breast pump functions as a technological solution to get breast milk from workers to their nursing babies, with people using the pumps during breaks from work.[65] Within a work-centric society, the technology has enabled rising expectations that childbearers should do both waged work and unwaged reproductive labour.

The Work Transfer

More than just causing stagnation in terms of saving time, since the seventies, new technologies have arguably *increased* some of the temporal burdens associated with healthcare work.[66] Combined with both a drive to contain costs and the desire of many patients to be treated at home rather than in an institutional setting, new technologies have facilitated the transfer of elements of this work from a relatively productive professional sphere to the low-productivity unwaged home.[67] Ventilators, catheters, morphine drips, and hemodialysis are just some of the devices that have moved into the domestic residence in recent decades. This constitutes a reversal from the earlier movement of this work from unwaged or low-waged amateurs and lay healers to increasingly well-paid (and masculinised) professionals.

One important driver here has been the widespread use of reimbursement based upon diagnostic-related groups (DRGs) – whereby hospitals are reimbursed a standardised amount for any given diagnosis, regardless of the cost to them. The result is an incentive system for hospitals to push patients out of the door as soon as possible, thereby lowering their costs and maximising their cut of the fixed revenues.[68] While America was an early leader in adopting DRGs in the 1980s, these have since become widely used around the world.[69] In the US, the introduction of DRGs meant that patient care suffered, fewer patients were admitted, and the time individuals spent in hospital care greatly decreased. Until the 1980s, hospital inpatient services 'were perceived as an unambiguous social good'.[70] Yet today, 'wherever data are reported, hospital inpatient utilisation has fallen sharply'.[71] As a result, whereas the average hospital stay in America was 7.3 days in 1980, by 2000 it was down to 4.9 days. The average stay for elderly patients was cut in half over the same period.[72] Supported as a cost cutting measure for hospitals, in 1985 the shift to unpaid home care was estimated to have saved the industry $10 billion in wages.[73] Similar trends hold across the rich countries, with the number of hospital beds (per 1,000 people) in decline since the 1970s and with people staying in hospitals for ever shorter periods.[74]

These shorter hospital stays aren't necessarily reflective of less healthcare work or quicker recoveries. In many cases, this work has instead been transferred across spheres and taken up by unpaid caregivers who are taking on tasks that would once have been performed by professional nurses (tube feeding, injections, changing catheters, monitoring blood pressure or glucose, concocting pharmaceutical cocktails, tending to wounds, etc.)[75] – tasks for which they have often been given only cursory training. In many cases, this work is trivialised as being far simpler and less skilled than it actually is.[76] The technologies of home care have become vastly more sophisticated, as devices originally created for care in the hospital have been adapted for home use – though in many cases, the home itself must be transformed into a sterile, hospital-like environment in order to facilitate the safe use of these technologies, with the risk of emergencies or malfunctions creating a 'pervasive sense of anxiety' for carers.[77] After all, the germ theory of disease was one reason why healthcare moved out of the home and into sterile environments in the first place. Carers are forced to engage in what has been called '"disability world-making", which involves solving problems with everyday objects, tinkering and hacking to make worlds liveable'.[78] Following the experiments with 'virtual care' during the COVID-19 pandemic, such experiences are likely to become generalised and normalised as healthcare systems shift more work into the home via remote monitoring and tele-health.[79]

The use of these technologies represents a significant extension of traditional domestic work. No longer 'just' cleaning the house and looking after dependants, women – and mostly it *is* women – are now being asked to take on highly technical medical tasks, leading to the rise of a carer who is both expert and amateur and who bears substantial responsibility while garnering little respect (and even less support).[80] By 1997, it was estimated that 26 million people in America were doing such unpaid healthcare work in the home, at an average of 18 hours per week.[81] And whereas professionals have (relatively) clear boundaries between their work and the rest of their lives, complete with breaks and mandated time off, household carers have little space for respite from the demands of care work.[82] The result is a proliferation of work for those with such caregiving duties. Far from reducing work, then, this shift is increasing overall workload by reducing productivity and making it the responsibility of unpaid carers.[83] Just as washing machines brought work back into the home, so too have these new medical technologies.

The transfer of work has also affected retail, with technology increasingly being deployed to outsource certain work to consumers.[84] The 1970s saw the continued development of self-serve culture, as customers were increasingly expected to do work that had previously been carried out by waged workers.[85] ATMs became widespread, self-serve gas stations popped up, and today, self-checkouts are increasingly ubiquitous – not least after the pandemic-fuelled push for social distancing.[86] Often mistaken for 'automation', these technologies are in fact *labour-displacement* machines used to shift work from a waged worker to an unwaged user. More recently, platforms have become another means to offload work to users: planning a trip or organising something like life insurance are tasks which used to be done by waged workers but are now provided as a user-led service through the internet. And government efforts to tackle climate change have in no small part hinged upon imposing 'sustainability work' upon households despite the relatively minor benefits to be gained from this approach.[87] The period of neoliberalism can therefore be broadly characterised as one of domestic stagnation in technological terms, combined with a growing number of devices being used to transfer activities from waged to unwaged spheres in an effort to save costs.

Why Did Technology Stagnate?

The neoliberal period has seen a drastic decrease in the pace of innovation, then. This is surprising in light of the sociological changes occurring at the same time. As more women left the home and entered the waged workforce, we might reasonably expect to see more demand for labour-saving devices in the home. Why did companies not take advantage of this expected demand and create new technologies? Or, put another way, why did a slowdown in innovation occur?

One possible reason is that it was part of a broader technological slowdown over the last fifty years. As Robert Gordon has argued, the 1920s to the 1970s was a period of one-off productivity improvements dependent upon a series of radical technologies created in the decades prior.[88] The entire economy benefited from these enhancements, and productivity surged to unprecedented (and unrepeatable) levels. Yet once those technologies became widespread, their marginal benefits dwindled – and more importantly, there were no new technologies emerging to replace them. Even the internet has been mostly underwhelming in productivity (labour-saving) terms, especially compared to earlier inventions such as electricity, the steam engine, or the telegraph.[89] So maybe it is no surprise that reproductive labour-saving technologies did not advance much when there was a general technological slowdown.

There is a second reason for this lack of innovation though – what we might call the 'maids over machines' principle – which derives from the fact that domestic labour-saving devices are often more expensive than the low-wage workers who might carry out the same work. For those who dream of a fully automated home, the unfortunate reality is that many of the tasks of domestic social reproduction are quite difficult to get a machine to perform. Folding clothes, for instance, involves complex image recognition in varied lighting conditions, sophisticated dexterity, and the ability to operate in an unstructured environment. These are all incredible challenges for machines, even to this day.[90] And tasks demanding such capabilities are common within the household: picking up laundry, tidying surfaces, dusting decorative objects, and so on. This is not to say that there is no hope that this work might to some extent be alleviated by technologies; one can imagine the construction of structured environments, for example, which might make such tasks more amenable to automation. The dishwasher, after all, is effectively a structured environment that enables a heterogeneous collection of dishes to be washed. In general, however, developing machines to automate this labour – if it is even presently possible – would mean an array of rather expensive consumer products. If one is wealthy enough to buy expensive labour-saving devices, one is also wealthy enough to employ domestic labourers, who have a proven track record conducting a varied range of household chores and who are responsible for their own maintenance and upkeep. One does not need to clean, repair, upgrade, or store a paid domestic worker. Who can afford a Roomba but not a cleaner? The choice for a household, then, is between an expensive machine and a cheap maid (or perhaps an unpaid spouse[91]). It is the human option that has routinely been chosen in this second period. As wages have stagnated for many, and as inequality has risen across many countries, it has become easier and more cost-effective for wealthier households to turn to servants.[92] The end result has been the creation of global chains of care as demand has risen for domestic labourers to replace wealthier women as they moved into the waged workplace.[93]

Digital Social Reproduction

Recent years have seen further minor developments in domestic technology. More easy-to-wash, easy-to-iron clothing is now available than ever before, continuing the reduction of labour required to keep clothes clean and neat. And while the tablet computer market has dwindled in recent years, these devices remain popular as a means of occupying children's attention (and enabling parents to enter public spaces with less fear of a tantrum).[94] The more interactive tablet has come to supplement that classic tool of childcare automation, the television. In America, for instance, screen time for young children doubled between 1997 and 2014.[95] And YouTube videos oriented towards children have significantly increased in length, in order to meet a demand for long spans of automated childcare.[96] Somewhat perversely, the more enjoyable aspects of childcare – engaging, playing, interacting with children – have been automated via screens, while the more routine and burdensome aspects have remained largely untouched.[97] Hence, we use domestic technologies for our children's entertainment, education, and enrichment, so that we can cook their dinners and organise their PE kits. Surely it should be the other way around.

While new labour-saving devices have been somewhat harder to come by, the past half century has seen at least one genuinely significant change – a change that, as with the furthest-reaching shifts at the *fin de siècle*, was infrastructural in nature. The home has become networked. Just as the arrival of running water, sewage systems, electricity, and gas fundamentally shaped what was possible within the home in the previous century, so too does the arrival of the internet influence domestic possibilities today. This infrastructure has set the scene for further transformations and is sparking a resurgence of interest in technologies of domestic social reproduction.

Outsourcing Housework

First, digital platforms have enabled and fostered rapid growth in personal services in a reversal of the decades-long decline of the servant economy. Coming to prominence with Uber (the taxi app that connects riders with drivers), a plethora of platforms have since emerged to offer a whole range of personal services 'that make it possible to substitute paid for unpaid labour, for example in food delivery, cleaning, personal care, childcare, running errands, gardening, dog walking, repair, building maintenance, filing and sorting and putting up shelves'.[98] As a means to outsource traditional household labour, digital platforms have been one of the most significant technological transformations in recent decades. They are not a reduction of work, of course, but rather a transfer of work from the household to the market.[99] In many countries, they have become quite widely used, reaching far beyond the upper classes. One European study, for example, found that in the seven countries examined a quarter of all households had used a platform to hire a domestic service.[100]

In the area of cooking, digital platforms have extended a pre-existing long-term shift of this work from the home to the market. Previously, the most obvious example of this has been people dining out more.[101] Studies indicate that in a number of wealthy Western countries, the time spent eating in the home has decreased since 1970, while the time spent eating out has increased.[102] As one economist puts it, 'The fast-food industry … must have saved housewives the world over trillions of hours of cooking and cleaning.'[103] In America, for instance, households are spending a growing proportion of their food budget on food away from home (see Figure 2.1). More and more of Americans' caloric intake is coming from eating out.[104] These changes are particularly prevalent as household income increases: both the middle class and the rich are far more likely than the poor to eat out (whether in fast food or full-service restaurants).[105] Indeed, for the wealthiest households, more money is spent on eating out than on food at home, suggesting that money – rather than desire – is often a core limitation to people moving a substantial portion of this work outside the home.[106]

Digital platforms are further reducing the household work involved by enabling a rapid expansion of food delivery services.

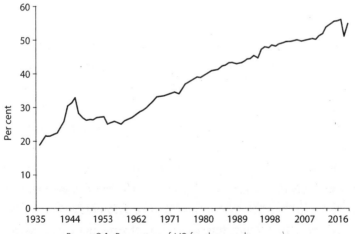

Figure 2.1: Proportion of US food expenditure spent on food away from home, 1935–2019[107]

Borne on the back of notoriously poorly paid and precarious workers, platforms like Uber Eats, Meituan, DoorDash, Grab, and Deliveroo have seen significant growth in moving food from restaurants to homes. These services have been particularly attractive to the overworked as a way to quickly grab a meal, and they appear to be largely the result of a shift from home cooking to delivery rather than from restaurants to delivery.[108] Such has been the success of digital platforms in this area that companies are now building 'dark kitchens' – micro-kitchens placed around a city for the sole purpose of producing food for the delivery market.[109] During the pandemic, use of delivery platforms surged further as consumers, unable to visit restaurants in person, instead ordered food in.[110] Some commentators have even gone so far as to predict the 'death of the kitchen' by 2030, as more cooking is moved from the home to industrialised food production.[111]

In another example of the outsourcing of food production, the use of convenience foods has risen, particularly as part of an effort to make life easier for the time poor.[112] Rather than making multiple trips to a supermarket to constantly replenish fresh ingredients, people have turned to purchasing commodities such as ready meals and frozen foods as a way to simplify their schedules. These foodstuffs make time easier to manage (what and when one eats is no longer tethered to what's ripening in the fruit bowl or about to rot in the fridge), but also reduce the time it takes to prepare food – which is why time-constrained people are more likely to use them.[113] As a manufactured commodity, these items have been subject to productivity increases as well, making them increasingly cheap over time. Overall, the time spent cooking and washing up has decreased since the 1970s, likely because of the increased time spent eating out, the greater use of convenience foods, and the adoption of dishwashers and microwaves.[114]

Digital platforms are similarly transforming the experience of shopping. While the trend for decades has been for shopping to consume ever more of people's time, the rise of online ordering and delivery in recent years may be symptomatic of a return to pre-1930s retail and its associated shift of work to the market. The move to online retail/e-commerce is a major transition and one that brings shopping increasingly back to the mail-order paradigm of the turn of the century. In both cases, individuals order consumer goods (via catalogues or digital platforms) and these items are then packaged up and shipped to them to arrive at their door. Shopping malls, department stores, and the high street have all been suffering as a result.[115] The work of transporting goods is not disappearing – instead, it's being put onto an army of low-paid workers – but in terms of *where* work is being done, it is a notable shift to the market. There is also arguably a reduction in the overall amount of transportation work involved here, given that the use of dedicated couriers could mean a more energy- and time-efficient approach than that of multiple individuals travelling to distant stores to bring goods home themselves.[116]

Globally, there are now estimated to be more than 1.5 billion people who shop via e-commerce.[117] The pandemic has accelerated growth of users as well, with e-commerce moving from 20 per cent to 35 per cent of all retail sales in the UK, and from 11 per cent to 16 per cent in the US.[118] Even countries that had held out against e-commerce, such as Italy, have adopted this new approach to shopping as a result of pandemic lockdowns.[119] If you exclude groceries, which require a different type of logistics given the perishable nature of many food products, e-commerce is nearing half of the remaining retail sales in the UK.[120] And while online groceries lag behind the rest of e-commerce, they are also growing rapidly in many countries.[121] The pandemic saw a major boost to this sector – doubling in the UK, for instance (albeit from a low level).[122] The past few years have seen hundreds of 'dark stores' open up: like dark kitchens, these are micro-warehouse hubs placed throughout a city for rapid grocery delivery that aim to replace corner shops and convenience stores.[123] Platforms are looking to expand their delivery services too, including items like prescription drugs and alcohol, while also promising increasingly rapid – and for workers, increasingly dangerous – delivery times. It is clear that household shopping is undergoing changes, with potentially significant shifts of work out of the home and into the market. While many millennials will have memories of spending an entire day of the weekend travelling around, getting groceries, and crossing items off our shopping lists, things are now increasingly being delivered directly to our doors.

As a means to outsource traditional household labour, digital platforms have therefore been one of the most significant technological transformations in recent decades, enabling and fostering rapid growth in the personal service industry. Crucially, though, none of this has necessarily meant any *reduction* in the total amount of labour that society contributes to a task; rather, the most important aspect has been the qualitative shift of work from the home to the market. The end result of recent socioeconomic changes – diminished time away from waged work in dual-earner households, expanding chains of care, and new platform businesses – has been a situation in which a growing amount of domestic social reproduction can now be outsourced to markets. As Barbara Ehrenreich notes, 'This is finally transforming the home into a fully capitalist-style workplace, and in ways that the old wages-for-housework advocates could never have imagined.'[124]

At Home with Platforms

If platforms are facilitating the shift of work to the market, the main area of domestic innovation in recent years has been the 'smart home'; a term indicating a constellation of devices networked together within an individual household. The idea for the smart home is not new – it has been around since at least the 1980s, with a number of companies building experimental houses to demonstrate what the 'home of the future' might look like. What is striking, though, is how little has changed of the imaginary since that time. Take, for instance, this 1987 description of a smart home:

> The main R&D effort is directed towards a control system integrating: remote registration of outdoor temperature and humidity, regulation of indoor air quality, temperature and environmental control in specified zones and light regulation. It includes control of an advanced security system, with motion detectors ... It also involves service/diagnosis equipment and makes use of voice recognition and voice information.[125]

Add in a connection to the internet and this description works equally as well for the modern smart home. Indeed, even in the 1980s, many of the devices themselves – TVs, fridges, coffee makers, and so on – had been around in their 'dumb' form for many years; what was novel was the idea of integrating them.[126] The smart home, then, serves a managerial function in relation to the various smart devices it contains, offering an overarching vision of every movement and environmental fluctuation, combined with digital- and voice-control systems to enable the use and remote coordination of these elements.[127]

At the same time, the reduction of housework has long been a priority for people imagining an ideal future home. The changes to the home emerging in the late nineteenth century, for instance, saw a number of feminist reformers advocating for an easy-to-clean house.[128] And from its origins, the smart home has been closely tied to notions of reducing housework. Indeed, the 'pursuit of more leisure time through domestic technology has long been a feature of (smart) home visions', and promotional materials for integrated technical systems frequently present them as simplifying and streamlining household processes.[129] Yet what is notably missing from these visions of the high-tech, hyperconnected smart home is housework itself.[130] Again, it would seem, massive infrastructural developments are transforming the character of work in the home, but labour-saving gains are not becoming a reality. Why might this be the case?

First, we would argue that these houses are frequently oriented towards *convenience*, rather than towards saving labour per se. This is a subtle distinction, but an important one. The idea of convenience bespeaks ease, removal of difficulty, and the lessening of annoyance, rather than a substantial saving of time or reduction of work. Convenience is less a matter of productivity, then, and more a matter of subjective user experience. It is also an idea that readily lends itself to operating at the micro scale – the scale on which many aspects of the smart home function. The automation of small tasks (e.g., turning on the lights as a person enters a room) and assistance with the management of the home (e.g., alerting the resident when they are out of milk) are all marketed as ways to alleviate the multitasking, harried nature of contemporary housekeeping.[131] This ultimately makes clear the ambitions of the smart home: reducing minor frictions in everyday life. In the words of one technology analyst,

An electric kettle or a vegetable peeler don't save hours of your day or free you from drudgery – they just remove a tiny piece of friction a few times every single day for the rest of your life. Today, the world of smart devices is trying to discover quite what other pieces of friction it might be able to address. By their nature, these often don't look like a problem at all until you automate them away – any more than adjusting your wing mirror by hand did.[132]

Far from fulfilling the perpetual dream of a self-cleaning house, then, the smart home looks to – at best – round off the edges of everyday irritations.

It is worth noting, however, that what are minor inconveniences for some can be much bigger hurdles for others, and the smart home may be more impactful for the latter group. Voice-based interfaces, like Amazon's Alexa, have found some favour with elderly people. Those with faltering eyesight (not to mention the blind and the partially sighted) may find it easier to get information by asking for it orally than by typing it out. Others with muscle tremors may find it easier to communicate a message through voice rather than through touch.[133] And our own personal experiences of carrying a baby on one hip and a toddler on the other have given us a newfound appreciation for hands-free interfaces – although we have admittedly yet to discover what happens when said baby and toddler learn to communicate fluently with smart devices for themselves.

However, these potential benefits also need to be set in the context of the new work that the smart home creates. This work arises in part from the need to integrate smart home devices into existing household behaviours and spaces. Robot vacuum cleaners, for example, save us the effort of manually dragging a Hoover over the carpet, but they also require that our spaces be arranged in very particular ways. Floors must be kept clear, potential obstacles repositioned, corners and crevices fenced off in case the device gets stuck, and staircases blocked to prevent potentially fatal falls for your Roomba. Rather than putting machines at the service of our living arrangements, we are adjusting our living arrangements to better accommodate our machines. Furthermore, the smart home creates a whole new series of technical tasks – updating devices, attending to notifications, getting appliances to work together, scouring the internet for quick fixes, and so on.[134] If you want a picture of the smart home future, imagine trying to fix a malfunctioning printer, forever. Households' resident IT experts can expect plenty more to do as we enter an era of digital housework.

Lastly, the work of the smart home, far from presenting a more balanced vision of reproductive labour, instead appears set to consolidate existing gendered hierarchies. Considering that in heterosexual households it is men who tend to take up the work of home IT maintenance under current technomaterial conditions, we are confronted with the possibility that the proliferation of digital housework may mean 'more work for father'.[135] Rather than encouraging an equitable redistribution of labour in the home, however, there is a risk that this would entrench existing gendered divisions between the work of 'digital' and 'traditional' housekeepers.[136] Moreover, this would replicate a characteristic of the existing division of reproductive labour in heterosexual couples whereby men tend to get the 'best' work. Already in housework and childcare, men tend to do work that is more autonomous, less routine, and more engaging than that of their female partners.[137] Much the same could be said of digital labour in the sphere of housework; those who lead on implementing smart home technologies often see it as a hobby – at least initially.[138] This work certainly has the potential to become a burden or annoyance over time, with users recounting how they wish the technologies would just work and not require endless supervision and maintenance, but it nevertheless demonstrates

that qualitative as well as quantitative differences in the performance of reproductive labour represent a substantial issue for
feminist post-work imaginaries. The equality of reproductive
labour is not just a matter of time.

Why then does the smart home appear increasingly ubiquitous? We should see this panoply of technologies not as a
response to consumer/user demand, but instead as a platform
capitalist-driven market. In the early twentieth century, manufacturers took newly affordable electrical motors and put them
into an overwhelming range of now motorised devices and
marketed them relentlessly. As Judy Wajcman notes, 'The drive
to motorize all household tasks – including brushing teeth,
squeezing lemons and carving meat – [was] less a response to
need than a reflection of the economic and technical capacity for
making motors.'[139] Today we are witnessing a similar dynamic
with smart home devices: the drive to make all household tasks
'smart' is less a response to need than a reflection of the economic and technical capacity for collecting data and producing
computer chips. As with the earlier period of motorisation, we
could see this period as an experimental stage where companies
throw innumerable smart devices at the wall in the hopes that
some of them stick.[140]

Whereas the drive to motorise household devices served a
simple profit logic of 'more devices = more sales = more profit',
smart homes are also underpinned by the unique imperatives
of platform capitalists. The first and most obvious point is the
extraction of data from domestic spaces. Whether the data has
an immediate purpose or not is immaterial as the relative cheap-
ness of extracting and storing it means companies can collect
it now in the hopes of finding a use for it later on. So smart
homes are becoming incredible data producers with the intimate behavioural patterns of households increasingly visible to

internet service providers, data brokers, and major platforms.[141] Some companies, such as Roomba, are openly embracing this shift by transforming themselves into data companies that promise unprecedented access to the internal layouts of homes.[142] It is unsurprising, then, to see a company like Amazon buy up these smaller but data rich companies.[143] Ultimately, for platform companies, 'home is where the data is'.[144]

Smart home devices – and particularly the voice-enabled hubs that are coming to centralise control over them – are also crucial to the platform-capitalist aim to expand, consolidate, and lock in access to their core services. It is the latter that are profit generating and the entrapment of users into a service also helps to ensure a long-term stream of income. As a result, platform capitalists are relentless in their push to embed their smart assistants and corresponding devices into homes. Amazon has been particularly prolific with the implementation of Alexa into myriad cheaply priced devices, ranging from microwaves to rings to clocks to eyeglasses.[145] Efforts like this have been supplemented by the provision of chips that make it simpler for others to add smart assistants to devices, as well as the general support being offered for third parties to use a particular platform's service. On top of this, deals with the devil are being made between platform capitalists, landlords, security companies, and police in an effort to further ensure these devices spread into homes – often against the wishes of users and renters.[146]

So while the smart home today reflects a similar dynamic to earlier periods of electrification and motorisation, the logics of data extraction inflect these historical patterns in unique ways. In the end, the smart home on offer today is a thoroughly capitalist product with predictable aims of profit, data, and control and with predictable lacunas when it comes to housework and the actual labour of reproductive workers in the domestic residence.

Far from being an emancipatory transformation of the home, the contemporary smart home is simply part of a long line of domestic technologies that have done little to illuminate or alleviate the burdens of reproductive labour.

Conclusion

We remain enmeshed in a world of domestic technologies whose potential to reduce work has gone largely unfulfilled. To be sure, there is evidence that this potential has played a role in facilitating women's entrance into the labour market.[147] But the capacity of these devices to significantly reduce household labour has been limited by the social organisation of the work, by the creation of new associated tasks, and by the general ratcheting up of expectations. The end result is that the Cowan paradox continues to hold, with hours spent on housework remaining broadly stable for all of the twentieth century. Prime-age adults spent twenty-six hours a week in 1900 on domestic work, while by 2005 that had only reduced to twenty-four hours a week.[148] For full-time housewives, the time spent on unpaid housework stayed steady at around fifty hours per week for the entirety of the twentieth century.[149] The gender shifts over this time have been notable, with women doing less work than before and men doing significantly more – but as one recent study discovered, there is no 'evidence that the diffusion of [domestic] appliances leads to any significant alteration in the traditional gender division of housework tasks'.[150] Technological impacts were minimal, as the far more important predictor of gender balance in unpaid domestic work is the employment status of women.

One key conclusion is that we do not have the technologies that we deserve. In a manner which is mutually reinforcing, the design of domestic technologies has been oriented both by a particularly gendered imaginary of how housework should be done and by a lack of input from the workers and users who are most involved with this labour process. The imagined figure here has traditionally been an individual woman – work was not imagined as being redistributed *within* the household, let alone beyond it, and a collective process of social reproduction was never envisaged. As a result of such constrained imaginaries, work that was reduced on the one hand proliferated and grew on the other, while alternative technologies lay undeveloped or unused because the social relations and infrastructures that they required didn't exist. Instead, convenience foods are packaged for individual families, appliances are built and priced for single family homes, and most domestic technologies spend the majority of their lifetimes stuffed in closets and tool sheds.[151] Even today, this gendered vision of domestic work continues to have a relentless hold on our imagination. Numerous purveyors of smart homes have created speculative futures filled with cutting-edge technologies – but always within a world of individual family homes and a conventional gendered division of labour.[152] Seemingly everything can change except the social relations surrounding domestic technologies. The dismal impact of domestic technologies in no small part lies here, then – with the social imaginary that orients the creation, deployment, and use of technologies. It is therefore not the case that technology is a panacea for post-work social reproduction – but neither is it a futile dead end. Technology might, under different social conditions, serve as an ally in the quest for temporal autonomy and for the recognition, redistribution, and reduction of reproductive labour.

3
Standards

As we have seen, a core paradox of technology used for social reproduction is that it rarely alleviates work. Rather than reducing the amount of time spent on work, more often than not it seems to lead to more work. One of the most significant ways in which work has been reasserted is through the ratcheting up of expectations. The more cleaning technology enters the home, the cleaner the home is expected to be. As kitchens are industrialised, the more complex and time-consuming food preparation becomes. As the flow of hot water is mechanised and bathrooms become a standard feature of homes, the more regular and extensive showering and personal grooming becomes, and so on. And all of these standards tend to become enforced through state representatives, advertising, and the weight of social expectations. While *capacities* for extending free time may have grown, social norms, standards, and expectations have evolved in such a way that these advances are minimised.

One can detect this tendency towards greater expectations even within the writings of some post-work thinkers. Indeed, it is interesting how frequently high (that is to say, extremely labour intensive) domestic standards are mentioned in post-work

theorising across a number of traditions. The German collective
Krisis Group, for instance, insists that the labour involved in
'the preparation of a delicious meal' will never be eradicated.[1]
Andre Gorz celebrates 'looking after and decorating a house
... cooking good meals, entertaining guests' and so on.[2] Kate
Soper looks forward to a world where 'cooking, sewing, and
mending – even cleaning – [become] more rewarding'.[3] And
William Morris's classic utopia *News from Nowhere* sees the work
of hospitality, tending to others, and making spaces beautiful
proliferate substantially. Upon his arrival in his new world, for
example, Morris's narrator encounters a group of women who
immediately interrupt what they're doing to wait on him hand
and foot. Upon instruction from one of their male peers, these
women 'bustled about on our behoof, and presently came and
took us by the hands and led us to a table in the pleasantest
corner of the hall, where our breakfast was spread for us'.[4] While
preparing food, decorating houses, looking after guests, and so
on can be a source of immense pleasure when conducted in a
self-directed fashion, placing these things at the centre of post-
work imaginaries can all too easily allow coercive obligation to
resurface in an unacknowledged form.[5]

Moreover, given that gender politics have gone largely unmen-
tioned in many post-work projects, the chances are fairly high
that women and others who have traditionally performed this
work will continue to be stuck with it in such a future society.
For those who wish to dispose of their time in ways other than
cooking, cleaning, and caring, it may be advisable to think less
about the heights of domestic splendour to which we will all be
able to aspire after the end of work and more about reducing
the disciplinary force of certain social expectations. While these
activities should not be eradicated for those who enjoy them, it
is our contention that restrictive norms should not be allowed to

petrify around reproductive labour and that ideas about socially acceptable living standards should be revisited. The post-work imaginary should be as excited by the prospect of high-quality canteens as it is about labour-intensive home-cooked meals.[6]

Standards of cleanliness, comfort, and parenting, as well as busyness in general, all have a history, as this chapter will show. Moreover, this history tends to have a *direction*: norms of 'comfort and cleanliness are subject to distinctive forms of escalation and standardisation'.[7] While this chapter will show that these tendencies are not unidirectional, it is nevertheless the case that norms around things like the cleanliness of the home, the presentability of the person, and the care of children have tended to become both more demanding and more universal. The result is that, even to the extent to which technologies of social reproduction may be capable of saving labour, they are put to use in the name of increased output and higher standards rather than the reduction of working time. How were these seemingly natural habits and norms constructed, and what's the alternative? Given the gendered dynamics around standards, a loosening of expectations is also an important way to reduce the burden of social reproduction and foster gender equality.[8] Our aim should not be to indiscriminately reduce standards, but instead to be aware of the ways in which our social systems *oblige* us to accept certain norms without subjecting them to conscious deliberation, so that we might imagine better ways forward.[9]

Never Clean Enough

We can begin by examining the escalating standards around cleanliness. Far from being an ontological given, our notions of what is clean and what is dirty are socially constructed. They are the product of a complex combination of scientific knowledge, social habits and prejudices, morality, civilisational discourses, and technological affordances. The idea of cleanliness is typically wrapped up with conceptions of the respectable. In fact, cleanliness was often presented as an absolute necessity to maintaining social order.[10] One of the first economists to study the home, John Leeds, claimed that 'the increase in cleanliness of home and person contributes to the growth of democracy ... Cleanliness is not only next to Godliness, but it is essential to the establishment of the Brotherhood of Man.'[11] Standards of cleanliness also play a role in drawing social divisions, with vague notions of an 'improper smell' often invoked in discrimination against other cultures. Soap was seen as one of the British Empire's great gifts to other countries. The Unilever company even made their company slogan the blunt pronouncement that 'soap is civilisation'.[12] Cleanliness comes to be seen as an expression (and reproduction) of social order, as a way to enter into 'respectable' civil society, and as an intrinsically civilising practice. Eugenicists made cleanliness a core part of their programme for "improving" racial stock – at least in the case of those they felt could be elevated to respectability.[13] Even revolutionary communes have placed a significant emphasis on cleanliness, with competitions held and inspection groups formed to ensure strict criteria were met.[14]

Cleanliness is also a mode of appearance within society; it is a way of signifying a particular status. It is not for nothing that the working class has often been represented as 'the great unwashed' and why cleanliness became such a marker of respectability.[15] Being dirty comes to indicate that one is unworthy. In many countries, the moral division between the clean and the dirty can take an acute social form. In India, for instance, higher castes will often hire members of lower castes to deal with the work of cleaning, with the latter deemed 'symbolically unclean and impure by birth'.[16] Similarly, Black women and immigrant women have historically been relegated to 'dirty' domestic work so that their white middle-class employers could keep their distance from the work of the household.[17] All of these multifaceted elements of cleanliness have played a role in various elements of housework – from personal hygiene to laundry to house cleaning.

Personal Hygiene

While our focus in this book is not on personal care, the history of bathing and showering is an illuminating example to introduce some of the changes undergone in the name of cleanliness. Notions of personal hygiene have been heavily tied up with conceptions of the body. When, in the sixteenth century, it was believed that the body was in fine balance between different humours, bathing was thought to open up pores and let in evils. Miasma-based theories of contagion, by contrast, saw disease being transmitted via the air, and so the removal of smells became particularly significant (with perfumes and other fragrances sometimes positioned as a way to combat these diseases). Bathing, in this episteme, was subject to conflicting advice: some conceived of dirt as a protective layer against airborne contagions, while others saw bodily odour as a warning sign to be dealt with.[18] With the germ theory of disease, however, cleanliness took on an unambiguous value as a signifier of health. Moreover, with germs being invisible to the naked eye, even the appearance of cleanliness could be insufficient to ensure good health – the path was thus opened for constant self-surveillance and obsessive germaphobia. Knowledge of disease and notions of hygiene and sanitation, alongside changing conceptions of the body, therefore all played a role in shifting standards of bathing and personal grooming.

Yet hygiene standards were also tied up with technological affordances. When bathing meant lugging water into the home, warming it up, and removing the waste afterwards, the sheer amount of work required limited how often baths could be taken. The rise of indoor plumbing and public water systems drastically altered the calculations here and enabled people to bathe more readily (though this was not without issues, as the first – wealthy – homes to get indoor plumbing were often plagued by poor construction and sewage issues that actually made them less sanitary).[19]

Lastly, in a story that will repeat throughout this chapter, the advertising industry played a major role in igniting the escalation of personal hygiene standards. Deodorants and antiperspirants were invented in the early years of the twentieth century but were met with indifference by most of the public. People had to be convinced of new problems like 'bad breath' and 'body odour'. Products like Listerine shifted from being disinfectants for medical surgeries to being solutions to the newly invented disease of halitosis.[20] Women were a constant focus of the new advertising industry, and ads started to play on fears of social embarrassment. As one ad bluntly put it,

> You're a pretty girl, Mary, and you're smart about most things. But you're just a bit stupid about yourself ... There are so many pretty Marys in the world who never seem to sense the real reason for their aloneness. In this smart modern age, it's against the code for a girl (or a man, either) to carry the repellent odour of underarm perspiration on clothing and person. It's a fault which never fails to carry its own punishment – unpopularity. And justly.[21]

Advertisers also struck at mothers' sense of responsibility for their children, squarely placing the blame on them if their family became sick. The Association of American Soap and Glycerine Producers – slyly rebranded in 1927 as the Cleanliness Institute – went so far as to produce children's books espousing the importance of clean hands and washing frequently.[22] While social norms around personal hygiene may have eventually risen up in any case, it was the soap and deodorant and bathroom furnishing manufacturers, in collaboration with the new advertising industry, which hastened the process.

Laundry

Laundering is perhaps the clearest example of incrementally increasing standards. If we go back to the 1800s, we find that most families rarely washed clothes – typically, only once every few weeks.[23] Yet with the introduction of the domestic washing machine, the frequency of laundering shot up. By the 1960s, most families were washing clothes multiple times a week. By some accounts, Americans are now doing laundry almost three times more often than they did in the 1950s.[24] Today, in countries such as Japan, it is common for people to do laundry every single day.[25] Laundry has gone from being 'a weekly nightmare to an unending task'.[26] How did this come to be?

The first reason, of course, can be found in the new technological affordances provided by the washing machine. The burden of doing a single load of laundry decreased dramatically with these technologies, thereby enabling the frequency of washing to increase. Yet while technology may provide opportunities, it does not determine changes. The possibility of more frequent washing also required the *demand* for more frequent washing. For this we need to look at the influence of both advertising and broader social norms.

Women's magazines were – and indeed, still are – a major vector for domestic advertising. After World War I, these magazines increasingly presented laundering as a labour of love – as something which a good housewife should desire to do for her family.[27] Indeed, in these advertisements 'the idea that women wanted washing machines because they saved labour [was] lost in stereotypes of women as acquisitive, emotional, frivolous, and houseproud'.[28] Emerging social norms also played a role, even as advertisers eventually moved away from heavy-handed guilt tripping. Workers who sought a job would likely have to interact with their upper-class employers, meaning that a particular style of self-presentation was required to get a job. Equally, as parents internalised these norms, they began to worry about how their children might appear to others. Ruth Schwartz Cowan, more attuned to 'the senseless tyranny of spotless shirts and immaculate floors' than most, nevertheless recounts her own experience of worry and concern about her children appearing dirty.[29] We might also draw a distinction between a culture which washes clothes once they are considered visibly dirty and a culture which washes clothes after they've been worn once. The Japanese, for instance, tend to fall into the latter category, while South Korea tends more towards the former.[30]

Standards of laundering have admittedly seen competing tendencies in recent years. On the one hand, it is clear that some of the 'extras' of laundering have disappeared. Expectations around, for instance, perfectly ironed and starched clothing have drastically diminished, even among the professional classes. Whereas once it might have been expected that a housewife would ensure her husband's shirts were immaculate for work, today this is largely unheard of. There has been a definite lowering of standards in this area (though we should also note the role played by new 'wrinkle-free' and 'easy iron' fabrics in reducing this work). Furthermore, professional settings now tend to permit more casual styles of dress and the vanguard tech sector has pushed a slacker aesthetic even for CEOs. The pandemic-accelerated turn towards working from home has arguably exacerbated some of these normative shifts around professional self-presentation as, for many, lounge and leisure wear became a regular lockdown uniform.

At the same time, though, the standards applicable to laundry have arguably increased, largely driven by detergent manufacturers. This industry remains big business, with a market size of more than $60 billion in 2020,[31] and is the focus of intense research and product development.[32] Every year sees the introduction of new products promising whiter whites, brighter colours, more subtle fragrances, and better stain removal. There is an expectation, fostered by the industry, that our clothes should always be as bright, fresh, and immaculate as they were on the day we purchased them. So while there have been some diminished expectations for the work surrounding laundry, it would nonetheless seem that social expectations continue to tend towards ever-cleaner clothes.

House Cleaning

Until the 1900s, the Western household for most people was predominantly a grimy place. Many nineteenth-century homes had dirt floors, with all the dust, mud, and resistance to cleaning that this implies. Wood-burning stoves sent soot into every nook and cranny. And the streets outside — filled with muck, horse manure, and refuse — were impossible to keep from being tracked indoors. Cleaning, as a result, was not done in any modern sense and the idea of a proper clean really only implied the annual 'spring clean'.[33] Yet even under these difficult circumstances, cleanliness was a marker of class status. Those who could afford it would hire labourers (typically immigrants and women of colour) to keep their homes as presentable as possible.[34] Meanwhile, working-class families sought to keep things clean as well, urged on by the social pressure created by norms.[35]

The late 1800s and early 1900s created new motivation for higher cleanliness standards, however. This drive was particularly underpinned by growing knowledge about how diseases spread and how they could be combatted. While the late nineteenth century consolidation of the germ theory of disease was the major impetus for higher standards of cleanliness, the hygiene and sanitarian movement had already begun by 1815. As the germ theory gained favour throughout the middle of the century, there was more and more pressure placed on individuals to maintain higher standards of cleanliness. A norm of higher cleanliness passed from the professional and upper classes – mediated via domestic scientists, sanitary engineers, and health professionals – down to working-class families.[36] Diseases were no longer seen as a necessary result of poverty; rather they could be combatted by sufficient scrubbing, washing, ventilation, and general attentiveness to the microbial environment of the home. Similarly, the responsibility for reducing disease moved from implacable matters of fate to suddenly being in the all-too-human hands of the mother. Expert advice not only insisted that women should desire to take control of this work, but often argued that any sicknesses that arose in the family would be their fault for not ensuring the house was kept clean enough. Even dust was, for a time, deemed to be a potentially deadly invader.[37] As a result, cleaning was supposed to be deeper and to happen more frequently, and expectations for the work of social reproduction escalated accordingly.

From the 1920s onwards, this drive for higher standards was further pushed by companies keen to sell a whole new range of consumer products to a growing mass market.[38] In the fevered visions of marketers, 'neglect of housecleaning [became] tan-tamount to child abuse [and ads] played directly to maternal fears and guilt'.[39] New technologies and cleaning products were promoted as enabling spring cleaning to happen every day. Ideas about hygiene were used to emphasise how important it was to keep a clean house and how, conveniently, their new consumer product would enable people to do just that.[40] Mothers were again a particular focus of these ads, often interpellated as personally responsible for the health of the family.[41] A 1932 Syracuse Washing Machine Corporation advertisement asked, 'How precious is your baby's health?' Guilt became a way to sell goods, and women's identities became increasingly tied into this work as well. Cleaning became 'an expression of the housewife's personality and her affection for her family'.[42] A dirty house was a sign of failure and caring as a practice was increasingly conflated with *being* caring as a disposition.[43]

These demands for cleanliness arguably peaked in the imme-diate postwar period. More recent decades have witnessed a significant decline in the time spent in domestic cleaning.[44] As women have moved into the workplace and men in mixed-gender households have neglected to 'pick up the slack', it would seem that the standards for what constitutes an acceptably clean house have diminished. Many have ceased to prize the pris-tine and immaculate home of the 1950s ideal and have instead found themselves at home in the rather more dishevelled and lived-in domestic spaces of today. Survey research backs this up: despite less time being spent on cleaning the home, people state they are more happy with the cleanliness of their home than in decades past.[45] Cleaning the home today is also much less likely to involve the range of specialised cleaning products that once guaranteed a spotless home.[46] And today we are seeing some reaction against the ultra-hygienic – with warnings that excessively clean houses might enable childhood leukaemia and that showering too often can eliminate beneficial bacteria.[47] In fact, if not done properly, efforts to clean the home can simply spread germs around.[48]

As with other standards, however, class position makes a difference here – upper-middle-class households may be spending less *time* on cleaning, but they are also spending more *money* on cleaners to ensure 'proper' appearances are maintained. The rise of 'cleanfluencers' is another emergent normative trend, positioning housework as a kind of self-care or therapeutic well-being trend.[49] And the COVID-19 pandemic certainly opened a new awareness of hygiene and fostered greater attentiveness to potential contamination via surfaces, interpersonal touch, and so on. Ensuring that people devoted sufficient time to handwashing became the initial focus of major public health campaigns, for instance – a focus that later shifted as knowledge about the airborne qualities of the virus developed. But at the same time, research shows that those working from home reduced the time they spent doing things like showering, shaving, and putting on makeup[50] – cleanliness being at least partially tied up with anxieties about social appropriateness, respectability, and how one is perceived rather than a straightforward expression of individual desire.

Ornamental Cookery

A similar pattern of rising and falling standards appears in the case of cooking. Prior to the 1900s, the work of food consumption was primarily oriented around the production of food rather than its preparation. Growing, tending, and harvesting that which would become food took priority over the creation of elaborate meals.[51] Instead, meals were functional and simple:

stews, breads, potatoes, and so on. This all begins to change over the course of the twentieth century.

Domestic Ideals

As the new century dawned, the emerging disciplines of domestic science and home economics encouraged housewives to systematically elevate standards, including those around cooking and meal taking. Some saw co-operative housekeeping, shared kitchens, and communal dining rooms as one way to ensure high-quality meals and proper nutrition, but there was also a new emphasis on productivity and systematicity within the single-family home. This drew upon an intensifying interest in industrial efficiency and the rationalisation of production. Home economist Christine Frederick, for example, advocated for the principles of scientific management to be brought within the home. Industrial engineer (and mother of twelve) Lillian Gilbreth similarly turned her attention to the domestic residence, applying 'Taylorist ideas of breaking down activities through time and motion studies, and increasing efficiency through ergonomic design. Human-centred domestic ergonomics resulted in kitchens in which 'everything lay within arm's reach'[52] – an idea that we will discuss in more detail in relation to architectural design in Chapter 5.

As ambitious as these plans were, however, their utility proved to be somewhat limited. As Ehrenreich and English put it,

> industrial scientific management techniques had almost nothing to offer the housewife. First, the scale of household work was much too small for the savings accrued by time-motion studies to mean much. The seconds saved by peeling potatoes with Frederick's scientific method ('Walk to shelf … pick up knife …' etc.) might add up to something in a factory processing thousands of potatoes but

would be insignificant in the preparation of dinner for four. Second, as later domestic scientists themselves realized, in the household, the manager and the worker are the same person. The whole point of Taylor's management science – to concentrate planning and intellectual skills in management specialists – is necessarily lost in the one-woman kitchen.[53]

Domestic science was not simply an attempt to save housewives time and effort, however. (Indeed, new practices of household organisation and management were more than capable of absorbing any time saved elsewhere.) It was also an effort to raise standards around things such as nutrition and food hygiene at a time when discoveries were being made about the role of vitamins and minerals in individual health.[54] If anything, Frederick saw the possibility of more free time as an existential quandary for middle-class housewives, whom she saw as searching for challenge, individual meaning, and a sense of purpose. Fortunately, she decided this would not pose a long-term problem, given that 'as housewives became more efficient, their standards would rise apace'.[55]

At the same time, the reformist efforts of turn-of-the-century domestic science (entangled as they were with ideas about 'good taste' and appropriate conduct) could also reproduce a parochial set of class values. In the hands of some of its white middle-class proponents, home economics advanced the idea that there was a correct way to lay a table, for example – one which didn't take into account different approaches to the act of eating or uneven access to resources.[56] In the US, early public kitchens sought particularly to educate the poor, and often struggled to persuade immigrant populations to give up their 'preferred national dishes and spices to the plain, institutionalised menu which domestic science dictated'.[57] The effort to increase food standards was particularly important for feminists in the 1900s, given the preponderance of malnutrition and food adulteration at the time. However, this effort was often bound together with a set of beliefs about respectability that neither saved time nor improved nutrition, but rather imposed a very particular set of expectations upon people.

By the end of World War II, cooking standards were reaching their zenith as men returned to their jobs and women were shuffled back into isolated homes. Experiences during the war also led to newfound appreciation for elaborate meals: 'War-time deprivations set the stage for postwar appetites.'[58] The ideology of domesticity and the housewife were dominant here, and cooking and cleaning came to be seen as not only the primary role for married women, but also as a key way for them to express themselves as individuals. At the same time, new technologies such as convenience foods and pre-packaged meals were becoming available as means to alleviate the work of cooking.[59] Rather than saving time, however, this technology was often marketed as a way to facilitate the creation of more varied and sophisticated meals.[60] Advertising, likewise, focused on the promise of allowing women to be better mothers and wives – rather than on any promise of reducing work.[61] Cookbooks and marketers of the time therefore insisted on using pre-packaged ingredients and meals as a *foundation* upon which to build.[62] The 1950s were, in the words of Roland Barthes, the time of 'ornamental cookery' – concerned with glazes and sauces and elaborate supplements to basic meals:

> Glazing, in *Elle*, serves as background for unbridled beautification: chiselled mushrooms, punctuation of cherries, motifs of carved lemon, shavings of truffle, silver pastilles, arabesques of glacé fruit: the underlying coat (and this is why I called it a sediment, since

the food itself becomes no more than an indeterminate bed-rock) is intended to be the page on which can be read a whole rococo cookery (there is a partiality for a pinkish colour).[63]

For the middle-class housewife, dinners were expected to be punctual and often elaborate. And dinner parties were common, with a plethora of snacks and drinks to be made available to guests, often cohering around some sort of theme.[64] What was technically possible in terms of culinary convenience, then, did not dictate the aspirational social norms around cooking and eating; the availability of TV dinners did not deflate the swollen (and profoundly disciplinary) expectations regarding gendered reproductive labour in the kitchen.

Foodie Culture

Social expectations surrounding the preparation of food have been changing for many years now. With the exception of France, most countries spend much less time on cooking in recent decades. In America this tendency has gone the furthest, with a typical individual spending only thirty minutes cooking and cleaning dishes per day (compared with fifty-two minutes for the OECD average).[65] Part of this change has to do with the rise, in the 1980s, of the microwave and the ecosystem of quick microwaveable products that the food industry produced around it.[66] But the decrease in time spent cooking is also the result of a change in the kinds of cooking undertaken. Indeed, when we look at countries more closely, we see a significant move away from the 1950s ideal of domesticity – in no small part because of the rise of the dual-earner family and the subsequent time pressures put on households. British households of the 1950s, for instance, often used to have hot cooked meals for breakfast; today they tend to rely on cereal. Likewise, lunches were often comparatively labour-intensive roasts or stews, whereas today it is more likely a simple sandwich (and a depressing, store-bought meal deal sandwich at that). If dinners once entailed multiple courses, today such extravagances are typically reserved for guests or special occasions.[67] In both cleaning and cooking, one could argue, labour-intensive norms are in decline.

However, there has also been a resurgent push for elaborate home cooking in recent years. Often pitched as a reaction to worries about industrial food production, increases in obesity, and general health and environmental concerns, this new 'foodie culture' has begun to generate impossible standards (as aspirational norms, if not daily realities). The main demands of this movement tend to be oriented around more organic food and more home-cooked meals as antidotes to commercial, packaged, allegedly chemical-infused food. The result has been major increases in things like farmers' markets (over 8,600 in America now) and organic food sales (increasing annually by 10–15 per cent for decades).[68]

The rise of this foodie culture is not just about health, either. There is cultural status attached to being a foodie – one is seen as being progressive and refined. Even children's eating habits become representative of the family's class status.[69] Are they appreciating sophisticated food? Eating their vegetables? Are they picky eaters? Baby food is particularly subject to social pressures towards organic, made-from-scratch meals. And yet, the aspiration to be a foodie (and to be seen as a foodie) involves an immense amount of work. At a minimum, it involves the work of finding and shopping for the appropriate ingredients, finding deals to make one's shopping list fit within a grocery budget, staying up to date on research around what is healthy, finding new recipes to try, testing meals out with families (and often seeing these rejected by children who would prefer chicken nuggets!) – and of course the labour of cooking the meals from scratch. While being vegetarian or vegan is becoming easier in many countries in the Global North, these choices still demand significant effort to ensure proper caloric and vitamin intake. Perversely, for some, the very existence of labour-saving technology is itself an imperative to spend more time cooking. Home cooking advocate Joel Salatin, for instance, says that in comparison to our great-grandparents, 'if our generation can't do at least as well with our 40-hour work week and kitchen tech, then we deserve to eat adulterated pseudo food that sends us to an early grave'.[70] In a classic case of moral blackmail, he goes on to say that children surely do not deserve this. Of course these invocations of great-grandparents rely on mythical ideas of the past. Most members of this previous generation were more likely to be eating stale and monotonous food, plagued by scarcity rather than enhanced by an abundance of fresh, organic produce. Yet these imagined pasts are motivating factors for much of the contemporary foodie culture. And despite the reduction in cooking and cleaning up time that most countries have seen, there are nevertheless strong social norms against this.

So while standards around cooking have to some extent declined from their postwar peak, particularly as an activity demanded of the individualised figure of the housewife, they have perhaps taken on a more dispersed form. Concerns around food today tend to focus less on the ornateness of the presentation, and more on the perceived nutritional and symbolic value of the meals being served.

The Rug Rat Race

When it comes to the work of childcare, two major changes loom large. First, women are significantly more likely to work for a wage today than they were seventy years ago (a point we will return to in more depth in the next chapter). This therefore restricts the time available for the delivery of unwaged care. The second major transformation is the widespread expansion of state support for childcare over the past few decades. Across the advanced capitalist countries, there has been growing support for childcare whether through cash- or tax-based subsidies, support for parental leave, or public provision of childcare services.[71] This is a striking development – with 'family policy spending [expanding] more than any other social policy domain' during an age in which the welfare state has been the subject of intense pressure to control spending.[72] In fact, 'the only welfare state expansions since 1990 have occurred in activation and in work/ family reconciliation policies.'[73]

The effect of this growing investment can be seen in enrolment rates for childcare provision. As of 2016, 33 per cent of young children (zero to two years of age) in OECD countries are in formal childcare, for an average of thirty hours a week, and the proportion of children participating has been growing in most countries.[74] Beyond the youngest children, the use of formal childcare increases significantly and has continued to rise in recent years. Between 1998 and 2007, participation jumped from 30 to 50 per cent.[75] And children are spending more time than ever before in day care and school programmes.[76] As it stands, 80 per cent of four-year-olds in most OECD countries attend preschool or some other form of early childhood care and education.[77] Figures 3.1 and 3.2 summarise this trend, with a focus on children who receive thirty or more hours of care per week. (These are children who are, in other words, receiving levels of formal childcare that might allow two parents to work full-time jobs.) While the shift to a wage work–centric, childcare-supporting regime of social reproduction remains an

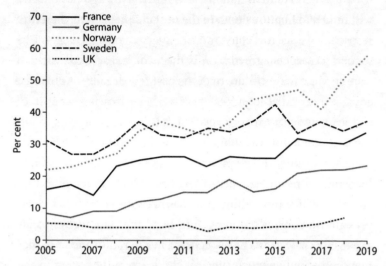

Figure 3.1: Proportion of children under age three in thirty or
more hours of formal childcare per week, 2005–2019[81]

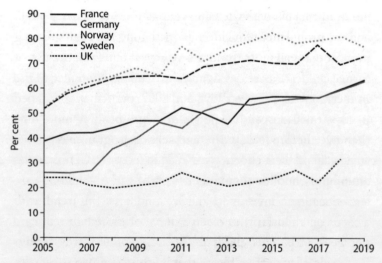

Figure 3.2: Proportion of children age three to school age in thirty
or more hours of formal childcare per week, 2005–2019[82]

'incomplete revolution',[78] there is nevertheless a significant trend within OECD nations towards a similar approach to childcare support.[79] We see this convergence, for example, in the so-called Barcelona targets agreed by EU heads of state in 2002, which sought to provide childcare to at least 33 per cent of children under three and at least 90 per cent of children between three and the mandatory school age.[80]

The impact of these two changes on how much time parents spend on childcare would seem to be obvious: with parents working more and governments providing more childcare, parents must be spending less time with their children. And yet against all expectations, hours spent in this activity appear to have been *increasing*.[83] American mothers, for instance, are spending about as much time on childcare as they were in the 1920s.[84] The nature of this time has changed, with more of it being devoted to interactive time, often concentrated into the weekends, and less of it devoted to passive childminding.[85] Yet the trend remains, with women appearing to reduce time spent on housework and men reducing paid work time and leisure time all in order to spend more time with children.[86] How could this be?

Little Strangers

In recent decades we have arguably begun to witness a shift in the domestic ideal. If women were once lauded as house-wives, and if their efforts were channelled into the upkeep of both family and home, the focus is now more specifically on *motherhood* and investment of time and effort into children. This reflects a long process of historical change in the relation-ship between parents (particularly mothers) and their progeny. Contemporary perspectives on childcare differ notably from historical understandings of the labour of raising children. As

Juliet Schor notes, even the idea of a 'deep biological bond' between mothers and children is a relatively recent invention.[87] A few hundred years ago, it was quite common for a newborn child to be referred to as 'it' or 'the little stranger'.[88] Childcare was not something a parent might devote themselves to but rather something done alongside other activities.[89] For wealthy families, feeding was often outsourced to wetnurses and parents had relatively little direct involvement in baby care.[90] Babies in all families would often be swaddled in such a way that they could be left alone for long periods of time. In poorer households, once children reached an appropriate age, they would likely become servants or apprentices, often in other people's houses. The lack of contraceptives or reliable abortion care meant *having* children was all too easy, while a lack of adequate nutritional or financial resources meant *keeping* children was all too difficult. The end result was that it was relatively common for children to simply be abandoned by families who could not provide for them.[91]

The nineteenth century saw major changes when 'the idealisation of mother love, vigilant attention to the needs of children, and recognition of the unique potential of each individual came to dominate child-rearing ideology'.[92] With these new ideas came new institutions (schools, children's hospitals, orphanages, and so on) as the functions of raising children (most notably, education, healthcare, and religious pedagogy) were gradually shifted outwards from the family to civil society and the state. While this moved some work outside of the home, it also meant that labour-intensive standards of childcare and education were simultaneously passed on through these institutions to working-class families (mothers especially), often via processes of social exclusion for those who failed to meet them.[93] This increased attention being paid to children was facilitated by the reduction in routine housework brought about by new domestic technologies.[94] By the twentieth century, the tasks of motherhood were coming to more closely approximate what we recognise today: breastfeeding, toilet training, trips to physicians, weighing children frequently to make sure they're healthy, attending school meetings, scheduling activities, worrying about germs and nutrition, and so on.[95] Women's identity was increasingly tied up with heteronormative and reproductive futurist expectations surrounding their ability to meet the social standards of motherhood.[96] Ultimately, modern childhood – where children spend their time largely devoted to education and personal growth, rather than work – is a recent invention that was not consolidated until after World War II. Even the term 'parenting' was not widely used until the 1970s.[97] We should stress that this is not to hold up seventeenth-century parenting as a lost ideal, but rather to demonstrate how standards have risen and produced more work.

Raising Human Capital

Since the 1980s, many countries have witnessed an increase in what we can broadly call 'intensive parenting'.[98] If cleaning and cooking have diminished in importance and the standards surrounding them have loosened, the opposite holds for childcare. Whereas 'back in the fifties, women were told to master the differences between oven cleaners and floor wax and special sprays for wood; today they're told to master the differences between toys that hone problem-solving skills and those that encourage imaginative play'.[99] Spending interactive time with children can be among the most pleasurable aspects of parenting, but under intensive parenting there is a single-minded instrumentalisation of such activities. From their earliest years, children are the object of intense focus. Parents are pressured to make sure their offspring are getting the right stimuli (even in the womb!), ingesting the proper (organic, home-made) nutrition, and receiving the parental attention and discipline required for a well-developed, high-achieving young person to emerge. As they grow older, the number of supposedly necessary tasks only increases as children (particularly more affluent children) are scheduled into multiple responsibilities: football leagues, piano classes, ballet lessons, programming tutorials, Chinese lessons, and more. The work of social reproduction extends as parents fill their time with researching the best activities in which to enrol their offspring, coordinating multiple schedules, ferrying children from one place to another, and often learning along-side their kids so that they can support their development. If and when these offspring continue on to university, more and more parents are remaining heavily involved in their lives – to the point where some universities report having to adapt to the demands of intensive parenting.[100] As a result, despite a decline in fertility and the expansion of waged work, parents are spend-ing more time than ever before on their children – particularly interactive and developmental time.

Why is this happening? In short, it can be considered a quite rational response to changing material conditions: rising ine-quality, a shift to 'human capital'-centric economies, and the intensified competition characteristic of contemporary capital-ism. Parents, anxious about a dwindling number of 'good jobs', aim to get their children into the top schools as a way to give them a chance in today's world.[101] If parenting in the postwar period was about creating emotional attachments between mother and child, parenting today is presented as a matter of cultivating human capital.[102] Such a goal involves sustained preparation and training in competition with other children – what some have called the 'rug rat race'.[103] Given the role of competition here, it is no wonder that countries with higher levels of inequality are far more likely to adopt intensive parenting styles.[104] Yet there are also anxieties about class status at play here. Children must be seen as being part of a 'good family' in order to meet children from other 'good families', with everyone deploying the appropriate signifiers to indicate their suitability. As one researcher notes, what is important about the food a middle-class parent serves at a playdate is not necessarily its nutritional value, but whether or not it's organic.[105]

Intensive parenting, in other words, is an important means of class reproduction. Wealthier families 'invest' more in their children in an attempt to reproduce their class position across generations.[106] As spending on children increases with family income, wealthier families tend to spend more and inequalities are reflected in children's development.[107] Research shows that families across classes are increasing the proportion of income they spend on childcare and education (versus toys and clothing),[108] but the imbalances between rich and poor families are only increasing. Whereas rich families once financially spent four times more than poor families on educational enrichment for their children, today that figure is closer to seven times as much.[109] Similar patterns hold for the amount of *time* that families spend on their children: as they move up the class system, parents tend to spend more time on their children.[110] Likewise, the hyper-scheduling of extracurriculars is predominantly an affliction of relatively affluent households. While parents of all kinds have increased the hours they spend on childcare, it is those higher up in the class structure who have most increased their time.[111] Similarly, it is largely middle-class families that are in a position to make labour-intensive efforts to foster and direct their children's development.[112] Hurdles that make reaching these standards more difficult – a lack of money, a dearth of time, or a child with extra developmental needs, for instance – don't remove the demand for the work of intensive parenting, they just place more guilt on those who can't perform it.[113]

This intensive type of parenting is also reflected – and reinforced – in legal form. A massively risk-averse culture has driven institutions to adopt rules and regulations that prohibit a wide variety of activities deemed to be too dangerous. Schools in many countries, for instance, reinforce particular ideas of parenting through the adoption of 'zero tolerance' policies on any type of disruption, with parents apt to be dragged in for 'a chat' if their child breaks these expectations. In America, custody laws similarly impose intensive parenting as a social norm. Those parents who spend the most time with their children are more likely to get custody of them, and time spent with children is also more likely to reduce any child support payments.[114] And for Black women and poor women, attempts to evade intensive parenting and grant their children increased independence are far more likely to lead peers and authorities to question the adequacy of their parenting. As a result, some mothers have 'far greater freedom to let their children roam independently without fear of losing them to foster care – not because they care more, but because their race and class largely exempt them from [child protective services'] scrutiny'.[115] (Notably, Utah had to pass a law clarifying that it was not a crime for children to roam freely.[116]) Through mechanisms such as these, the social norms of contemporary parenting acquire the heft of state punishment. While other standards around social reproduction have declined somewhat since postwar peaks, then, the demands of childcare have shot inexorably upward.[117]

Fix Up, Look Busy

In the early 1900s, sociologist Thorstein Veblen famously delineated the existence of a 'leisure class' whose class status was, in no small part, expressed by their ability to withdraw from work. The aristocrats of the feudal era had been able to separate themselves from the daily grind, and many from the new capitalist classes followed in this tradition. Whereas the lower classes – quite literally, the *working* classes – were forced to work in order to survive, the upper classes were able to extract themselves from the 'spiritual contamination' of work.[118] Instead they signified their social status through overt expressions of idleness, frivolity, and consumption. Ownership over fixed capital enabled them to sit idly by and live off of passive income from their property, while the workers struggled to make ends meet. As Veblen writes, for the leisure class 'abstention from labour is not only an honorific or meritorious act, but it presently comes to be a requisite of decency'.[119] Few who were wealthy enough would deign to be seen engaged in drudgery.

Conspicuous Busyness

Today things are rather different.[120] Whereas aristocratic idleness may once have been a marker of high social status, today it is work and busyness which provide the social norm that many elites strive for. While it overlaps with expressions of wealth and conspicuous consumption, the ideal being sought here is the appearance of being important, valued, self-disciplined, and in demand. This expectation of busyness is expressed in the first place via longer working hours. Unlike most of the other standards that we have discussed in this chapter – but in line with Veblen's thesis around the norms of the upper classes – the standard of busyness applies perhaps most strongly to the affluent.[121] In the US, for instance, while there has been a general increase in long (fifty-plus-hour) working weeks, this has been concentrated particularly among salaried professional and managerial workers.[122] There are also greater expectations surrounding longer working hours. In part, this appears to be a result of the shift to service-based economies, where the productivity of any given worker is increasingly difficult to discern. Instead, workers have learned that *performances* of productivity can be a key means by which to demonstrate their contributions to a company. People who don't put in long work hours come to be seen as the odd ones out. And those with caring responsibilities tend to be disproportionally affected by these expectations, as they often find that they do not have the time or resources to meet them.[123]

This is not only an affliction of the professional classes, though, as people from lower classes also find themselves increasingly working long hours, though typically due to holding a number of different jobs.[124] There is a material compulsion to the growth of multiple jobs – namely the stagnating wages facing many workers and the rise of a gig economy that evades labour laws – but there is also an ideological infrastructure emerging to justify this situation. Celebrations of 'hustle culture' are becoming a key means through which greater expectations of busyness are being normalised. In these celebrations, typically expressed via social media content, perpetual positivity is the order of the day in the face of endless struggles to get rich. Typically, everyone else is presented as lazy – unwilling to work on weekends! sleeping in late! – and the secret to success is revealed to be a simple matter of ever more work.[125] As one freelancer platform infamously put it in their marketing, 'You eat a coffee for lunch. You follow through on your follow through. Sleep deprivation is your drug of choice. You might be a doer.' Adhering to hustle culture means taking up side hustles (and monetising hobbies) whenever possible. In the UK, for instance, microwork on digital platforms has become a key way to supplement the income from other jobs.[126] Given the imperative to work all the time, to gather more and more side hustles, to constantly be productive, it's no surprise that some of those committed to hustle culture end up feeling guilty when they're not working.

The drive to be busy continues, spreading beyond formal working hours. We see this in the demand and expectation that increasing proportions of employees must be constantly connected to their workplaces – accessible through any and all technological means available.[127] The distinctions between remunerated work and domestic life, once considered characteristic of wage labour under capitalism, begin to blur here, with the former coming to impinge upon our mental space during our supposedly free time. There is also evidence that the affluent classes feel increased pressure to make the most of their leisure time. This has resulted in wealthier households turning towards more and more expensive replacements for existing leisure goods and services. In many such households, 'inconspicuous consumption' has taken hold, where individuals may purchase leisure goods with the hope of using them some day.[128] And it has also led to leisure consumption occurring at a more rapid rate – an attempt to fit more into a finite period of time.[129] The imperative to be productive has taken hold in our free time as well.[130] For many of us, we cannot simply rest and relax, but must instead always be doing something – making *good use* of our time. Activities like watching television or playing videogames are all too often deemed to be a waste of time. Even our free time has to be productive.

Why has the leisure class become the harried class, then? One of the most plausible explanations centres on a shift in the importance of education, cultural knowledge, social skills, and other 'human capital'. If the leisure class was the beneficiary of property ownership and an idle return on rents (broadly speaking), today's harried class is more often than not dependent on human capital that requires constant work in order to generate an income.[131] This helps explain why it tends to be those in jobs that reward these sorts of skills – managers and professionals – whose roles are more likely to involve long hours.[132] Those who are fortunate enough to make it into these positions still then have to perform the requisite labour in order to receive their salaries. On top of this, there is the generalised cultural intensification of the work ethic. In a transformation of the original Protestant work ethic and its positing of work as a calling that could enable social mobility, today we have the work ethic as a key medium of self-expression in itself.[133] Working hard is a norm ingrained not only in our workplaces, but in our homes and throughout the general fabric of our lives.

Conclusion

Given the shifting focus of standards and the endless nature of housework, unpaid reproductive labour tends to fill whatever temporal container it is placed within.[134] There is always something more that can be done, and the ratcheting up of standards is a key mechanism through which this temporal vacuum is filled with, well, vacuuming. This is particularly the case for childcare, with supervision of young children requiring almost constant low-level attention. As one 1940s advertisement put it, once the clothes are in the washing machine, 'I'm free [sic] to take care of the children or do other housework.'[135] And it has been suggested that given the lack of value attached to work done in the home, women often see the performance of long hours as a way to indicate their own (non-monetary) contributions to a family.[136] The end result is that housework has a nasty habit of impinging on whatever free time we might desire.

In the face of these norms, there is a degree to which we can, as individuals, recognise and consciously deliberate about the uses of our time. Are we creating a spotless house because we want one, because it serves a functional purpose, or because social norms compel us to do this work? An important part of such reflection is to overcome the guilt that is often felt by people who fail to meet unreasonably high social standards: mothers who are unable to spend all their free time and active attention on their children or parents who can't afford the time or money to cook healthy meals from scratch. And there are plenty of immediate benefits that can be gained from individual choices to reduce expectations. Rethinking parenting, for instance, could mean more free time for parents and more play time for children. The rise of intensive parenting has led to children spending less time in unstructured play and more time in rigorously structured activities – and the play that they do have increasingly involves highly vetted activities, friends, and food.[137] One school in America even cancelled the annual kindergarten play because it would have meant two days of focusing on something other than work.[138] A revival of children's free time would benefit everyone. As one child put it, 'I wish my parents had some hobby other than me.'[139]

At the same time, individual efforts run into implacable structures. The norms governing reproductive labour are not ephemeral but rather embodied within real social structures that have real social consequences if ignored. Children who aren't intensively parented, for instance, risk losing out on the opportunities that this model of parenting aims to provide. Despite the problems and time intensity of this approach, many understandably adopt it because they want to see their children succeed. Class distinctions also play a significant role in the continued setting of norms. Middle-class notions of cleanliness, bourgeois images of elaborate meals, and capitalist pressures to 'invest' in one's children and to put on conspicuous displays of busyness are all part and parcel of our class-based societies. On top of this, as we have seen, marketing has routinely been a key agent in the creation of new 'needs' and higher expectations. And these social expectations take on the weight of legislative force when representatives of the state come to adjudicate their performance.

The welfare state has long served a disciplinary function in terms of ensuring adherence to particular standards. Receipt of many benefits, for example, entails significant surveillance by figures of the state: 'Health inspectors, school inspectors, and social workers – largely women – [have] enforced social reformers' bourgeois notions of morality, hygiene, appropriate social roles for working-class people, and most centrally, acceptable family–household configurations.'[140] The judgments (actual or anticipated) of these figures are a key disciplinary force behind standards of cleanliness and conduct. This can manifest itself in minor ways, such as when a UK primary school placed an injunction against parents doing the school run in their pyjamas.[141] But it can also be expressed in much more harrowing ways, such as the removal of children from families and their placement into often underfunded and inhospitable foster care systems. The role of the child welfare system is particularly prominent here, for while it is ostensibly in place to safeguard the young from their not-always-supportive families of origin, in actuality it is increasingly notorious for imposing standards far beyond safety and well-being in its assessment of home environments. We can see this in recent developments such as the directive in Texas that child protection services should 'investigate the families of trans children who receive gender affirming care',[142] as well as in the kinds of 'warning signs' that can instigate investigations. A child might 'seem unkempt or unattended. A parent might be observed smoking marijuana. A house might appear dirty' – none of which need necessarily speak to the unfitness of the caregivers involved. In the US, investigations of child neglect are largely focused on poor families; yet instead of offering material assistance, households are drawn into a regime of intensive surveillance, and children are threatened with removal from their homes.[143]

Social reproduction under conditions of capitalism means that 'the task of teachers, nurses, and social workers is the production of not just any "life" but that of a docile, exploitable worker, and that this reproduction of labour power by employees of the state can't be divorced from state repression'.[144] The imposition of particular, sometimes seemingly arbitrary, standards of self-presentation, hygiene, and behaviour are part and parcel of this. Individual choices about standards therefore run into significant limits, particularly when various norms are embedded into law (as many childcare norms are). More than individual deliberation, we need to transform the structures which impose these standards. We ultimately need to create the means through which we can collectively determine and self-legislate the sorts of norms to which we might want to commit ourselves.

4

Families

We have seen in previous chapters that technology and social norms interact in complex ways to either restrict or enable free time when it comes to domestic reproductive work. Underlying the organisation of this work lies the family (or more precisely, the family as a social unit archetypically comprised of a conjugal couple and their dependent children).[1] While there is considerable lived diversity in terms of how people actually organise their domestic lives, this paradigmatic form continues to be widely celebrated in Western countries as a cultural ideal and reinforced by a broad set of state policies.

Yet, in terms of reproductive work, the family is wildly inefficient and a vast repository of gendered inequalities. Although the amount of unpaid housework that women perform has been gradually declining since the 1960s,[2] and despite men (slightly) increasing their share (see Figures 4.1 and 4.2), the family continues to embody a marked gendered division of labour.[3] In fact, for every country in the world for which we have data, women spend more time than men on unwaged work – on average 3.2 times as much.[4] In 2015, for example, 60 per cent of unpaid care work in America was done by women.[5] Between 1985 and 2004,

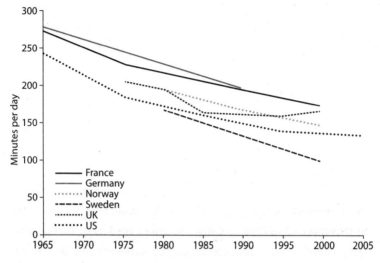

Figure 4.1: Total Housework Time, Women[9]

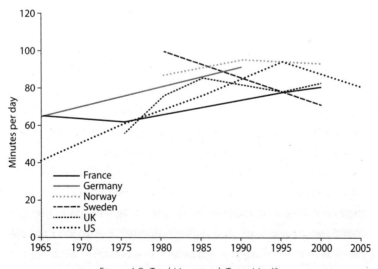

Figure 4.2: Total Housework Time, Men[10]

employed women in America saw no change whatsoever in the number of hours they spent doing unpaid social reproduction.[6] In the UK, meanwhile, women do 60 per cent more unwaged labour than men,[7] and even in the most gender-equal countries, such as Norway and Denmark, women continue to do nearly 1.5 times as much. In the current best-case scenario, the average Swedish woman does 1.6 years more of this labour than the average man over the course of her lifetime.[8] In all these examples, women remain responsible for the bulk of unwaged social reproduction, even as their hours in the waged workplace are brought increasingly in line with men's.

Temporal inequality within the family is also not just a matter of minutes and hours. Given that some forms of work are more burdensome than others, there are crucial *qualitative* differences to consider when it comes to the organisation of unpaid labour.[11] In many nuclear families, for example, mothers take on the bulk of nocturnal caregiving – responding to children's nighttime needs for nourishment or comfort. Studies of dual-earner couples found that women were 'three times more likely than men to report interrupted sleep if they had a child at home under the age of one, and stay-at-home mothers were *six* times as likely to get up with their children as stay-at-home dads'.[12] Fathers, on the other hand, tend to spend more of their caregiving time in the comparatively enjoyable work of 'talk-based, educational, and recreational activities rather than routine physical and logistical tasks'.[13] On top of this, most of the time fathers spend caring for their children takes place when mothers are also present, while mothers were much more likely to look after children on their own – making the latter more intensive.[14] Looking beyond childcare, the temporal inequalities continue: women tend to take on more repetitive tasks (such as laundry, cooking, or cleaning) while men involve themselves in less routine activities (such as DIY projects or shopping). The way in which this work is conventionally distributed within heterosexual families thus actively promotes a rest and relaxation deficit for particular kinds of caregivers. It is largely women who are left sleepless, harried, and starved of a life beyond the demands of caring for others.

As this would suggest, women across the world almost always have less leisure time than men – on average, thirty-three minutes less per day, or nearly four hours less per week.[15] The official statistics for the UK arrive at a similar conclusion: men currently have five hours more free time per week, and this inequality has been increasing over the past fifteen years.[16] Further imbalances become apparent when one considers the *character* of that free time. Measures of leisure are almost always measures of the primary activity undertaken at any given point in time (that is, of the main activity in which somebody is engaging at that moment). This neglects the fact that people may be doing more than one thing at a time and therefore that the quality of free time may differ.[17] For example, according to a standard time-use survey, a mother who is watching television while also passively supervising a toddler playing nearby would be coded as enjoying her free time. Yet obviously this situation also involves some element of childcare work and in any case is a quite different type of free time than that experienced when one's dependents are not present. This is one reason why those heavily engaged in social reproduction work tend to have a different experience of time.[18] This work involves frequent interruptions and demands persistent background attention. Given that men spend a greater portion of their leisure time not in the company of their children, it is little surprise that researchers find they have *better quality* free time than women: they are more likely to have longer periods of leisure, with fewer distractions, restrictions, and interruptions.[19]

However, while it is of critical importance that we recognise and reckon with temporal inequality as a feminist issue, an acknowledgement of the continued unequal distribution of reproductive labour *within* the family can only get us so far. It is to the family form itself that we must turn if we wish to expand and extend free time. The nuclear family is particularly ill-suited to many types of care work, such as childrearing. An 'insoluble conflict is built into the nuclear family. Children are a twenty-four-hour-a-day responsibility, yet parents have legitimate needs for personal freedom, privacy, and spontaneity in their lives.'[20] The end result is a time crunch for parents of young children, with needlessly negative impacts on everyone involved. The family also involves an absurd duplication of effort:

> Out there in the land of household work there are small industrial plants which sit idle for the better part of every working day; there are expensive pieces of highly mechanized equipment which only get used once or twice a month; there are consumption units which weekly trundle out to their markets to buy 8 ounces of this non-perishable product and 12 ounces of that one.[21]

Similarly, women's co-operatives in the early twentieth century lamented that nothing was 'so silly as the present waste of time and money of each household doing its own wash'.[22] As we have seen in previous chapters, the delegation of reproductive labour to separate homes – and, typically, to atomised housewives – meant a major reduction in the labour-saving potential of early domestic technologies. The industrialisation of the home went hand in hand with an individualisation of its labours. The duplication of work that occurs as a result has fostered a number of dissenting voices arguing that there must be a better way to organise this socially necessary work, which has in turn led to several imaginative, speculative, and in some cases, realised alternatives that we will examine later in the book.

For now, however, these issues of inequality and inefficiency take us to the heart of temporal politics and to the importance of extending any fight for free time beyond the waged workplace to people's own homes. Qualitative as well as quantitative differences in the performance of unpaid housework and care work represent a substantial issue for feminist post-work imaginaries, and dismantling the structural obstacles prohibiting a more equitable distribution of this work is particularly crucial. A major part of this involves confronting and challenging the gendered expectations surrounding caregiving practices within the family as a hegemonic form for the management of social reproduction under capitalism. But it also means questioning the nuclear family as the ideal reproductive unit for an emancipatory post-work politics and as a bastion of resistance to contemporary cultures of work. The family has shown itself to be isolating, exclusionary, labour intensive, time consuming, and deeply unfair – and yet it has retained an impressive grip upon the cultural imagination. How did the nuclear family become hegemonic, and how does the division of labour that it engendered continue to shape the ways in which so many of us live our lives?

The Birth of the Breadwinner

Our story begins with the expansion of capitalist industrialisation in the nineteenth century. In the two centuries prior, women were still largely responsible for care work and housework, but three important qualifications make clear the differences in how reproductive work was organised during this period.

First, reproductive work was often done communally and the majority was done for others (either as unremunerated help or for an income) rather than for oneself. The idea of a housewife working alone in support of her family was somewhat alien to this period. Secondly, women spent a relatively small portion of their working time on care work and housework – around 30 per cent of their tasks involved such work. The narrow specialisation of women into a particular set of reproductive activities was something that would only come later. Far from there being a rigid division of labour, all members of a household participated substantially in most areas of work.[23] Lastly, the household as a reproductive unit was not synonymous with a biological family. For many, the household was often filled with extrafamilial members and a 'family' was not defined so much by blood as by labour relations; it consisted of those who lived and worked together.[24]

However, the expanding market sphere introduced a series of new demands on wage workers, setting a rhythm and pace of production that was ultimately at odds with this pre-industrial organisation of reproductive labour. The demands of capitalist competition drove production to specialised locations (factories, at first) outside of the domicile, making it more difficult for wage labourers to perform unpaid family work in the home.[25] Conversely, unpaid work – including the organisation of household finances and of the various wage workers (children and adults) within the family – became increasingly complex, time consuming, and thus less conducive to the performance of wage labour outside the home. For some time, these competing demands led to a crisis of social reproduction among the urban working classes, as women and children were intensely exploited alongside men in factories, before returning to the decrepit housing they shared.[26] The eventual fix for this unsustainable situation was for households to withdraw their married female members from external employment (unless finances urgently required it). While women often worked full-time in the years before marriage and childbearing, they tended to largely withdraw from wage work if and when their domestic situations changed. Labour force participation for white women in 1890, for instance, dropped 'from 38.4 percent to 2.5 percent when they married'.[27]

Based in the home, these married women increasingly saw the assorted responsibilities of the household come to dominate their time.[28] As the activities of production migrated ever further from the domestic residence, 'the household was left with only the most personal biological activities – eating, sex, sleeping, the care of small children, and (until the rise of institutional medicine) birth and dying and the care of the sick and aged'.[29] The specialisation encouraged by the emerging regime of reproduction meant that, increasingly, daily life would be experienced as divided into two domains: a market sphere dominated by concerns over competition and efficiency, and a household sphere of unwaged and often unrecognised work that was deemed to be a space of intimacy and respite from the outside world. A formal separation was materialising between the market and the household.[30]

This is not to suggest that these separate spheres were hermetically sealed, however. Married women continued to generate income but favoured arrangements that were more compatible with their specialist household commitments – by taking in boarders, doing laundry and piecework, working the commons, and so on.[31] In this way, some of the tensions between the need for income and the demands of unpaid work could be (at least partially) mitigated. When needed, married women could also function as what we might call an intrafamilial reserve army of labour. This is a separate idea to that of capital's reserve army of labour – a term referring to those un- or underemployed people who can be drawn upon by capital when workers are needed and who are relied upon as an implicit threat of replacement if wage workers demand 'too much'. Rather, the idea of the intrafamilial reserve army refers to a repository of potential wage labour within a family, drawn upon during times of need by the household unit and thereby increasing the family's ability to adapt and survive in the face of changing circumstances. In the late 1800s, this was a crucial part of the role played by working-class wives, who made intermittent returns to wage work when the household depended on it (such as in cases where a wage-earning partner died or faced unemployment or illness).[32]

As the nineteenth century drew to a close, men's wages were rising, the use of child labour was dwindling, and women were finding it more difficult to earn a non-wage income.[33] As a result, the work of husbands and fathers was taking on proportionally greater significance for families' overall income. Studies have shown, for instance, that for working-class households, the male wage labourer was responsible for 70–80 per cent of the total family wage.[34] To be sure, this dependency upon a single wage varied in relation to a household's socioeconomic position (with the poorest families still reliant upon income being generated by all members), and different countries experienced this process of proletarianisation at different times and speeds. But the overall tendency was for greater dependency on the wage of a male head of house as alternative sources of income dwindled.

These changes in material circumstances were complemented by a shift in the ideological infrastructure surrounding gender, work, and family. Given that married women's waged work was often driven by desperation and urgent need, it is not surprising 'that working-class culture adopted the image of the married woman at home as the sign of the health, stability, and prosperity of a household'.[35] While relatively few working-class families could achieve this ideal, the expectation that a male breadwinner should be able to support his entire family gained significant traction around the turn of the century.[36] Trade unions, for instance, came to rely upon the idea of a family wage as a means to bargaining for higher wages – with the added bonus that it signalled to progressive bourgeois allies that the working-class was also seeking the same family form.[37]

It is crucial to emphasise, however, that throughout this period the lived reality of households was far more diverse than the emerging norm would suggest – particularly for working-class families, immigrants, and ethnic minorities, who lived more often in extended households or closely networked groups. As Marx and Engels noted at the time, 'in its completely developed form this family exists only among the bourgeoisie'.[38] Into the twentieth century, many Black families also continued to demonstrate a 'flexible and elastic kinship' characterised by households that 'failed to conform to the pattern daddy-mommy-child', and particularly by temporary and transient domestic partnerships, extended families, and women breadwinners.[39] Against such diversity, the domestic ideology positioned itself precisely as a marker of race, class, and status distinction. While the male breadwinner family form brought with it significant benefits for the working class, through improvements in living standards, and formed a key foundation in further political struggles, it also demands to be seen as the 'means by which the workers' movement would distinguish itself from the lumpenproletariat, black workers, and queers'.[40] Despite inevitable variations in lived experience, the breadwinner/homemaker model, marked by a structural separation of market and household spheres, was nevertheless solidifying.

There was a widespread convergence towards such an approach across the late nineteenth and early twentieth centuries, as the accessibility of this arrangement 'expanded dramatically for white American and European wage workers in the 1880s and 1890s, and became the dominant family form in many stable working-class neighbourhoods'.[41] Both the working- and middle-class versions of the family depended upon the separation of unpaid reproductive labour from remunerated productive work and upon the sharp gendering of this separation. By 1900, the ideal had established itself 'as the normative aspiration of the European working classes'.[42] And by World War I, 'the urban proletariat had assumed its modern form, and "the traditional family", as we think of it today, had taken shape'.[43] Whereas families in the Victorian era tended to take on highly class-specific forms – with '[f]ertility, housework, gender roles, and the experience of childhood and youth' all varying widely – twentieth-century families 'continued to confirm and reproduce class differences, but ... began to do so by channelling people into institutions, values, and behaviors that were largely similar'.[44] A particular form of the family – a nuclear unit with a male breadwinner, a female homemaker, and non-wage-earning, biologically related children at school – started to become hegemonic.

A New Politics of Time

The increasing separation of men from the daily realities of intrafamilial social reproduction was in turn bound up with a decrease in domestic responsibilities and growing temporal inequality when it came to unwaged work. A new gendered politics of time was emerging. In the pre-industrial period, work was largely performed outside, whether by men or women, and was temporally regulated by natural rhythms that blurred demarcations between 'work' and 'life'.[45] The emerging spatial division between a workplace and a home, however, led to a growing distinction between work and leisure – for men, at least – and an increasing desire to keep the space of (male) leisure unencumbered by work of any sort. Many fathers found that the organisation of their days and weeks was dictated by the rhythms of wage labour, meaning that they sometimes 'saw their children only on Sunday, and their wives for only five minutes a day'.[46] The home was idealised 'as a leisure centre to which men could retreat after work, sanctioning their abstention from domestic labour'. The men of the nineteenth century therefore tended to do less in support of their wives at home than might have been the case in previous eras. Indeed, it appears that during this period men spent 'very little time at home beyond eating and sleeping, preferring to pass the time after work with male friends in pubs and clubs. Those who involved themselves in housework were widely considered to be eccentric or effeminate.'[47] The very design of the home came to reflect an increasing insistence that all associations with work be banished. Furniture, decor, colour scheme, and so on were all intended to present the home as a space of non-work.[48]

Unpaid family workers, however, were to a significant extent exempted from the rigid temporal logic of the clock and the calendar. Married women's 'time was less regulated by linear time, and they were becoming the only family members who were thought to have time for family. As a result, women became not only the principal managers of family time but its main symbol.'[49] The upshot of this was that mothers (and women, more broadly) became closely associated with family time. Because intrafamilial housework and care work operate according to a less regulated and predictable timetable than other forms of labour, there continued to be a lack of temporal boundaries around unwaged reproductive work during the nineteenth century. While those labouring within their own homes may have enjoyed greater control over the pace of the working day, they did so at the expense of any prospect of a real *end* to that day. The conditions for a clear-cut conclusion to or refusal of work were simply not in place. There was therefore a growing entrenchment of gendered temporal inequality, with many men becoming increasingly protective of their discretionary time, without necessarily recognising that those around them did not experience this kind of sharp delineation between the times and spaces of labour and leisure.

The generally stricter demarcation for men between the time of work and the time of leisure enabled struggles around that demarcation to become a key focus of the labour movement: 'Workers begin to fight, not against time, but about it.'[50] Shorter working hours were now a possible priority. For instance, the 1866 congress of the International Workingmen's Association (the First International) focused on 'les trois huits': eight hours for work, eight hours for sleep, and eight hours for what we will. However, 'in their eight hours of leisure, working men, even their socialist vanguard, were not thinking of doing much work at home.'[51] Meanwhile, for women the work of the home was being repositioned not as toil but as a deep-seated and natural expression of their very essence.[52] That is to say, this work ceased to be understood as labour at all but was rather positioned as a form of autonomously chosen activity that conveniently coincided with the daily needs of the reproductive unit.[53] This duality of spheres was given concrete expression in labour struggles as well. When women's co-operative groups sought to collectivise their labour and purchase industrial technologies for things like baking and laundering, men chaffed. A financial investment in machines was at odds with men's idea that this work is just provided for free.[54] The duality also played out when some Canadian trade unions were arguing for reduced working time in the 1950s. For men, the shorter working week was deemed important for rest and relaxation, as well as for self- and political improvement. For women, meanwhile, the shorter working week was seen as a way to further enable housework and provide more time to spend with their families.[55] The rise of separate spheres – however much they blurred in practice – was accompanied by a new politics of free time.

Peak Family

As the twentieth century progressed, further developments helped to shore up breadwinner/homemaker hegemony across the Global North – including, perversely enough, specific challenges to it. In the United States, for example, the fallout from the Great Depression saw married white women once again being called upon to act as their household's reserve army of labour. Many were compelled by circumstance and profound economic need to take up paid employment wherever they could find it, despite the work available often being considered undesirable. During the 1930s, large numbers of women

sought employment, as their husbands were laid off or took wage cuts. Yet even while married women increased their employment from 29 to 35.5 percent of the female labour force, public acceptance of such employment plummeted. Federal laws and business policies discouraged the hiring of married women and mandated that they be the first fired in cutbacks; twenty-six states passed laws prohibiting their employment.[56]

In the face of low pay, unfavourable conditions, and widespread social opposition, women's waged work came to further be seen as something best avoided. In the context of the times, female employment was very often 'an act of desperation rather than a free choice. Many women who began their families in the 1940s and 1950s associated their mothers' employment during the 1930s with economic hardship and family failure. They looked forward to establishing a different pattern in their own marriages' – one that more closely followed the breadwinner/homemaker model.[57]

This sense of women's employment beyond the home as an imposition (rather than an opportunity) was partially reinforced by the arrival of World War II. Again, women found themselves compelled to enter into wage work and were often prevented by circumstances from pursuing the kind of family life they might have imagined for themselves. This time, however, both the employment available and the social conditions under which it was pursued were radically different. Huge numbers of women entered into formal waged work, supported by both material and ideological scaffolds that were explicitly intended to facilitate their labour force participation. Many governments developed significant systems of assistance for the social reproduction of families. For example, the United States federal government funded more than 3,000 nurseries during the war.[58] In the UK, wartime nurseries were also opened and expanded – from 14 in 1940 to more than 1,300 by the end of the war.[59] These and other efforts offered many women a taste of what comparative economic freedom and more satisfying paid employment might look like, but under conditions which, once again, were not of their choosing.

In the long run the war appears to have expanded horizons for women, but in the short term women were led to retreat from full-time work.[60] Much of the support put in place for social reproduction under wartime conditions was unceremoniously rescinded.[61] There was an 'almost universal reimposition of sexual segregation and pay differentials by companies after the war'.[62] There were also concerted efforts made on the part of politicians, academics, and cultural propaganda to get women to restrain themselves to a quiet domestic life.[63] These discouraging factors intersected with the 'pent-up desires of both women and men to start a family, producing an idealization of family life that may have slowed down and certainly concealed the steady rise in the number of married women workers'.[64]

Perhaps most crucially, the welfare states constructed in the wake of World War II's devastation were explicitly reliant upon the breadwinner/homemaker model and made significant efforts to enforce this approach. As William Beveridge wrote in his famous report (a report that would go on to inform the construction of numerous welfare states), 'The great majority of married women must be regarded as occupied on work which is vital though unpaid, without which their husbands could not do their paid work and without which the nation could not continue.'[65] Such postwar efforts were not the first time that states had constructed gendered policies, of course.[66] The American New Deal of the 1930s, for example, instituted a two-track welfare system.[67] One track provided unemployment insurance and old-age insurance without question, receipt of which was untarnished by stigma – but which excluded most women and minorities. (The latter exclusion was explicitly designed to force Black women in the south to remain bound as domestic servants and sharecroppers.)[68] The other track offered less assistance, was highly stigmatised, mandated means testing to receive it, and included programmes aimed to help support women with children. But even the latter track excluded most women of colour, who were deemed to be undeserving recipients.[69] In the postwar period, many (though not all)[70] welfare states took up similar dualistic approaches to the provision of benefits which typically provided the best welfare (insurance) to male workers, while (unemployed) women received only minimal assistance.[71] The Netherlands, for instance, allowed women to work part-time in the 1950s and 1960s because such positions weren't accorded full social welfare benefits.[72] Assumptions about who was working and who was a homemaker structured everything from benefits to housing policy to pensions.

Other aspects of the welfare state directly channelled women into unwaged domestic labour, thereby further enforcing a particular family form. In some European countries, for instance, women were given rights to take leave from work, but without any guarantee that they could get their job back – effectively facilitating women leaving, but not re-entering, wage work.[73] And as we've seen in relation to standards, the postwar welfare state may have had some benefits for white male workers, but for women (particularly women of colour) it often meant a loss of control over their lives – more efforts by the state to influence how they lived. Heteronormativity was embedded in many policies from the beginning, and a number of welfare programmes featured requirements which in some way restricted the sexual and domestic lives of their recipients. Council housing provision in the 1960s in the London borough of Lambeth, for example, only offered space to those with children – and 'cohabiting men [were] presumed to be the breadwinner' for the rest of the household.[74] Efforts were made to channel people into marriage (sometimes in the belief that atypical family forms were themselves causes of poverty and crime).[75] Tax breaks and immigration rights associated with marriage have also been key motivators for many to say their vows.

In the US of the late 1950s, too, the Aid to Dependent Children welfare programme was increasingly limited to those considered 'deserving', with

> multiple exclusions serving to define the boundaries of state-subsidized reproduction. 'Man-in-the-house' rules allowed states to refuse benefits to women who lived with or were in a sexual relationship with a man, deeming him the proper substitute for the paternal function of the state; 'suitable home' laws allowed welfare case workers to deny aid to unmarried or immoral women; 'employable mother' laws, often invoked in the South, designated African American women as indispensable workers outside the home and therefore excluded them from the domestic ideal of white motherhood.[76]

As Melinda Cooper puts it, 'In practice, public assistance programs were qualified by a panoply of state administrative laws that strictly policed the moral and racial boundaries of the Fordist family wage.' The hegemony of the nuclear family is underwritten by this new standardisation and its imposition of sexual and racial norms, and it is here that a restrictive reproductive imaginary finds the social and cultural conditions necessary for its flourishing.[77]

This was the era of peak family, then. If the first half of the twentieth century had seen this model spread as an ideal, the immediate postwar era saw the 'family arrangements we sometimes mistakenly think of as traditional [become] standard for a majority of Americans, and a realistic goal for others'.[78] Across Europe and America, one encounters widespread concord in terms of how best to organise social reproduction, manage resources, and generally live one's life (even among those who are unable, for one reason or another, to conform to such a pattern).

Work for All

Although the paradigmatic family achieved significant satura-
tion in the mid-twentieth century, and in spite of ongoing state
efforts to maintain its centrality, the dominance of this model was
in fact rather short lived.[79] In some countries, the first shifts away
from this form were almost immediate. After a brief postwar dip,
female employment in America began to climb again as early
as 1947, and by 1950, 21 per cent of all white married women
were in the labour force.[80] A similar trend can be detected in
Europe, with married women's employment declining at first,
before gaining pace in the 1950s.[81] In fact, despite this being
the mythical era of the stay-at-home housewife, women were
typically spending *more* time engaged in wage earning activities
than had previously been the case.[82] Such changes became ever
more significant as we moved from the postwar settlement to
the period of neoliberalism.

For many households, dual employment was not a straightforward matter of preference – a breakdown of the appeal of a male
breadwinner ideal – but was in fact significantly motivated by
economic conditions.[83] The economic crises of the 1970s and the
subsequent attacks on the workers' movement 'ultimately made
it impossible for most working-class people to afford to keep an
unwaged housewife out of the labour market'.[84] Already by the
late 1970s, commentators were beginning to notice a gradual
fading away of the family wage.[85] Women were no longer acting
as an intrafamilial reserve army of labour – a resource to be kept
out of the waged workforce wherever possible and drawn on
only in emergencies. Rather, they increasingly found themselves
pressed into permanent active service. By the 1990s, most American households were dependent on two earners for maintaining
their living standards.[86] In the absence of decent wages and

affordable necessities, women – as they always have – sought to contribute to their families' income. As such, the demise of the male breadwinner model must be understood in relation to the disintegration of the economic conditions that enabled that form to become temporarily hegemonic; the family is itself partly reflective of the material conditions of the economy.

It becomes further apparent that women's increasing hours in the wage workplace are the result of something other than unfettered personal preference when one considers the role of the state in this process. Whereas the postwar welfare state instituted a strict divide between the unwaged work of women and the waged work of men, the contemporary neoliberal state seeks to expand the labour force through an increasingly insistent demand that *everyone* be made dependent on waged work – equal opportunities exploitation.[87] If the postwar welfare state had helped to decommodify workers by reducing their dependence on the market,[88] the contemporary welfare state aims to 'recommodify them by supporting market competition rather than replacing it'.[89] A large part of this effort has been through labour activation policies designed to push and pull people into work, through both negative activation policies (e.g., cutting benefits or reducing their length) and positive activation policies (e.g., job training).[90] Anything that is seen to disincentivise waged work must be reduced or removed. As a result, the generosity of unemployment benefits has been cut in most countries.[91]

As part of this general approach, targeted efforts have been made to coerce *women* in particular into the workforce.[92] In 1968, for example, Sweden explicitly moved from a dual roles model (built upon an assumed sharp gendered division of labour, in which women would take time off from paid employment to look after children) to a universal breadwinner model.[93] Today, nearly every welfare state of the Global North follows this

approach, facilitated again by welfare cuts that have increasingly pushed women into waged work.[94] In the America of
the early 1970s, for example, cuts to welfare for women with
children meant that mothers struggled to survive on dwindling
benefits; Black mothers in particular found themselves driven to
engage in political struggle for the means to sustain themselves.[95]
American welfare reform in the 1990s further focused on getting
people away from benefits and into work, leading to increases in
women's employment.[96] Most notoriously, changes introduced
in 1996 involved a work requirement for single parents receiving payments and set a time limit on receipt of the benefit.[97] In
the UK, meanwhile, income support for single parents used to
apply for children up to sixteen years of age; now it only applies
for children up to five, with the explicit expectation that parents
of school-age children will take on waged labour. That's over a
decade's worth of support for single parents unceremoniously
rescinded. A variety of other welfare changes in the past twenty
years have also aimed to steer British mothers specifically into
employment, with considerable success.[98]

The age of the male breadwinner/female homemaker is well
and truly over, then (see Figure 4.3). These changes hold across
every advanced capitalist country (although with some continuing to lag in absolute terms). For instance, the number of
two-parent households where the mother stays at home while the
father works decreased from 46 per cent in 1970 to 26 per cent
in 2015.[99] In America, the proportion of *mothers* working more
than fifty weeks per year went from 19 per cent in 1965 to 57 per
cent by 2000.[100] The collapse of the male breadwinner model has,
however, meant slightly different things in different countries.
Sweden, for instance, has facilitated full-time employment of
women, but most often in traditionally feminised sectors such
as childcare or nursing. Places like the UK and the Netherlands,

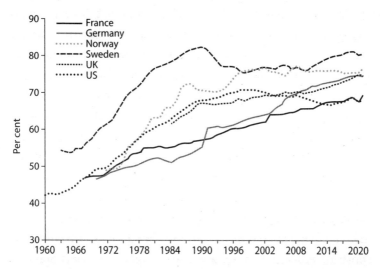

Figure 4.3: Women's participation rates in the labour market, 1960–2020[102]

by contrast, have removed labour regulations and channelled women into more part-time and temporary positions. The US, meanwhile, has enabled more opportunities for women to do full-time work in traditionally masculinised sectors but at the cost of excluding the poor, the less educated, and women of colour.[101] While the paths have differed, the results have been the same: the demise of the male breadwinner model.

Under Pressure

We might be prompted to wonder if this shift is really such a bad thing. Certainly, as one of the stated aims of many feminist movements, the gradual demise of a male breadwinner approach has had some significant benefits. Most obviously it has meant the declining dependency of married heterosexual women on the income-earning potential of their male partners and there-fore increased financial independence. The (partial) erosion of the traditional gendered division of labour has also thrown the naturalisation of reproductive labour into new light. Few, with the exception of some contemporary arch-reactionaries, would now pretend that cooking, cleaning, and other domestic tasks are an uncomplicated 'labour of love'. And as Wally Seccombe notes, the rise of female employment has meant an 'undercutting [of] men's customary prerogatives as breadwinners (above all, the right to treat the home as a leisure centre, abstaining from housework and childcare)'.[103]

However, the positive outcomes of the end of the male bread-winner model – a modicum of freedom from direct spousal financial control, cultural access to forms of work that might prove (under the right conditions) to be relatively stimulating and satisfying, the potential social and political benefits of cooperating with others on a shared endeavour beyond the isolated and isolating domestic residence – are tempered by less welcome factors. First, the demise of this model hasn't enabled a proliferation of better alternatives; instead, households have been forced into an increasingly desperate dependency on the market. A celebration of equalised access to (and dependency upon) wage labour is therefore highly limited as an approach to addressing the contemporary challenges of social reproduction.

Second, the result of this breakdown (or reintegration) of spheres has not been gender parity, be it in terms of homemaking or breadwinning. The male breadwinner ideal may have loosened its grip in recent decades, but its influence can nevertheless still be felt on lived domestic arrangements across the wealthy nations. There continues to be a gender imbalance in terms of hours spent in waged and unwaged work, for example – one which reflects a conventional division of labour.[104] As such, we should not assume that women being drawn into wage labour necessarily equates to a complementary lessening or redistribution of their reproductive burdens. Once again, we also find that the state has had a significant influence here. In practice, with governments often failing to provide sufficient services to balance waged work and care, any espoused policy ambitions towards a universal breadwinner model are compromised.[105] Studies suggest that while a *genuinely* universal breadwinner model is prevalent across much of Scandinavia, this is rarely the case elsewhere.[106]

Rather, a 'one-and-a-half earner' model has emerged, the most common form of which involves a household member working part-time who – when needed – also takes up responsibility for unwaged care work.[107] Given structural inequalities such as the gender pay gap, women remain the ones who predominantly cut their working hours to take up caring responsibilities, leading to a reassertion of 'traditional' family imaginaries and their associated temporal inequalities.[108] Indeed, it's worth noting that a more clear-cut breadwinner/homemaker model reappears at pinch points for care work, such as when dependents are very young or in poor health. We saw this clearly during the early stages of the pandemic. During lockdowns, the home became a concentrated hub for a wide variety of caring tasks which are more usually provided elsewhere – either by the public sector (in the case of education, adult day care, some kinds of medical care) or by the market (early years childcare, domestic cleaning, hot food preparation, and so on). Many households found themselves required to take on additional kinds of caring responsibilities during the pandemic, and family members, typically women, frequently picked up these responsibilities in addition to paid work. With schools and nurseries shut down, globally more than half a trillion hours of childcare were pushed back into the home, to be taken up largely by women.[109] While an exceptional case, the pattern nonetheless holds more generally. When babies need looking after, women are far more likely to exit the workforce to take this on; when a family member needs long-term care, it is again women who are more likely to put their jobs on hold and become unpaid carers. We also saw earlier how technologies are enabling more and more of this work to be pushed back onto the family – just as various welfare states are making family provision a central plank to their long-term-care policies. A so-called 'sandwich generation' has arisen with caretaking responsibilities for both their younger children and older parents. The end result is that while the dual breadwinner model may be the current norm, the family remains the carer of last resort – and when called upon to perform this function, a traditional male breadwinner model often re-emerges.

A final key point to make here is that, just as previous family forms were characterised by a particular politics of time, so too is the current universal breadwinner form. Whereas the previous period could be seen as typified by a struggle over men's working hours and women's boundaryless work, today the key aspect tends to be a universal sense of growing time pressures. On one level, these pressures are the result of the fact that the total amount of (waged and unwaged) work being performed by individuals has been growing for much of the Western world since the 1970s.[110] The popular success of books such as *The Overworked American* and *The Second Shift* in the 1990s was due in large part to the fact that they gave expression to a common sentiment: that free time is disappearing and that life is becoming more harried.[111] From the 2000s onwards, in particular, there is a widespread upwards trend in total working hours.[112] We are seeing growing workloads for many breadwinners, regardless of gender. Yet a focus on individual workers also obscures the reality of new temporal pressures on the *household*, particularly in its dual-earner form. The 'vicissitudes of scheduling and the intricacy with which our lives are tied to others can only be fully understood by treating the household, rather than the individual, as the unit of analysis'.[113]

Looking at the household as a unit helps us to understand the rise in recent decades of subjective feelings of time pressure that appear to outpace any objective increase in work time. People report feeling like they have less time than ever before.[114] This has been backed up by studies in numerous rich countries which have shown major increases in the amount of people who report feeling rushed and pressed for time.[115] Part of the reason for this is that people are dealing with increasingly disjointed schedules; the standard nine-to-five job is no longer dominant, and people are working much more flexibly. The result is that coordinating timetables between different people and activities is becoming ever more difficult.[116] Even if one is not working longer hours, more time is spent trying to coordinate those hours together, and we feel less in control of how time proceeds.[117] Equally, our time increasingly involves multitasking, and free time becomes something where both waged and unwaged work often impinge on our psyche. We may watch television, for instance, while idly typing up a report, responding to work emails, cleaning the house, or (as discussed earlier) passively minding children. As such, this time can hardly be considered straightforwardly 'free'.

These new feelings of time pressure are also partly the result of having a much higher proportion of families being either dual earner or headed by single parents (which typically means single mothers).[118] In both instances, there is no unpaid worker – or half breadwinner, for that matter – available to run point on social reproduction. Therefore, 'feelings of increased time-pressure have an objective foundation for an increasing proportion of the population', particularly in the case of households with children. Families with children are much more likely to feel stressfully short on time than those without, and single parents are much more likely than those in dual-earner households to experience this acute sense of pressure.[119] Forty per cent of full-time working mothers in America report feeling rushed *all the time*.[120] And there is a clear pattern of decreasing free time for parents, with women facing the brunt of the loss.[121] For instance, American mothers have seen their free time decrease from a high of 37.7 hours per week in 1975 to 31.4 hours per week in 2008. Fathers saw a similar decrease from 35.7 hours in 1975 to 32 hours in 2008.[122] Lone mothers are particularly burdened, with around 30 hours a week less discretionary time than childless dual-earning households.[123] If a previous era had a gendered politics of time in which men sought clear boundaries and restraints on work while women were positioned as inexhaustible labourers of love, today seems to present a messier, but no less oppressive, set of constraints on our time. Ultimately, the politics of free time cannot be considered separately from the form of the household.

Conclusion

These circumstances bring home a few key ideas particularly clearly: first, the fact that the family is an adaptive form – it has persevered as a dominant unit of social reproduction, refracting changes in the economy through its own dynamism. As this chapter has argued, an anomalous spell of relative conformity and stability has now drawn to a close. Working-class families, people of colour, and migrant families have seen the greatest moves away from the nuclear family model from the 1960s onwards.[124] Marriage is now less common across the OECD countries, with the marriage rate dropping from 8.1 per 1,000 people in 1970 to 5.0 in 2009, and the divorce rate doubling during the same period.[125] This has meant fewer married women: between 1970 and 2014, the proportion of married adult women in America declined from 72 to 55 per cent.[126] Since the 1980s, the proportion of children born to unmarried mothers has doubled in America and tripled across the OECD.[127] There has been a major increase in single-parent households as well.[128] Single mothers in America now comprise 26 per cent of all families with children (increased from 12 per cent in 1970) – and a striking 54 per cent for Black families (the result of America's racist system of mass incarceration).[129] These figures are expected to rise across the OECD in the coming decades as well.[130] Nuclear families now tend to make up less than 60 per cent of intergenerational households in the Western world.[131]

Changes in family forms and marital norms are reflected in shifting patterns of co-residence as well. Average household size in the high-income countries is now below three – 'a level without historical precedent'.[132] As part of this trend, single-person households make up a significant and growing portion of the population (more than 30 per cent of households in places like France, Germany, and the UK – and as high as 40 per cent in places like Finland and Norway).[133] The diminishing size of households lends new urgency to feminist arguments about the needless repetition of domestic work. If it was absurd that individual *families* should each cook their own food and run their own washing machines, what are we to make of solitary *individuals* each doing this work? Adding to temporal concerns, there are also growing ecological concerns about the energy and resource wastefulness that such arrangements can involve.[134]

The second key point is that the family remains the carer of last resort – and therefore the repository of residual necessary labour. From the perspective of the state, for instance, the family was the obvious structure to which to turn in order to manage an immediate, pandemic-induced reproductive crisis, as it could be expected to pick up the slack when other options were taken off the table. This was frequently thanks to household members stepping in, behind closed doors, to take on additional responsibilities at considerable cost to their own well-being. The pandemic situation also illustrates a shift in the generally accepted role of women as shock absorbers within reproductive units – as the people assumed to be the most resilient part of a most resilient social form. We have seen over the course of this chapter that, throughout the history of the family under capitalism, mothers have served as an invaluable reserve army of labour for their households. Today, we would argue, the emphasis has shifted from women as an intrafamilial reserve army of *wage labour* to women as an intrafamilial reserve army of *unwaged care*. In an emergency, women in mixed-gender households are expected to cut back their hours in employment to step into caring roles – to tend to ailing elders, chronically ill family members, or very young children, for example – rather than to step out of reproductive specialism and into wage work. The absence of sufficient non-familial resources – whether through affordable market-based care, public provision, or voluntary efforts – means that the family takes on the brunt of this work.

This has long been a struggle, even for those nuclear families most catered to by welfare systems. Yet in the face of the growing prominence of other family forms, these challenges are becoming even more significant – particularly given the lack of recognition of non-traditional families from states. Many policies remain oriented towards the nuclear family (tax policies, immigration policies, and so on) and stubbornly refuse to recognise the diversity of ways in which people organise their lives today. The reproductive crisis is not just being felt by those who reside within family-households. Indeed, it is being borne most acutely by those who are *not* currently members of conventional nuclear units of social reproduction – those who have long been denied access to, or who have to some degree chosen to build their lives outside of, the privileged and exclusionary institution of the family.[135]

So, where does this changing picture of family, gender, and work under capitalism leave us? This is an issue to which we shall return in our conclusion. For now, we can say that there are profound tensions across the reproductive regime as it stands, with the ghost of the breadwinner/homemaker model continuing to butt up against more recent assumptions that everybody who can work for pay will work for pay. At the same time, the under-provision of public resources for care means that it is carers, the cared-for, and the *should*-be-cared-for who find themselves at the sharp end of this situation. From our point of view, it is hard to see any route out of the current reproductive crisis that doesn't extend to a fundamental rethinking of the familial reproductive regime – one that questions sedimented assumptions about the proper role of the family, the home, social standards, and domestic technologies.

5

Spaces

The domestic sphere has, for too long, been denuded of a sense of political opportunity. Despite a rich heritage of domestic design and community planning, contemporary feminists in the Anglosphere have largely come to accept the 'spatial design of the home … as an inevitable part of domestic life'.[1] More generally, the single-family residence has become an aspirational norm – an achievement to be celebrated and strived for. Whether one embraces it wholeheartedly or attempts to resist it, the conventional family home shapes the possibility space of our intimate lives. We call this tendency 'domestic realism'[2] – the obstinacy of domestic imaginaries in the face of otherwise extensive visions of sociotechnical overhaul. Domestic realism names the phenomenon whereby the isolated dwelling (and the concomitant privatisation of household labour) becomes so accepted and commonplace that it is almost impossible to imagine life being organised through any other form. That this should be the case despite many people's lived experiences of the pressures and difficulties attendant upon home-based reproductive labour (not to mention of domestic violence and abuse) makes such an attitude all the more remarkable.

But there are many possible forms of domestic arrangement – both spatial and relational – aside from the atomised and depoliticised family residence that we most closely associate with the idea of home today. Indeed, it is important that we understand the built environment and its infrastructures not only as means of registering and consolidating dominant political positions but also as potential sites for intervention and as territories for contestation. Interrogating the spaces of reproductive labour may be one way of contributing to the construction of a new kind of explicitly feminist post-work common sense.

In what ways might changes to the built environment help to foster and support this reinvention? Reducing the amount of work that a house can generate has rarely been a key concern for designers, developers, or planners (as our discussion of the smart home in Chapter 2 began to illustrate). Certainly, addressing the politics of the gendered division of labour has not been a mainstream priority for home builders in the era of domestic realism. Nevertheless, there *have* been a number of intriguing architectural interventions and small-scale experiments throughout the twentieth century. What can we learn from these historical examples?

Laying the Foundations

The house is by no means a novel problem. From the *fin de siècle* to the end of World War I, the spatial politics of the domestic dwelling had substantial cultural visibility. These decades were a period of significant spatial change within industrialising nations – one in which alternative means of organising the built environment seemed possible and one where key questions about the design and function of housing were still to be settled. Many feminists recognised domestic space as the nexus for a number of crucial political issues.[3]

The Russian Commune in the Early Twentieth Century

One of the most notable moments of experimentation was in the spaces opened up in the immediate wake of the Russian Revolution. The Soviet regime had inherited a vast housing crisis from its Tsarist predecessor. As cities grew rapidly, overcrowding became widespread and strangers were increasingly forced to live together.[4] Ambitions towards the establishment of a new form of daily life – or *novyi byt* – were set against this background of deprivation. Revolutionary ideology was inseparable from material limits, and from the Bolsheviks' point of view, communal housing had the advantage of addressing both.[5] Such housing would be an efficient use of space, would help bring about a collective style of living, and would thus 'form the foundation of a new socialist person'.[6] Certainly, it seemed to open the door to the house commune, which was widely touted as the most appropriate form of communist housing and the future of shelter in Russia. As many urban residents were already living in cramped and shared spaces, turning dwellings into communes seemed like a relatively simple step.[7] In a further key advantage, communal facilities such as laundries and kitchens would better enable domestic work to be shared and rationalised, thereby giving women more time to participate in civic life and productive work.

Enthralled with the possibilities wrenched open by revolutionary fervour, architects and urban planners created grand utopian visions for future housing and cities. The commune was central to many of these (though ultimately, few were ever built).[8] According to many of its theorists and advocates, the new socialist *byt* involved three crucial spatial components:

communal laundries, communal childcare facilities, and communal kitchens.[9] Moscow's first custom-built house commune, finished in 1929, offered luxurious facilities of this kind and many more. One popular women's magazine of the period enthused about its

> communal kitchen, with the latest in domestic equipment, the separate dining room overlooking what would soon become a garden-courtyard, and the steps leading out to a veranda; about its creche and kindergarten, its mother and child corner, its consulting room where children would be regularly checked over by a visiting paediatrician. There was a laundry, a club, a stage for amateur theatre productions, a library, reading room, and hairdressing salon [and on the roof, a solarium, which could] be converted into an open-air cinema after dark.[10]

The shifting of certain private responsibilities into the public realm represented more than a development in domestic architecture; it was a challenge to the conventional family and an attempt to transform the organisation of social reproduction in its entirety. For some, the ambition was that life would be entirely socialised: 'There would be no kitchens for individual use, no shops selling food products, no individual child care, and no rooms in which husband and wife could carry out any semblance of family life.'[11] Women were to be liberated into the public realm via the wholesale eradication of the family.[12]

House communes rarely had the space or the resources to set up adequate common facilities, however. It is no surprise, then, that journalists who set out to report on co-operative housing at this time frequently discovered that most people were living in more traditional family-centred ways and that communal living had little support.[13] In response, the government tried to get people to see the entire 'socialist city' as their home: 'Citizens were encouraged to stroll en masse through their city parks, squares and boulevards, make use of communal recreational facilities, and see their "living space" as simply somewhere to sleep.'[14] Public resources, such as the Moscow Metro and its impressively spacious stations, became showpieces of public luxury. Coverage in weekly news, culture, and entertainment magazines tended to neglect the housing crisis in favour of celebrating municipal amenities. The message for Soviet citizens was that their home was now the entire city and not just a cramped room in an apartment.[15]

This idea of the city as one's playground was combined with efforts at a more local provision of shared resources (such as laundries and kitchens) within specific housing schemes. The Narkomfin Communal House of 1928–1930 is one high-profile example of such communal luxury. The Narkomfin was a 'transitional' development located in Moscow which generally sought to encourage the principles of communal living while nevertheless offering a range of different accommodation types (from self-sufficient family apartments to smaller kitchenless units to dormitories with shared showers and beds that folded into the wall). Within the development, a covered walkway connected the living block to a communal block containing a gym, library, communal kitchen, and dining area.[16] A third building housed the laundry, and there were originally plans for a fourth building that would contain a crèche. The idea was that the children of the complex would effectively live in this building, with a team of professional staff overseeing them while their parents engaged in work and social lives.[17]

Challenges in terms of the management of reproductive labour were quick to appear, however. Many of the original female residents of the Narkomfin building had independent careers and pursued the newly established ideal of women eschewing domestic life in favour of contributing to the project of building socialism.[18] The problem remained, though, as to what to do about housework and care work once these women had been 'liberated' into wage labour. Policy makers and social reformers typically viewed domestic transformation as a matter for women. There was very little discussion of shifting men into unpaid domestic work – not surprising given the significance accorded to public work.[19] But the effect of enlisting women into the world of work *outside* the home without equally enlisting men into the world of work *within* the home (and before adequate public infrastructure was in place to take over this work) was, predictably enough, to increase the burden on women. Waged women were faced with less time for sleeping or eating properly and subsequently experienced more exhaustion.[20]

The first Five-Year Plan (1928–1932) intensified the housing crisis in Russia. Industrialisation drew more people to the cities, which led the regime to turn further towards the idea of communal housing. However, given the ongoing massive state investment in industrial development, the new *byt* was not considered a priority and few financial resources were made available to support it.

[The] house commune and the transformation of *byt* had been promoted largely on the grounds that they would lead to the demise of the traditional family and liberate women from domestic responsibilities, especially child care, but this had turned out to require a level of expenditure which the authorities, given their current economic priorities, would not commit. If women were willing to provide domestic services for free, they should not be discouraged from doing so, and they were more likely to provide these services for their own families.[21]

The tide thus began to turn away from communal living and the socialisation of domestic labour as the basis of *byt* reform.

In May 1930, the Central Committee of the Communist Party decisively pivoted, issuing a directive condemning the 'full socialization of family life' and 'fully communalized living patterns'. By the time of its completion, the Narkomfin Communal House was already being 'relegated to the dustbin of history as a peculiar and archaic manifestation of a bygone era'.[22] While the building continued to house residents, the ideas which framed it were disappearing. Before long, the communal facilities had been removed and the site reconfigured to fit more traditional lifestyles.[23] At the same time, state institutions stopped investing in housing co-operatives. Rural communes were transformed by the process of collectivisation, while the flood of rural migrants into cities brought with them dispositions that were further disinclined to communal living.[24] Workplace housing (in the form of factory barracks) took greater hold, and citizens continued to rub along in fractious proximity within overstuffed apartments. Now, however, people's experiences of cramped living conditions were stripped of the veneer of ideological correctness. Literature espousing means to rationalise housework or agitating against bourgeois households stopped being published and fell out of circulation.[25] A new vision of the Soviet good life emerged, centred upon the conjugal heterosexual couple and their children, which was reflected in the 1937 tightening of restrictions on divorce and abortion. While the city and the nation remained the home of the citizen, a new emphasis on the hearth and the single-family apartment (still largely unavailable to the average worker) displaced elements of communal luxury.

A period of profound domestic experimentation in Russia – characterised by unappealingly inflexible (if always contentious) ideas about where and how people should live and with whom, and by stubbornly poor living conditions for many, but also by more admirable ambitions towards luxurious public spaces and magnificent shared resources – was brought to a definitive close.

The Anglo-American Home in the Early Twentieth Century

Like Russia, America was undergoing considerable industrialisation and urbanisation at this time, and this had a profound effect on the shape and organisation of the home. However, in contrast with the Soviet situation, dominant ideas of 'right living' in the US and UK involved a sharp spatial demarcation of households. Anxieties particularly around cleanliness drove changes in the organisation of the home and its associated labours. New knowledge about contagions and how they spread meant that late Victorian suburbs were seen by the middle classes as providing a form of 'spatial health insurance' – protection against immigrants, the poor, and other supposed vectors of disease.[26] The single-family home was a sanctuary against 'unruly neighbours'.[27] The suburbs likewise represented 'enormous gestures of withdrawal from cities that were perceived as unhealthy, dangerous, and crowded', while the architectural trappings of individual homes (porches, hedges, front gardens, and so on) offered a system of filters between private domestic space and unpredictable public space.[28]

Despite the perceived benefits of such measures, however, the single-family home did have its dissenting voices. Feminists of the period recognised that it was remarkably resource intensive, demanding not only masses of fuel and equipment, but also the endless repetition of specific tasks (such as those involved in cooking and cleaning). The hold that this kind of isolated domestic residence had over the middle-class imagination worked to entrench the irrational privatisation of reproductive work and encouraged an obscene squandering of time and energy.

As such, many domestic reformers turned towards ideas of collectivity and interconnection in their approach to housing, drawing inspiration from fast-developing city centres rather than their peripheries.

We can get a sense of this from the work of the American writer and domestic reformer Charlotte Perkins Gilman. As Gilman remarked, 'Our houses are threaded together like beads on a string, tied, knotted, woven together, and in cities even built together; one solid house from block-end to block-end; their boasted individuality maintained by a thin partition wall.' Furthermore, residents were dependent upon shared infrastructure: 'Water is a household necessity and was once supplied by household labour, the women going to the wells to fetch it. Water is now supplied by the municipality, and flows among our many homes as one.'[29] With the arrival of sewers and telephone lines, water pipes and electricity cables, many reformers naturally alighted upon infrastructural solutions to household problems. Proposals for the collective management of domestic labour – common facilities, co-operative housekeeping, and communal living – capitalised upon (and were inspired by) these existing trends and emerging technological potentials.

The idea of shared domestic infrastructure enjoyed considerable popularity during the early decades of the twentieth century,[30] and many people found themselves drawn to the benefits of communal life.[31] There were numerous attempts at lived experiments as well as a variety of more utopian theories espousing the wonders of this approach. In cities such as London and New York, mansion flats 'were built with communal heating, waste-disposal, and water facilities. Some offered deep-freezes and laundries in the basements'[32] – luxurious innovations for the time. In some urban areas of the US, the apartment hotel – which offered shared facilities and serviced rooms for long-term habitation – began to flourish. The Ansonia building on New York's Upper West Side, for example, was erected between 1899 and 1904, and offered high-end residential spaces with a collectivist bent.[33] It was made up of kitchenless suites of various sizes and boasted considerable amenities. These included everything from healthcare facilities (a doctors' surgery, dental office, and pharmacy) to an on-site florist, barbershop, and tailors. There was even (for a time, at least) a city farm on the roof, providing residents with fresh eggs free of charge each morning. At the same time, a great deal of domestic labour was outsourced to an expert, professionalised workforce, to whom the residents could pass messages via pneumatic tubes in the walls. While the Ansonia was clearly premised on an idea of opulence for the affluent rather than anything akin to a Soviet idea of public luxury, it nevertheless serves to illustrate the nascent ascendency of alternatives to the single-family home in this period. A different domestic imaginary, in which a degree of collectivity was desirable even for the rich, was very much a live possibility at the time.

Ideas of communal living held promise for those further down the class spectrum, too. In the early 1900s, 'a group of enterprising Finnish immigrant women, working as domestic servants … pooled their wages to rent an apartment to use on their days off'. Over time, this modest initiative grew into the Finnish Women's Co-operative Home – 'a four-storey building with sleeping accommodation, lounges, club rooms, a library, a restaurant and an employment agency'.[34] A $5 per-member-per-year shareholder's fee helped cover costs – and outside of war time, the employment agency was capable of turning a modest profit, allowing members to reap a dividend. Domestic work was handled by a dedicated housekeeper and cook, and residents were expected to do nothing more than make their own beds in the morning and pay their dues. Furthermore, the co-operative (to its credit) didn't impose many burdensome restrictions upon members' conduct. As a 1918 report in the *New York Tribune* put it, 'There are no rules to be observed in the home except those which any girl of decent inclinations or education would naturally observe.' Members were free to entertain guests of any gender and to enter the building at any time of the day or night. The co-operative's unique features meant that it could stand 'absolutely on its own feet, a monument to the vision and perseverance and intelligence of the Finnish women ... engaged in domestic service'.[35] It continued to operate until at least the early 1920s.

If initiatives such as apartment hotels and co-operative homes sought to collectivise the work of social reproduction by bringing people into shared space, other approaches sought to *retain* the atomised single-family home while rationalising the labour processes within it. Reformers such as Christine Frederick, for example, believed the correct application of science to the home could improve the domestic workers' condition.[36] Her (hugely popular) writings throughout the 1910s explicitly engaged with the conventions of engineering and scientific management, including applying insights derived from the efficient organisation of factory production to labour within the home – a tendency which also came to characterise a number of the Soviet communes. This involved efforts to redesign domestic space by, for example, adjusting the heights of worktops to ensure that tasks could be performed with the minimum amount of stooping and extraneous movement. On the face of it, Frederick's efforts to rationalise the layout of the home (and particularly the kitchen) might be seen as an endeavour to ameliorate the worst of the domestic burden, helping reproductive labourers identify the most efficient, labour-saving, and least-burdensome ways to perform their work.[37] However, this approach also brought with it a plethora of new kinds of pseudo-managerial work, meaning that time spent in one form of domestic activity (the elbow-grease heavy tasks of cleaning or cooking) was immediately eaten up by another (the organisational labour of administration, record-keeping, and strategic forward planning).[38]

Frederick had transformed the housewife into a manager[39] and offered her 'status by association with what many intellectuals at the time saw as the key motors of social progress, science and industry'.[40] While her proposals have the distinct advantage of making 'efficiency and the notion of time-saving in kitchen work a socially acceptable goal for women', they are arguably organised more towards the cultivation of prestige via professionalisation than they are towards the fight for free time.[41] The work demanded by the home is neither reduced nor redistributed in her proposals; indeed, it only comes to be recognised because it is brought more closely in line with the masculinised, middle-class activities of industrial management. But while Frederick's work often aimed to impose the capitalist rationality of wage labour onto domestic space in a way that was less than productive, these kinds of ideas nevertheless hold a grain of emancipatory potential, as we can see when we consider more progressive experiments.

In 1914, for example, the New York Feminist Alliance proposed the building of a Feminist Apartment House – one designed to prioritise the elimination of the worst burdens of domestic drudgery. More than just offering opportunities for co-operative housekeeping, the complex was configured to make shrewd use of spatial hacks to reduce the need for certain kinds of cleaning labour. Within the Feminist Apartment House, 'all corners would be rounded, all bathtubs would be built in, all windows would pivot, all beds would fold in to the walls, and all hardware would be dull finished' in order to reduce the labour of dusting, sweeping, polishing, and so on.[42] In this case, design was conceived of as one way of making the waged or unwaged reproductive labourer's life less onerous and was a tool to be combined with other, more collectively minded approaches.

While it was undoubtedly an era of expansive imagination and concrete experimentation, it is nevertheless worth noting that many of these early twentieth century Anglo-American alternatives were plagued with shortcomings. One of the more notable lacunae was the lack of consideration given to the specifically gendered nature of social reproduction. For domestic reformers such as Gilman, their work rarely examined the issue of *who* would do the housework (aside from sometimes suggesting that it should fall to professionals). That feminists of this period sought to intervene within the spatial organisation of domestic life before agitating for greater male involvement in housework and care work says something about the assumed intractability of gender roles. There were also significant issues around class politics. Many projects of domestic reform were driven by white bourgeois home economists, who often neglected the fact that the urban working classes had existing (and far less positive) experiences of co-living and shared facilities, given the appalling tenement conditions prevalent at the turn of the century.[43] These spaces were plagued with an 'insufficiency of light and air due to narrow courts or air shafts, dark hallways with no lights or windows, overcrowding of buildings on lots, fire hazards in design and use, lack of separate water-closets and washing facilities, overcrowding, and foul cellars and courts'.[44] Indeed, British working-class women often ended up seeing the proposals of middle-class reformers as ignorant impositions.[45]

In a US context, domestic reform was often undertaken as a project of disciplining the poor, making immigrants more

American, and inculcating an ideology of 'right living' that was modelled after the aspirations of the white middle classes. Practically, 'it meant thrift, orderliness, and privacy instead of spontaneity and neighbourliness'.[46] Similar disciplining functions were embodied through the efforts of progressive intellectuals and reformers to establish legal protections from damp, mouldy, cramped housing. While well-meaning, such efforts were intertwined with ideas around eliminating social vices, which meant that any material improvements tended to be 'overshadowed by the abuse and harassment that accompanied the police presence inside private homes'. In the early 1900s, 'the police were given great latitude in the surveillance and arrest of black women and tenement residents', with the result that housing reform was often entangled with the imposition of bourgeois norms surrounding behaviour, conduct, and ways of living (particularly in terms of sexual morality).[47] Moreover, these reformers tended to ignore or overlook the already existing informal networks created by working-class women, Black people, and immigrant groups.[48] As the example of the Finnish Women's Co-operative Home demonstrates, projects of collectivised social reproduction were by no means limited to middle-class social reformers. Co-operative domestic arrangements in, for example, the Chicago settlements of the 1890s in fact worked to facilitate the organisation of trade unions and helped to discourage strike breaking.[49] There are many different approaches to dislodging domestic realism, then – some more emancipatory than others.

In the end, vested capitalist interests (namely, the American hotel industry) helped to put an end to luxurious, collectively resourced, equitably organised living arrangements as a feasible labour-saving alternative to today's domestic realism. A series of lawsuits in mid-1920s New York sought to cut down on the competition posed by apartment hotels; the industry argued that such complexes could not be considered real hotels since they had permanent, not transitory, residents – and as a result, they should be regulated by the stricter rules around apartment buildings. By 1929, the Multiple Dwelling Law had been passed, piggybacking on anxieties about overcrowded and unhealthy tenements in the city. The regulation stated that apartment hotels were to be regulated as apartment buildings, with the same rules to hold around the scope and occupancy of the spaces. These policy changes compromised the economic viability of kitch-enless apartments within such complexes, and after the stock market crash of the following year, few such apartments survived.[50] Here, the material interests of a distinctive and powerful lobby contributed to the quashing of potentially emancipatory co-operative living arrangements.

These experiments in co-operative housekeeping and the collectivising of reproductive labour often took place in a context of privately funded developments or speculative building projects (particularly in America). In many cases, commercial pressures led to their abandonment, or to their reorientation away from original socialist feminist ambitions. Looking towards continental Europe, however – particularly in the interwar years – we find domestic proposals emerging from a rather different context and facing rather different pressures.

Housing for the Masses

Social housing first emerged in the late nineteenth century as a response to the transformations being wrought by capitalist industrialisation. The shift of rural populations into cities was a particular spur; cities strained under the influx of workers, with shanty towns, slums, and overcrowded housing increasingly prevalent.[51] Social housing was an answer to these problems, and the interwar years saw European governments become directly involved in constructing alternatives to conventional single-family residences. We look here to the 1920s, with Europe facing the task of reconstruction in the wake of World War I and with an emerging desire among some designers to use this moment to move beyond class distinctions.[52] The possibilities afforded by social housing at the time – namely, extensive building, mass adoption, and opportunities for the implementation of radical new spatial imaginaries – meant that housing projects held considerable appeal for avant-garde practitioners across disciplines. Urban planning was inexorably entangled with ideas about society, community, and futurity, and social housing was produced not just as a response to housing shortages, but also as a way to show how a more socialist, classless society might look.[53] Politicians, architectural theorists, and municipal planners alike explored radical ideas about how space could be reorganised to build such a world.[54]

The Frankfurt Kitchen

In the city of Frankfurt, architect Ernst May was appointed head of the department of housing and city planning, where he proceeded to oversee the creation of 15,000 housing units by the end of the decade.[55] One of the key characteristics of these new dwellings was their innovative approach to domestic design – an approach substantially informed by earlier discussions about scientific management within the home. Around two-thirds featured the so-called Frankfurt Kitchen, created by the architect Margarete Schütte-Lihotzky in 1926[56] – a particularly notable development, given that most homes of the time did not include a dedicated kitchen space.[57]

Schütte-Lihotzky's aim (much like Frederick's before her) was to apply techniques aimed at efficiency in the waged workplace to the unwaged – in short, to take seriously the idea that domestic work was *work* and to Taylorise the home. Time and motion studies were deployed to estimate the ideal size of a kitchen – big enough to enable work, while small enough to minimise movement.[58] The preferred, galley-style layout in turn reflected studies of how housewives moved through spaces while cooking and cleaning.[59] The overall aim was to construct an easier to use, less time consuming, and generally more pleasant working environment for reproductive labourers. In keeping with the principles of scientific management, this sensitivity to ergonomic design emphasised the role of the kitchen not as a sentimentalised 'heart of the home', but rather as a rationalisable workplace. In so doing, the Frankfurt Kitchen gestured towards the possibility of reducing some of the temporal and physical burdens associated with housework. Indeed, Schütte-Lihotzky was at pains to emphasise that her design was intended to reduce the time spent on domestic work and enable women to be liberated from it.[60]

However, this vision was not without its problems – problems which substantially diminished its post-work potential. The diminutive dimensions of the galley layout, for instance, saw children sent out to other rooms when the kitchen was in use, meaning that it was harder for their mothers to keep watch over them while preparing food or cleaning up. The assembly line assumptions of scientific management were ill-suited to the multitasking reality of social reproduction. Moreover, as with many early twentieth-century proposals aimed at eliminating drudgery, there are certain gendered assumptions embedded in the Frankfurt Kitchen that contradict Schütte-Lihotzky's stated ambitions. Since the space was deliberately designed for use by one woman – with sizings, heights, and ergonomics all oriented towards this imagined worker – the kitchen actively constrained possibilities for the sharing of domestic work.[61]

Schütte-Lihotzky's efforts placed clear restrictions upon redistribution as a means of transforming housework. Within the Frankfurt Kitchen, there is (quite literally) no room for change.

This example does, however, provide insight into the role of economies of scale when redesigning domestic spaces. Its initial successes were only made possible through governments embarking on large social housing projects. The top-down imposition of a new domestic imaginary (one explicitly advanced with the goal of increasing people's discretionary time) enabled a standardised, mass-produced model to be swiftly adopted by a large number of households. It was certainly rolled out more quickly and effectively than any effort relying on individual homeowners could have been.[62] While this top-down approach can (and did) easily lend itself to problems, it nevertheless points to the fact that, in particular contexts, social housing has enabled the widespread adoption of new, forward-looking ideas to mitigate reproductive labour. We find something similar in the second of our European examples – Red Vienna.

Red Vienna

Vienna, like Frankfurt, was subject to a housing crisis and a rebuilding effort after the devastation of World War I. A census from this period indicates that up to three-quarters of domestic dwellings in the city took the form of tiny apartments that were frequently without electricity, gas, running water, or their own toilets and that suffered from poor lighting and ventilation. Moreover, rental properties were in extremely short supply, and homelessness was rife throughout the city.[63] As Vienna looked to regain its equilibrium after the war, the municipality sought to take a more active role in addressing the city's housing crisis. Designed and built as part of a swathe of municipal reforms instigated by the Social Democratic city council between 1919 and 1934, these ambitious housing schemes can be seen as part of a deliberate political strategy for transforming reproductive infrastructure. The plans were uniquely utopian and far-reaching; the developers 'were consciously the harbingers of a new socialist world, one that both prioritised working-class needs and fostered more communal ways of living'.[64] Wider efforts at nationalising and municipalising reproductive services such as healthcare and education were tethered to this housing programme via the situation of collective resources.[65] Large-scale apartment complexes were equipped with healthcare facilities, gyms, kindergartens, libraries, lecture halls, workshops, laundries, gardens, and a wide range of other resources – measures funded via progressive taxation targeting luxury goods like cars and champagne, as well as the services provided by household servants.

These design choices were explicitly related to ideas regarding the drudgery of domestic labour, with socialist feminists arguing that domestic work should be professionalised and that communal apartment living could help to further alleviate the burdens of their work.[66] This was often framed in the most emancipatory terms, with architects (including Schütte-Lihotzky) arguing that large housing schemes with shared facilities would give working-class women more time for political organising and civic engagement. Indeed, promotional images of Red Vienna's individual apartments tend to depict 'a family at rest ... Girls in particular are shown engaged in intellectual pursuits; reading, studying, lost in thought'.[67] Furthermore, as Eve Blau remarks, the private space of the apartment was not typically the focus of these illustrations:

> The city produced and published a far greater number of images of the communal laundries, libraries, clinics, child-care facilities,

kindergartens, public baths, gardens, parks, playgrounds, swimming and wading pools, theatres, lecture halls, and the like, emphasizing that the new political and economic life of the proletarian city was to be shaped not in the private space but in the public and communal space provided in the new buildings. Not only are the laundries, clinics, and other communal facilities shown in full operation, but they are also depicted as the sites of technological, sociological, and scientific innovation in the new socialist city.[68]

As with the new Soviet *byt*, then, the emphasis was very much on private sufficiency and public luxury. The radical gender political potential of these attempts at building a socialised life, along with the possibilities of diverting understandings of luxury towards the communal, offer tantalising resources for twenty-first-century post-work feminisms.

However, we must not downplay the problematic elements of the Viennese project, nor overlook the barriers that prevented its expansion and ultimately stopped it in its tracks. First, there were failures (or at least limitations) in terms of the way communal services were implemented. While the official promotional material and ideological arguments presented a world where women were largely relieved of domestic labour, the realities were somewhat different. Nurseries, for example, failed to operate in a manner maximally helpful to working-class parents: they 'only accepted children at age four, so younger children needed alternative care; some opened at 8:00 AM, though the average workday began at 7:00 AM; some did not provide lunches; and most closed for extended holidays'.[69] There were related issues in terms of the city's high-spec collective laundries – facilities that were considered something of a showpiece. Households were only allocated a single washday every month, meaning that residents were expected to complete this chore (perhaps

the heaviest activity of domestic labour at the time) to somebody else's timeframe, under conditions of work intensification.
What's more, the only men permitted to enter these spaces
were those employed as laundry supervisors. While this rule
was in place so that women could remove outer clothing so
as to wash them at the same time, the effect was to enforce a
rigidly gendered division of labour.[70] Men could not help with
the monthly wash, even if they were willing. As with the case of
the Frankfurt Kitchen, then, we see that the post-work promise
of interwar social housing experiments is very much marred by
the obstinacy of gender ideologies.

The Red Vienna experiment was ultimately quashed by the
rise of fascism. In 1934, the fascist government eviscerated
the labour movement, removed Vienna's administration, and
replaced them with its own commissioners. These commissioners
were quick to reverse the municipality's efforts to redistribute
wealth through progressive taxation, and the experiments with
social housing were mostly abandoned.[71] But, for all these issues,
the communal facilities of Red Vienna's large apartment buildings did encourage the recognition of reproductive work, if not
its gendered redistribution. Under the conditions created by
Viennese interwar social housing, those assigned cultural responsibility for reproductive labour no longer worked in isolating
arrangements that cloistered them entirely from public view.[72]
With the introduction of such facilities, 'laundry was removed
from the private space of the apartment to a more communal
space outside the home – a space, moreover, that was ... shared
with other women, and that was bright, centrally located, and
actually equipped with labour-saving machinery'.[73] Recognition
and acknowledgement of this form of activity is arguably one
key strut in efforts to minimise its temporal burdens; it must first
be *seen* as work if it is to be *refused* as work.

Therefore, while Red Vienna's problems show that there is no architectural quick fix, it nevertheless offers us a compelling example of missed futures.[74] It illustrates that the fight for a better quality of life should not just concentrate upon single-family dwellings, the facilities available within individual households, and the leisure time these might free up, but upon a broader idea of communal luxury. The influence of the socialist building project can still be detected within Vienna today. Although the city is not immune to the pressures of a global housing crisis, it nevertheless continues to build significant swathes of affordable and high-quality social housing every year.[75] Social housing in the city continues to include shared amenities such as swimming pools and saunas, in keeping with Red Vienna's historical favouring of communal spaces and collective resources.[76] Today, most Viennese citizens still live in municipally owned or otherwise subsidised housing, with the city itself serving as 'Austria's biggest landlord'.[77] Having the municipality play such a significant role in the provision of accommodation has had a notable effect on the housing landscape of Vienna as a whole. Nevertheless, a vision of the collective provision of social reproduction has not taken hold across the wealthier nations. In order to understand why, we need to consider how the single-family home – and the supposed 'ideal' of suburban living – came to dominate. How did we get from a moment of apparent possibility in the first half of the twentieth century to the entrenchment of domestic realism in the second?

Shelter against Communism

As the twentieth century progressed, a new dwelling paradigm appeared: mass home ownership. In the nineteenth century, with the exception of the wealthy, most people rented their homes.[78]

And in the immediate aftermath of World War II, home ownership remained a minority position in most countries. Yet by the
end of the century, home ownership had become the dominant
form of dwelling in nearly every rich country.[79]

As many have noted, the rise of home ownership has been
crucial to contemporary capitalism because of its role in speculative finance, property development, and, more recently,
asset-based welfare.[80] But there is another less-remarked-upon
reason home ownership has been promoted under neoliberal
capitalism. As 1940s property magnate William J. Levitt pointed
out, 'No man who owns his own house and lot can be a Communist. He has too much to do.'[81] Beyond just economic impacts,
therefore, housing has been used to perpetuate a particular
configuration of values around hard work, busyness, individualism, self-reliance, and family structure. In other words, housing
– specifically home ownership and the American model of single-
family residences spread out across large suburban areas – has
been a linchpin for capitalism not only through its economic
functions, but also through its impacts on temporal autonomy
and the domestic organisation of reproductive labour.

How did this space of counter-communism emerge? A huge
number of dwellings were built in America in the years after
World War II, spurred on by the baby boom. This new housing
largely took the form of single-family residences, often designed
without input from either architects or prospective residents,
and typically offering little access to neighbourhood resources.
Instead, 'these houses were bare boxes to be filled up with mass-
produced commodities.'[82] Labour-saving devices that had once
'been architectural, such as built-in compartments with brine-
filled pipes for refrigeration or built-in vacuum systems for
cleaning, both used in many apartment hotels', were increasingly
scrapped and replaced with discrete household appliances.[83]

These consumer goods, proliferating as they did across innumerable atomised single-family homes, were capable of securing their manufacturers a significant profit, all while entrenching the privatisation and individualisation of housework.

Suburban housing certainly encouraged – and continues to encourage – a colossal squandering of human time, effort, and labour. Consider, as just one example, the amount of driving it demands. The rise of the suburban dream house in the mid-twentieth century saw social reproduction become increasingly dependent upon personalised means of transit.[84] With facilities geographically dispersed, women in particular found themselves spending increasing portions of their time ferrying dependents to and from homes, shops, schools, doctors' surgeries, leisure spaces, and so on. The spread of the automobile and the rise of the supermarket were both facilitators of postwar suburban living, as well as necessities imposed by this type of housing.[85] (As such, it is not surprising that a growing concern with time has partly driven the move from suburbs back into central cities.)[86] This was part and parcel of a wider ideological shift taking place during the postwar period, whereby the dream house took over as the ideal space from earlier visions of an ideal city.[87]

When it came to the domestic imaginaries of the postwar suburbs, then, there was precious little acknowledgement of the spatial elements of social reproduction. Indeed, the commercial housing industry was hugely successful in promoting a particular (and highly limited) image of home – one capable of displacing some of the previously ascendant ideas of shelter which prioritised not the single-family dwelling but the city, the neighbourhood, and the residential co-operative.[88] On top of this, as Levitt well recognised, owning a single-family home was a major source of *new* demands for work. Owner-occupiers now had to worry about repairs, were incentivised to think about how to spend time improving the home, and in suburbia, found a growing need to take care of sprawling lawns. Owning a home, in Levitt's ideal, precisely meant being too busy to think or act politically – too much free time might lead to communism!

Exporting the Home

As the twentieth century rolled on, postwar American domesticity itself became a weapon in a propaganda war. In a famous 1959 meeting, Richard Nixon and Nikita Khrushchev visited a model ranch house – typical of American dwellings at the time – included in a Moscow exhibition demonstrating the American way of life.[89] It was the General Electric show kitchen that sparked the so-called Kitchen Debate, with the two men using the exhibit as a means by which to espouse the ideologies of their respective countries. Khrushchev highlighted the in-built obsolescence of American design: 'Your American houses are built to last only twenty years so builders could sell new houses at the end.' Nixon, meanwhile, stressed capitalist individualism, consumer choice, and labour-saving innovation, declaring that 'in America, we like to make life easier for women'. He also asserted the importance of 'diversity, the right to choose, [and] the fact that we have 1,000 builders building 1,000 different houses'.[90] These claims about America's supposed achievements don't hold much water: we have already seen that women's work had not decreased, and the nature of capitalist housing developers is such that they tend to copy and paste a few floorplans to mass produce hundreds of sprawling identical developments.[91] Nevertheless, this moment of ideological conflict and national self-imagining served to cement the kitchen as a nexus where political, social, and technological differences found expression, while foregrounding some of the ways in which the house could be positioned as a defence against communism and unamerican values.[92]

American home ownership was used for more than just ideological posturing during the Cold War, however. In the wake of World War II, there was a global housing crisis, one caused by a lack of new construction, the mass movement of people, and the large-scale destruction of housing stock, shortly followed by a surge in births.[93] Housing supply was undergoing a severe shortage, and many countries were looking for ways to rectify this problem. Into this breach, American foreign policy looked to export the idea of mass home ownership as a way to ingrain capitalist values within developing economies. While many other developed countries offered assistance and advice for building housing, American programmes were uniquely focused on expanding home ownership (as opposed to collective ownership or the improvement of living standards) and market-led construction (as opposed to government-directed construction).

Interventions into housing were chosen on the basis of their strategic importance in the battle against communism. Taiwan, for instance, was deemed a key bulwark against Chinese communism. Here, American-supported housing aid was structured in ways which were supposed to jumpstart a local housing industry as a foundational sector that might lead to more capitalist development. Housing aid was also targeted towards crucial segments of the workforce – those who might revolt and shut down logistics networks, for instance – with the goal of expanding home ownership among these workers and demonstrating what capitalism could provide.[94]

Central to the planners' vision was the idea that home ownership would instil a self-help mentality in owner-occupiers that would foster a capitalist culture of individualism and self-reliance.[95] And echoing Levitt, the expansion of home ownership was seen as an important way to keep potentially restless workers busy – by giving them incentives to focus on repairs and improvements to their home rather than political agitation. In Taiwan, at least, the programmes were partly successful; offering housing support to model workers encouraged employees to significantly increase their productivity while simultaneously reducing any inclination to sabotage and steal from their workplace.[96] The American export of home ownership was therefore, in no small part, an intentional expansion of capitalist social relations.

But we should be careful not to strip homeowners of their agency here. Clearly, this vision of right living appealed to people for a reason, whether in America, Taiwan, or elsewhere. Suburban houses tended to offer fresh air and open space, for example, and in the postwar years they were made financially accessible to young families who had been yearning for privacy, stability, space, and autonomy after the forced mucking-by-together of the wartime years. Particularly in America, home ownership was also an expression of racial biases, with the growing suburban areas an expression of white flight, all backed up by the government; for instance, 98 per cent of the dwellings insured by the Federal Housing Association in 1952 were in 'white-only' areas.[97] 'Restrictive covenants' were widely used in many places as well, which imposed strict rules on home buyers about what the property could be used for and even to whom it could be sold.[98] Suburbia expressed a desire for sanctuary – from disease, from the working classes, from the racialised Other.

At the same time, however, we must recognise that a suburban cultural ideal was also aggressively promoted and meticulously maintained. Domestic life after the war 'became an art form carefully constructed and marketed by a whole new industry: a form of art therapy for a traumatized nation, a reassuring image of the "good life" to be bought like any other product'.[99] This industry was hugely successful in promoting a particular (and highly limited) image of home. And this image became, through juridical reinforcement, intertwined with a particular idea of the family as well. For example, 'the focus of single-family zoning laws shifted from the use of the land to the identity of the users', resulting in zoning authorities defining the family (and therefore those people who were permitted to live together) in terms of blood, marriage, or adoption relations.[100] Some laws went so far as to describe the degree of relatedness or consanguinity that would be required: for example, some allowed nuclear family members and a grandparent to constitute a family, but not adult siblings or cousins. The postwar years, then, can be seen as a time of opportunity foreclosed – a period in which American culture laboured to construct and consolidate domestic realism in the sense we experience it today.

Communal Counter-Imaginaries

While the nuclear family home held sway over the collective imagination in Europe and North America throughout the latter half of the twentieth century, it is not entirely true that there were no alternatives on offer. The grand, government-backed experiments of the first fifty years largely dissipated, but there were a number of both smaller experiments and would-be counterhegemonic imaginaries that arose throughout this period, from ambitions to transform the suburban residence into a fully automated dream home to the popularisation of the high-tech, masculinised bachelor pad.[101] Here, however, we wish to concentrate on one particularly influential example: the countercultural commune.

Exodus and the Countercultural Commune: Drop City

A concern with the refusal of social convention motivated much of American counterculture in the mid- to late 1960s, with the hippie movement famously embracing music, mind-altering drugs, and free love as vectors for expanding experience. To this extent, it represented a powerful anti-work tendency – one centred on the refusal of a certain type of disciplinary regime and the taking up of an alternative set of anti-authoritarian values. The movement believed that revolutionary change could stem from shifts in 'consciousness, in familial structures, in ways of living'.[102] This extended to experiments in communal settlements and domestic spaces – experiments which came to enjoy substantial cultural visibility, in part due to the attentions of mainstream media. During this time, there were up to a million Americans who 'dropped out' and moved into communes.[103] As such, these countercultural practices were invested with huge potential for cultural transformation – potential which has now largely slipped from view.

Despite a certain attentiveness to pleasure and enjoyment, however, many of the intentional communities that sprang up in rural areas of the US provided a rather rough and ready existence. Wheeler's Ranch and the Morning Star open land communes in northern California, for example, were populated with 'makeshift tents, wood frame structures, and canvas or plastic covered shelters' put together by their residents.[104] Some communes came to develop their own distinctive DIY aesthetic and 'futuristic vernacular architectures'.[105] The most influential of these was probably Drop City – an improvised encampment-come-'libidinal utopia', formed in rural Colorado in 1965.[106] The settlement was made of colourful geodesic-type domes, inspired by Buckminster Fuller and erected by art students without any architectural expertise or formal building experience. These structures were built from materials like chicken wire, bottle tops, and scavenged automobile parts – waste generated by American consumerism, which Drop City's residents sought to usefully repurpose. Although the dwellings held a certain visual appeal, the settlement remained 'a bizarre formal exemplar of worrisome structural soundness, uncomfortable, at times unhealthy, and by most measures socially dysfunctional'. As such, it makes for an oddly ascetic kind of post-work utopia. And yet, the 'dropout colony' can perhaps lend more to our attempts at imagining post-work spaces than other, slicker architectural fantasies of the period.[107] As a space intended to encourage detachment from a hierarchical mainstream culture dominated by the work ethic and restrictive social norms, Drop City might be said to imperfectly prefigure a world that could, should, and might well be otherwise.

The communes of sixties counterculture set themselves against conventional forms of life under capitalism – the nuclear family and wasteful, isolated suburban home as much as prevalent models of consumption, ownership, social hierarchy, and waged work in service of the profit motive. To this extent, they offered a post-work imaginary – but only in a very particular sense. The fundamental re-engineering of ways of being is hardly the agenda of the indolent, and an exodus from the work dogma demands to be seen as an intensely laborious and deliberate process. The dropping out encouraged by Drop City could not have been achieved without a fair amount of labour and dedication, and the supposedly work-shy acid communards who lived there might just as easily be characterised as hard-working.[108] Indeed, one critic suggests that early residents displayed 'a euphoric diligence more reminiscent of medieval Gothic stonemasons ... than of the hippie stereotype'.[109] The refusal of work, as exemplified by countercultural communes, did not extend to work in its most general sense, then. Far from representing a move away from any and all effortful endeavour, they must instead be seen as expressions of human creativity, collective inventiveness, and co-operative striving. They represented a type of post-work which operated not through the dramatic reduction of necessary labour, but instead through a transformation of the purposeful structure which guided this work: from an oppressive demand by the market to a freely chosen activity. This is exodus as a process that 'demands an affirmative "doing"' rather than a passive withdrawal.[110] With this in mind, we can see how some of the radical communes of the 1960s and 1970s might be positioned as materialisations of a post-work imaginary, despite the tremendous amount of commitment, effort, and energy they demanded from their residents.

There is much by which to be inspired here. But any enthusiasm one might feel for this historical moment of promise must be tempered by critical awareness of its flaws and failures. Care, in particular, posed an unresolved problem for many rural hippie communes. While children and their parents did live in Drop City, it wasn't an ideal environment for gestational and reproductive labourers – nor, indeed, for anybody else who was required to think beyond the most minimal and unobtrusive kind of physical needs. In fact, even though most of the close-knit community of permanent residents were young and able-bodied, many nevertheless chose to retreat to the city (or grad school) in the winter as the hardships became less bearable. Here we encounter the idea of exodus in a different sense. What of those less able to withdraw or with nowhere else to go? It is hard to imagine the frail or the vulnerable thriving in this environment, especially as it came to be plagued by food and water shortages, occasional spikes of violence, and bitterly cold winter weather. Drop City offered communalism without communal abundance, unable to cater for the needs of everybody. As such, its post-work imaginary was only fit for some.

Further issues become apparent when we dig deeper into the

commune's organisation of social reproduction. The invention of new forms of life associated with countercultural strategies of exodus was rarely understood as extending to reproductive labour. As one early Drop City resident put it, 'For being such an out-there, on the cutting-edge community, the gender division was remarkably traditional ... I never saw a guy wash a dish. [The one other female resident] and I both had children in diapers, so we spent a good deal of our time doing laundry.'[111] These experiences were repeated elsewhere in the intentional communities of 1960s America. As Mark Fisher sardonically put it, 'hippie was fundamentally a middle-class male phenomenon. It was about males being allowed to regress to that state of His Majesty the Ego hedonic infantilism, with women on hand to service all their needs.'[112] Although ostensibly espousing the refusal of work and the casting off of conventional values and social hierarchies, the counterculture's understanding of emancipatory social relations and of what counted as work displayed a remarkable failure of imagination and political will. If the acid commune has some utility as a 'promissory note',[113] we must nonetheless be careful *not* to mistake it for a blueprint.

Exodus and Separatist Communities: The Landdyke Movement

Of course, the countercultural communes of the sixties and seventies took a variety of forms, and not all experienced the same issues or approached them in the same ways. Perhaps the clearest examples of intentional communities transforming the debate around a gendered division of labour can be found in lesbian separatism – the construction of women-only communities which sought to avoid interactions with men.[114] Particularly interesting here is the landdyke movement, which was created when elements of second-wave feminism took up ideas from the

hippy counterculture.[115] Many separatist communities from this
period faced challenges common to those experienced by mixed-
gender hippie communes, given that they were also committed
to a withdrawal from the social mainstream and to the refusal of
its culture of work. Just as Drop City depended upon a make-
do-and-mend approach that recycled the detritus of American
consumerism, so too did many landdyke communities feature
DIY construction, unreliable infrastructure, and poor conditions.

   In the sixties and seventies (as today), residents of separatist
communities tended to live in 'marginal housing, including small,
owner-built cabins, decaying farmhouses, converted livestock
outbuildings, school buses on cement blocks, roughshod shelters made of strawbales and tarps, RVs, renovated log cabins,
owner-built adobe shelters, older mobile homes', and so on.[116]
Furthermore, they eschewed much agricultural technology and
adopted a more labour-intensive approach to self-sufficiency.[117]
As such, the landdyke commune can hardly be said to represent a straightforwardly post-work imaginary. Rather, as with
other countercultural communes, lesbian separatism of this
kind represents not a refusal of work, but the reimagining of
necessary labour on new, more agential terms. Difficult work
under trying conditions could come to be seen as a form of
temporal sovereignty given the ways in which it was opted into,
organised, and performed. Where lesbian separatist communities differed from many other countercultural communes of the
period, however, was in their sustained and explicit attentiveness
to moving beyond a gendered division of labour – an attentiveness that provided residents with access to (and responsibility
for) forms of work from which they would otherwise be culturally insulated and/or excluded. Separatists 'sought to alter
the subjection of women to capital (through wage labour) and
to men (through daily reproduction) by enabling women to

choose a life free from both modes of exploitation and to live a self-sufficient rural existence with other women'.[118] While other types of commune sometimes recognised the gendered division of labour as a problem (or at least paid lip service to that idea), few achieved such a thoroughgoing engagement with its abolition, given the ways in which expectations and obligations are necessarily transformed when men are taken out of the equation.

Separatism's approach to rethinking the division of labour was ambitious and all-encompassing. In Womanshare (a lesbian separatist community in Oregon in the mid-1970s), residents

> wanted to share all forms of labour, enabling each woman to gain a diversity of land skills and allowing her time and space for creative pursuits as well as ditch digging. They wanted to grow food organically, live simply, and fulfil as many of their own material needs as possible using simple technologies, to reskill re/productive life, challenge consumer culture, and engage in ecologically appropriate lifestyles.[119]

Living without men in rural settings necessarily rewrote the scripts of gendered work. Under these circumstances, even residents who may have had no experience in tasks like repairing tools or cutting down trees were given the opportunity to develop these skills. Care work was still required in these communities, of course, and women duly performed it – but without any expectation that this should be their primary purpose or natural duty. While these utopian projects undoubtedly centre liberation not *from* but rather *through* work, separatism did (and does) involve a partial liberation from 'women's work', via both its collectivisation and the eradication of its coercively normative force. Indeed, many of the participants in these communities have 'indicated they were able to "become" lesbian more fully on the land than they would have in a city, meaning that their identities as lesbians were strongly tied to their transcendence of gender roles and that such roles were more likely broken on the land'.[120] Such comments speak meaningfully to the performative role that work plays in the ongoing construction of personal identity (and, particularly in this context, one's navigation of the heterosexual matrix).

The discourses surrounding lesbian separatist communities, then, arguably lend themselves to anti-essentialist accounts of gender. One is not born but rather becomes a lesbian – and this process of becoming lesbian is deeply intertwined with work (as a force which makes and remakes the gender-sexuality nexus). However, this generates uncomfortable definitional questions for communities that seek to be available exclusively to women-loving-women: 'If women can do and be anything, then who are women? What makes them different?'[121] It is from such questions that lesbian separatism's notorious struggles with transphobia emerge. Separatist communes build their community around a position within the heterosexual matrix that they seek to undermine, meaning that 'some of the gender ideas or ideals that women use to create that sense of "like us" are gender essentials drawn ... from particularly raced bodies performing a particularly historic and cultural form of gender'.[122] In other words, if gender is no longer operational in conventional ways, then the gender difference around which such communities are based needs to attach itself to a different anchor, and in certain instances it locates this anchor within a fantasy of sexual dimorphism.[123] By staging an exodus from the gender binary via the exclusion of one of its supposed poles, lesbian separatism at times finds itself in the paradoxical position of seeking to unmake gender through its rigid, biologised enforcement.

We would also flag at this point that some of the general

criticisms applicable to withdrawal as a political tactic are also relevant in the case of some late twentieth-century lesbian separatist communes. As with the forms of exodus enacted by the acid communards, we must recognise that separatism can never be absolute – and that *economic* separatism in particular is impossible under current conditions. Cathy McCandless made this point in 1980, when she remarked upon what she viewed as the non-existence of lesbian separatism:

> I know of no individual Lesbian or Lesbian community that is not economically involved with men in some way. All of us buy things from the businesses rich white men control, live in buildings they 'own', use products made with forced or underpaid labour from materials they stole from Native people throughout the world.[124]

Not only is complete withdrawal logistically impossible, but one could also argue that it is politically *undesirable*.[125] This perspective is in keeping with some of the critiques levelled at lesbian separatism by women of colour in the sixties and seventies, who found the tactics of withdrawal to be a barrier to alliance building. This is evident in the remarks about separatism included in the Combahee River Collective Statement of 1977, for example, which rejects the idea that a person's gender necessarily negates the possibility of political alliance. The authors declare that lesbian separatism

> leaves out far too much and far too many people, particularly Black men, women, and children. We have a great deal of criticism and loathing for what men have been socialized to be in this society: what they support, how they act, and how they oppress. But we do not have the misguided notion that it is their maleness, per se – i.e., their biological maleness – that makes them what they are. As Black

women we find any type of biological determinism a particularly
dangerous and reactionary basis upon which to build a politic.[126]

As the statement notes, 'Although we are feminists and lesbians,
we feel solidarity with progressive Black men and do not advocate the fractionalization that white women who are separatists
demand.'[127]

McCandless expresses this kind of idea particularly forcefully
in her work, describing separatism as 'the political equivalent
of sulking': 'I have known any number of white Lesbians from
the middle and higher-than-middle classes who considered
themselves true separatists merely by virtue of the fact that they
didn't associate with men. That's what I call the social definition
of separatism, by the way, and I think it's basically bullshit.'
In her anti-racist analysis, the refusal to fraternise with men is
unhelpful in part because for most women, their survival does
and will continue to rely upon interacting with men.[128] Constructing one's politics around a withdrawal from male society
therefore risks abandoning other women without doing anything
to change the wider sociopolitical conditions in which they find
themselves. This limit of exodus is apparent in both the mixed
hippie communes and the separatist landdyke communities of
the rural Unites States, where taking off inevitably involves
leaving people behind.

As we know, domestic realism was not ultimately overthrown
by the communalism of the separatists or the hippies. While
some communities are still operational, Drop City and the vast
majority of initiatives like it proved to be relatively ephemeral
experiments, failing to outlive their moment of sociosexual
upheaval. This may well have been because, as sites of exodus,
they were not always effective at ensuring their own scalability.
They were often intended as prefigurative spaces, aiming to

offer a taste of post-suburban utopia in the here and now (or at least, a utopia for the young, the healthy, the able bodied, and the middle class with minimal caring responsibilities – that specific and limited range of people who might be best able to thrive in a space like Drop City). As such, they consciously operated as enclaves within the society from which they sought to withdraw – bastions of alternative values which were yet to flourish elsewhere – and the interventions they staged were in certain respects hyperlocal to the point of being site-specific. The 'simple positing and practising of a new world is insufficient to overcome' the structural forces preventing its generalisation.[129] Or, as Mike Davis puts it, 'demonstration projects in … rich countries will not save the world'.[130]

It would be wrong to entirely dismiss these kinds of exodus, however. While countercultural communes and other intentional communities are necessarily small in scale and often times fleeting in duration, they can nevertheless enact a profound influence on politico-popular culture. The figure of the hippie dropout and the militant lesbian separatist alike are widely recognised today, and the myth of the commune continues to shape our understanding of prefigurative alternatives (for good and ill). Sites of exodus have had an outsized influence that belies their material form and the scale of their immediate ambitions, and this influence was actively cultivated by a radical self-publishing tradition and by mediated networking efforts among the communards themselves (books, zines, listservs, media appearances, and so on). There are many ways to expand political imaginaries; although beset by issues – not least in relation to social reproduction, gender, and sexual politics – the communes of the sixties and seventies did a great deal to transform how we think about living together.[131]

Conclusion

In more recent years, we have seen the emergence of further alternatives to the single-family dwelling – namely, profit-oriented developments targeting aspiring professionals. Drawing disingenuously upon radical rhetoric – invoking the commons, for example, or even communes – these neoliberal co-living spaces have emerged in many major cities around the world over the course of the last decade.[132] Such developments offer relatively bijou living spaces in return for more extensive communal resources, ostensibly realising some of the dreams of earlier housing experiments. Given their profit-driven nature and their typical location in expensive urban centres, however, these co-living spaces remain unaffordable for most. Instead, they are tailored towards younger single workers, striving to climb the career ladder – a domestic WeWork for professionals seeking to network and be more productive.[133] As such, communal amenities are typically things like bars, co-working spaces, and fitness centres rather than crèches or long-term-care centres. And, like their much more radical commune cousins, they represent only a 'tiny niche' of the available dwelling options; investors continue to prefer funding more conventional housing forms.[134]

Housing today has become first and foremost a financial asset, whose function 'bears little or even no relation to its ability to perform as a dwelling, any more than a collectible car's value is related to its usefulness as a means to go shopping'.[135] The result of this has been, on the one hand, an explosion of luxury housing in many cities around the world and, on the other hand, a dearth of affordable homes for most.[136] The full implications of the financialisation of housing and the ensuing affordability crisis – from poor living conditions to dangerously (even murderously) low-quality buildings and land banking to houses used solely as investment vehicles being left to rot – have been widely discussed.[137] Our interest here is in pointing to the chilling effect that this has upon the diversification of available models of domesticity and, therefore, upon the possibility of reimagining the home from a post-work feminist perspective. As Richard J. Williams points out, in a 'highly developed market economy, buildings are commodities as much as lived spaces; their cost and enduring value as investments inhibit experimentation'.[138]

As long as housing is seen and treated predominantly as a commodity and an investment vehicle, there will be major barriers to the creation of more emancipatory and politically radical housing forms and to efforts to uproot domestic realism. The idea of widely designing the home for political purposes – let alone specifically to alleviate the burdens of domestic work – seems increasingly distant. The affordability crisis also means that fewer and fewer people are able to own a home at all – and that large numbers therefore have little to no say over how residences should be constructed or renovated. In fact, despite immense efforts to establish home-ownership societies, the reality is that this has become an impossible dream for many, particularly younger generations. There has thus been significant growth in private rentals and, increasingly, in outright homelessness.[139] In this context, the desire for single-family – and even suburban – housing should not be put down solely to ideological blinders. Yes, single-family residences and home ownership have been mobilised as tools to expand and consolidate capitalism against communist ideas. The house and lot are not only economic assets but also subjectivity-producing technologies. They function to induce and sustain generalised political compliance through highly individualised (but widely distributed) distraction. Yet we should be wary of sweeping aside the real desires for privacy, space, and control that contemporary home ownership affords (albeit in often perverse, unequal, and unsustainable forms). Rather than simply denouncing one housing form and prescribing another, then, the goal should be to find ways of maximising people's control over their own environments and facilitating meaningful decision making in terms of where and how our domestic lives are lived.

The rich moment of possibility at the turn of the twentieth century, when housing seemed open to fundamental rethinking, is largely over and done with. There remain, to be sure, pioneering groups and individuals who continue to experiment with both the social and spatial relations of the home. However, many of these experiments are piecemeal, limited in scope, or lacking in material support. Indeed, some experiments appear to be as isolated and atomised as the single-family homes they criticise. These limitations are not necessarily failures, and many spatial interventions succeed when considered on their own terms. If the aim is to challenge domestic realism, however, and to initiate a programme of material counter-hegemony in the name of decisively breaking open people's available options with regards to their intimate lives, then a wider-reaching cultural shift is required. We will need to undermine the various cultural, political, and legislative supports that artificially bolster and 'preserve the privileged status of the male-headed family and the single-family house' and that work to suppress the possible flourishing of any alternatives.[140] After all, given that 'there are so few alternatives to conventional housing at present, we really do not know what different households would actually choose if they had a real choice'.[141] How can we enable people's choices without allowing this to rigidify into something more prescriptive? How can we recognise and respect the pull that housing and urban design have over all of us while also finding ways to better acknowledge that the home is not simply a refuge, but also a (highly gendered) workplace?

6
After Work

'The promise of abundance is not an endless flow of goods but a sufficiency produced with a minimum of unpleasant exertion.'[1]

— G. A. Cohen

Freedom and Necessity

Time has been at the heart of this book — as it must also be at the heart of any post-work, postcapitalist world. The goal of such a society is to expand the realm of freedom, enabling people to meaningfully ask (and answer) the question 'what should we do with our time?'[2] But such a question requires that our time be our own — that it be *free time*, or to put it in the classic terms of the workers' movement, *time for what we will*. Under capitalism, vast quantities of our time are *not* our own. In order to avoid starvation, homelessness, and debt, we are required to sell our time to another. Access to our means of subsistence is conditional on securing a wage and on giving over nearly one-third of our so-called 'working lives'. Real freedom therefore requires, as a first condition, what Aaron Benanav calls abundance: 'A social relationship, based on the principle that the means of one's existence will never be at stake in any of one's relationships.' It is only with the assurance of such a situation that everyone will be able 'to ask "What am I going to do with the time I am alive?" rather than "How am I going to keep living?"'[3]

Real freedom also requires the absence of domination (that is, of arbitrary interference from another) – a point made in recent years by socialist and labour republicans.[4] Unlike more liberal ideas of interference, republicanism notes that domination can occur even if the dominant choose to never exercise their power; the very possibility of arbitrary interference is sufficient. Patriarchal structures, for example, can shape the way in which women think and behave, even if all the actual men in their lives opt to act ethically and equitably. For socialist republicans, domination also characterises workplace and market relations under conditions of wage labour.[5] In the former, workers can be made subject to arbitrary interference from their bosses, while in the latter, *everybody* is made subject to the whims of an impersonal market force against which they have no recourse.[6] In putting their focus on such cases, socialist republicans emphasise those relationships in which our means of existence – our livelihoods – are at stake. Such forms of domination must be overcome as prerequisites for real freedom, whereupon we can ask ourselves: what should we do with our time?

This real freedom takes a positive form – not merely the freedom *from* constraints or domination, but also the freedom *to* engage with and assemble things like identities, norms, and social worlds. In other words, the realm of freedom is not one devoid of obligations. It is the realm of projects to which we commit ourselves – individually and collectively – for their own sake and by which we '*recognize ourselves in what we do*'.[7] Such freedom complicates any clear-cut distinction between everyday ideas of work and leisure given that these projects can and will require immense efforts. As Marx wrote, 'Really free working, e.g. composing, is at the same time precisely the most damned seriousness, the most intense exertion.'[8] But this activity, though potentially demanding, frustrating, and onerous, will be free insofar as we commit ourselves to it for its own sake rather than being coerced into performing it by material need.

What then of the work of social reproduction? After all, such work makes clear that there is also a realm of necessity[9] – of activities related to the fact that we are living, social beings – which will be present in any possible society.[10] This work is necessary insofar as it is determined by both biological and social needs. These needs are, to a degree, historically variable; what is deemed necessary for life in the twenty-first century is very different from what was deemed necessary 200 years ago. Furthermore, the unavoidable character of certain basic needs does not exclude efforts to organise the provision of those needs in better – more pleasurable, fulfilling, sociable, efficient – ways. We need to eat, for example, but the process of producing, harvesting, cooking, and serving food differs significantly from culture to culture and can be significantly transformed. Improved working conditions have of course been a primary demand of the workers' movement since its inception and greater control over the production process is a key promise in postcapitalist thought.

Yet the work of social reproduction occupies an interesting position in regard to the distinction between a realm of necessity and a realm of freedom.[11] It is determined by needs (therefore of the realm of necessity) but can simultaneously be determined by free choice (the realm of freedom). We can find an example of this from own lives in childcare. Even deep in the weeds of nappy changing and sleepless nights – when the oldest is sick, the youngest won't settle, and the middle child is having a tantrum – we can recognise that we are engaged in a project that has largely been freely chosen. We are thus undertaking individually unfulfilling tasks as part of a larger satisfying end. The same goes for the act of cooking, in which many people take pleasure and pride. Labouring over a hot stove may not be intrinsically fulfilling, but it can take on the quality of being a freely chosen activity in the arc of a larger self-directed goal. What these examples show is that even necessary labour can be free given the right conditions.

With that in mind, we are now in a better position to describe the project of post-work. The goal is to reduce necessary labour (or 'work') as much as possible while expanding freedom (or 'free activity') as much as possible. This might occur through the technological reduction of work, the sharing of burdens, or the management of expectations, but also through transforming our relationship to the activities we undertake. In a post-work world, the burdensome work of social reproduction would be minimised, while the pleasurable aspects could become the focus of more freely chosen commitments. At the moment, we tend to have the opposite situation – we sit children in front of televisions so that we can cook functional meals to scarf down among a hectic schedule of other obligations. We can do better.

Taking the distinction between the realm of necessity and the realm of freedom as our guide, then, this chapter will set out a vision for what a future organisation of social reproduction based around post-work ideas might look like. Such a world presupposes that people's basic needs are met since freedom cannot be realised when people are preoccupied with bare survival or limited by the life choices provided by capitalist employers. This is, instead, a world of *post-scarcity* – not in the sense of an overabundance of commodities, but rather of a world in which access to life's essentials is no longer contingent on selling one's time to another.

Principles

Our goal here will not be to set out a blueprint for the future – as if such a task wasn't impossible – but rather to elaborate principles and suggest some concrete possibilities for how to move forward. Given what has been discussed so far, we think there are (at least) three key principles which might guide the construction of a better world: communal care, public luxury, and temporal sovereignty. Here we will unpack each of these ideas in turn, before sketching out some suggestions for how they might combine to enable a post-work future for social reproduction.

Communal Care

Our first guiding principle is communal care, or what has been variously described as 'promiscuous care',[12] 'care in common',[13] and 'family abolition'. This latter term has a particularly long and controversial history. As Marx and Engels noted in 1848, 'even the most radical flare up at this infamous proposal of the communists', alluding to the fact that abolishing the family had gained a firm foothold in the socialist imaginary of the nineteenth century.[14] The idea had a resurgence in the 1970s with second-wave feminism, and in more recent years it has again become visible as a key demand for communist radicals.[15] The term continues to be imbued with 'explosive emotional freight', however, and invoking it is now a surefire way to activate a particular set of (often rather conservative) critical reflexes across the political spectrum.[16]

It is for this reason that we favour the term 'communal care'. Without patient and extended unpacking, 'family abolition' can all too easily conjure up totalitarian images of children being torn from their parents and sent to dormitories (a situation which has arisen in several Western democracies – see Canada's treatment of Indigenous children and the United States' approach to 'child welfare').[17] There have also been understandable defences of the family from those who identify it as one of the few resources of practical care available under capitalism.[18] We hope that the term 'communal care' will serve as a more expedient shorthand than 'family abolition', then, by clearly foregrounding what is really under discussion: not the immediate demolition of a highly valued (if unevenly distributed) safety net, but the emancipatory *transformation* and *expansion* of caring relations.

The arguments motivating the idea of communal care are numerous and come from a surprising range of political positions – from Plato to Marx to David Brooks.[19] As many have noted, the family has been – and too often still remains – a bastion of patriarchal power. It is also a powerful intergenerational mechanism for the concentration of wealth and the perpetuation of related inequalities. Marx and Engels proposed eliminating inheritance in light of this, and even John Rawls believed a society of equal opportunity to be incompatible with the existence of the family.[20] And while many people enjoy a happy and fulfilling family life (we consider ourselves very fortunate in this regard), others have found themselves in families that are hostile, unsupportive, or dangerous. Globally, 27 per cent of women have experienced physical or sexual violence from an intimate partner, making the home one of the most dangerous places in the world for women.[21] Family-based elder abuse is similarly widespread across many countries.[22] A Japanese study from the mid-1990s, for example, found that half of the caretakers surveyed had abused their relatives, while a third admitted feeling hatred towards those they cared for. And, of course, the family has long proved inhospitable to those who are not cis-heteronormative. As Hil Malatino notes, a significant percentage of LGBT people 'don't have families, full stop. We lost them somewhere along the way. They rejected us. We had to escape them to survive.'[23] This is reflected in the high rates of homelessness and parental abuse suffered by queer youth upon coming out.[24] The family is often idealised as a safe space, a harbour in a hostile world – but for millions of people it is far from that.

These are hardly insignificant criticisms. For the specific purposes of this book, however, the most relevant objection to the family is that it is a system of privatised care overburdened by the demands placed upon it. It is hard to argue that the family is an adequate vehicle for care when members of nearly 20 per cent of nuclear families are estranged from each other.[25] Indeed, as we discussed in earlier chapters, this institution is demonstrably inefficient in terms of organising the reproductive labour of society, and can also act as a kind of buffer onto which capitalists push increasing amounts of work and responsibility. These sorts of pressures lead the family into ever more twisted expressions of its ostensible functions. The dramatic rise in domestic violence during pandemic lockdowns serve as recent evidence of this; as families retreated from the threat of the outside world, their members found themselves tragically unable to escape each other.[26] (Here we see that it is not always the domestic sphere which represents a haven from the public realm; rather, the public realm can be a haven from the domestic sphere.) All of this suggests that the family cannot and should not be the sole mechanism by which we seek to meet our society's caring needs.

Communal care offers a twofold approach to redressing these issues. First, it seeks to undo the legislative, cultural, and economic incentives which channel caring relations into one single container – that of the nuclear family. As we saw in our chapter on the family, a series of cultural norms and legal regulations means that the established family form affords significant benefits to those who take it up, while those who seek (or are forced) to

adopt alternative caring arrangements find things much more
difficult. Care is therefore subject to an 'intricate orchestration
of artificial insufficiency'.[27] The goal is to undo these coercions.
As Richard Seymour writes,

> Insofar as 'the family' is an ideological mystification which sanc-
> tions conservative social goals, the idea is to de-naturalise it. Insofar
> as 'the family' is an anti-social project of the state, and of capital's
> organic intellectuals, to both encourage market dependency and
> render people docile and accountable to the state in various ways,
> the goal is to reverse it. Insofar as 'the family' is a kinship-based
> household unit which has been made to bear responsibility for
> care and reproductive labour that could be socialised, the goal is to
> expand the realm of choice and loosen the coercive incentives that
> foster familial dependency.[28]

At present, people do not have much freedom when it comes
to the caring relationships they enter into. As the old saying
goes, 'You can choose your friends, but you can't choose your
family.' But what if we could? Or what if we could imagine the
provision of adequate care in terms of comradeship, mutual aid,
and other forms of collective provision rather than just those of
biological kinship?

The second key tenet of communal care is the creation of
alternative institutions that might better serve the responsibilities
now assigned to the family unit. The point is to disaggregate
the functions that have been combined within the family (often
awkwardly even at the best of times) – to create a whole series
of new institutions and ways to meet the needs that the family
is supposed to address. Should a parent really be expected to
meet all the caring needs of a child – for education, friendship,
guidance, mentorship, and so on? The same holds for spouses

and lovers; should our partners really mean *everything* to us? Family abolition (as communal care) says no and argues that we can create an ecosystem of caring institutions to better serve these diverse needs.[29] The aim is to 'transform not the family – but the society that needs it'.[30] In such a radically reconfigured world, protection is 'offered outward, rather than hoarded'.[31]

Public Luxury .

Our second guiding principle is public luxury. What can this mean in a finite world? Surely there are insufficient resources to ensure that luxury is universally available? And besides, luxury is typically conceived of as a positional good – a pure status object, desirable precisely because so few can access it. As such, the very idea of public luxury – that is to say, luxury that is accessible to all – might strike us as a contradiction in terms. But we can contrast this version of luxury with another – one based on ideas of *quality* rather than exclusivity, and on life beyond mere necessity. After all, 'nothing is too good for the working class.'[32]

In our cities this would involve infrastructural extravagance: some space of our own in which personal needs could be met, massively augmented by a revived commons. We can easily imagine a free time infrastructure that provided 'great urban parks, free museums, libraries, and infinite possibilities for human interaction'.[33] Such provisions would ensure that freedom is not just empty time, but rather something with which people have opportunities to develop their capacities and pursue collective projects.[34] While public provision, particularly in the US and UK, is often seen as a last resort – low-quality back-ups for the poorest in society – public luxury demands more, and might easily draw inspiration from places like Helsinki's lavish Oodi Library, Moscow's famous metro stations, or the stylish public housing of Vienna. The demand for such public luxury could be the rallying cry of a revived twenty-first-century social democracy.

As we saw in earlier chapters, the current organisation of social reproduction via single-family homes is significantly wasteful, and the domestic technologies now available are designed for individual consumers rather than for collective efficiency. A public luxury model would counter this, providing the infrastructure needed for the collectivisation of some domestic work – its removal from the home. Efficiencies of scale could be established, and appropriate technologies designed by and for the people who use them. Moreover, the localisation of reproductive services within neighbourhoods and communities would ameliorate much of the travel time currently required by, particularly, dispersed suburban living.

Finally, public luxury would mean that freedom could be expanded through communal ownership of tools – an approach which would generalise access to important but rarely used household items, rather than letting expensive kit gather dust in exclusionary regimes of private property.[35] The availability of collective options need not be a prohibition on individual or more labour-intensive approaches, of course. As Martin Hägglund notes in a telling discussion of dishwashers,

> The point of expanding the realm of freedom is not to decide in advance which activities should count as free, or to prescribe that living labor must be replaced by dead labor to the maximum degree possible. On the contrary, the point of expanding the realm of freedom is to enable these questions to be genuine questions – the subject of individual and collective deliberation – rather than being determined for us by our material conditions. When we have a dishwasher, doing dishes by hand is not a necessity but a choice.[36]

We could extend such notions more broadly, too: mass food production has not prevented people from growing their own food, mass clothing production does not mean that people can't continue to weave their own fabric and sew their own garments, and so on. The emergence of collective options certainly changes the calculations involved in taking on such activities, but it is only when a particular approach ceases to be obligatory that one has the opportunity to *freely choose* it. Growing your own food, designing your own clothing, and so on can then become autonomous activities rather than a matter of daily survival.

Having choices is a key part of what freedom entails. Public luxury, therefore, demands that we make time-saving options available to everybody, without insisting that they *must* be taken up. (Nobody, for instance, is suggesting that people be forced to give up home cooking or be forbidden from raising their own children.) As we will discuss below, the complex interplay of norms and goals within a postcapitalist world also means that public luxury might involve the adoption of simpler forms of technology. This would represent not a reversion to some imagined prelapsarian utopia, but a technologically literate, ecologically aware approach akin to that adopted by some intentional communities. We are talking here of the consciously determined use of technologies – a far cry from the capitalist-determined use of technologies we experience today. Public luxury must be a basic and essential element of attempts to think about emancipatory futures, then; we must accept nothing less than everything for everyone.

Temporal Sovereignty
In the realm of freedom we are faced with the question of what to do with our lives – or in other words, with having sovereignty over our time. As Hägglund writes, 'If it were given what we

should do, what we should say, and whom we should love – in short: *if it were given what we should do with our time* – we would not be free.'[37] Under capitalism, there is little deliberative space available for asking what we should do; the question of freedom is foreclosed in advance. The majority of us must give up forty hours or more per week in exchange for survival, typically selecting from a narrow range of possible jobs where decisions over what we do on a daily basis ultimately lie outside of our hands. Capitalism clearly regulates our time during working hours, but its impact also extends beyond the production process and into society as a whole. Its regulative force extends systematically, from the decisions facing individuals, to the paths taken by ecological processes, to the demands placed upon imperialist conflicts, and so on.

As Cordelia Belton has explained, the organising principle of 'value' under capitalism directly regulates the trade-offs between competing possibilities in our lives and does so in ways which conflict with many of the values we might hold dear.[38] On an individual level, by making all commodities, activities, and experiences commensurable with each other, value places significant limits on what we can choose to do with the time we have. Taking a day off wage work might mean more time with a loved one, for example, but it might also mean a smaller paycheque; letting a child play outside instead of having them learn a new language might mean more fun for everybody, but could equate to less preparedness for a future world of work; ordering a takeaway might provide a night's respite from cooking and cleaning, but it also means less money to pay bills at the end of the month. Pertinently, for this book, the choices available in free time become subject to the same calculative deliberation performed under the metric of value. Value significantly shapes the relationships between such choices; it makes the ostensible decision about what to do with our time that much clearer by making our options that much narrower. We saw this in the standards chapter, too: intensive parenting is a rational response to the incentives presented in wildly unequal societies; rising cleaning standards were fostered by advertisers seeking to sell more products; busyness appears as a virtue in a world dominated by the work ethic; the ideology of the housewife served a useful purpose for a society reliant on devalued domestic labour; and so on. To be sure, capitalism is not the sole factor behind these phenomena, but it is nevertheless a major force behind their social significance and the constraints that they impose upon people's lives.

Under postcapitalism, this situation changes substantially: capitalism's imperative to accumulate for accumulation's sake no longer operates as the regulative meta-norm to which all other norms must conform, and these norms can no longer be warped by its gravitational pull. Newfound free time – new in both a quantitative and a qualitative sense – opens up the problem of freedom. Keynes famously set the question out thusly: 'For the first time since his creation man will be faced with his real, his permanent problem – how to use his freedom from pressing economic cares, how to occupy the leisure, which science and compound interest will have won for him, to live wisely and agreeably and well.'[39] Yet Keynes' 'problem' is only intelligible outside of a society organised by capitalist ideas of value – a society where the possibilities imposed by value's systemic domination are no longer operative and where the question of evaluating trade-offs opens up.

To be clear, temporal sovereignty doesn't mean simply being at liberty to spend our time on whatever we might individually desire, as though we were monads capable of separating ourselves from any social or natural ties. We are social beings, and temporal sovereignty therefore means authoring our own norms and obligations to the collectives in which we live: 'Being free is not a matter of being free *from* a social world but of being free *to* engage, transform, and recognize yourself in the social norms to which you are bound.'[40] Temporal sovereignty also means that the question of what we should do – and how we should do it – is perpetually open to contestation. This is particularly crucial when it comes to the often implicit social norms that frame much of our decision-making. These norms can embody forces of domination, as we saw in the chapter on standards.[41] Norms around things like cleanliness, manners, and self-presentation, for example, impose gendered expectations about the arrangement and conduct of unpaid domestic labour.[42] Expectations about intensive parenting, likewise, tend to particularly fall upon women, along with any guilt that follows from failing to meet these frequently impracticable criteria. More broadly, as we saw in the family chapter, gender norms still impose a greater share of unpaid domestic labour upon women – even in the most gender-equal societies – with all the associated negative impacts this has on free time.[43]

All such norms must be subject to contestation in a future society, and this will demand sustained democratic engagement with others – indeed, we are, on some level, *always* collectively building social norms and projects to answer the question of what we should do. This means that another key facet of temporal sovereignty is that we create the deliberative structures we need – the 'institutions of freedom' that allow us to negotiate and determine collective projects.[44] This also involves building mechanisms that allow for individuals to determine their own separate paths.[45] After all, a post-work, post-scarcity, postcapitalist world is not one devoid of contestation and conflict. There will always be different values to choose from. Indeed, it is only after the collapse of the regulative meta-norm of capital accumulation that any meaningful deliberation between values becomes possible.

Social Reproduction after Capitalism

So what might a post-work future look like with respect to the necessary labours of social reproduction? Crucially, this work would be distributed equitably – from each according to their abilities, to each according to their needs. Sharing necessary labour is essential if we are to ensure that *all* have the capacity to develop their own projects of freedom – otherwise some will continue to lose too much of their time (that is to say, their lives) to work.[46] Long gone would be the days in which domestic labour was considered 'women's work' or in which 'dirty work' was the preserve of immigrants or women of colour. As an immediate (if small) step towards this, we might consider something like Nancy Fraser's 'universal caregiver model', which aims to support everyone as individuals with social reproduction responsibilities.[47] This approach fosters equality by taking the rhythms of caregiving as standard, taking seriously people's combined responsibilities for both production and reproduction, and recognising the need for flexible and part-time work. Government policies could aim to facilitate transitions between the workplace and the home, provide support for public and community-based systems of care, and generally seek to break down the traditional gendered division of labour in a way that doesn't impose more wage work on everyone. In a post-work world, we can imagine a more thoroughgoing sharing of society's necessary labours: where everyone is not only supported to do this work, but where the equal sharing of this work is taken as a duty and a contribution to a society of freedom. Only at this stage would everybody have equal opportunity to develop their own projects.

While everyone with the capacity to do so would contribute to the necessary reproductive labour of their communities, people would no longer find themselves automatically funnelled into certain roles. Rather, work – detached from fixed conceptions about the appropriate identity of the persons performing it – would be relatively freely chosen (with positive incentives for particularly difficult or demanding types of work), and there would be fewer barriers to moving between roles (over the course of a day, a week, a year, etc.). In short, work would no longer determine the social or self-identity of the worker. There would undoubtedly remain some degree of specialisation (on the basis of factors such as personal talents, interests, and aptitudes as well as social needs), but the division of labour would never-theless be much more flexible and everyone would contribute to the routine drudgery required to maintain their societies.[48] All people would have an appropriate *share* of work to perform, rather than simply a *job* to perform.

Yet we should recognise that the redistribution of reproductive labour is not a post-work panacea. While it would certainly mean less work for many, it would undoubtedly also mean *more* work for some and, on an aggregate level, would do little to impact the total quantity of work required. A post-work project must go further in its attempts to maximise freedom. As a first step towards facilitating a *reduction* of labour, the legal and cultural apparatus which privileges the privatised care of the nuclear family would need to be rescinded. As Michèle Barrett and Mary McIntosh put it, we should work towards 'weakening all the pressures that compel people to live or stay in nuclear family households' by challenging 'state policies that currently privilege "the family" at the expense of other ways of living' –

those around child custody, power of attorney, social security, and so on.[49] This wouldn't have to mean the *withdrawal* of those benefits that currently accrue to biological families, but rather the *extension* of those benefits to different kinds of relation; they might initially go beyond the merely marital or parental to more fully encompass bonds forged by friendship, community, or extended kinship. Friends, for example, could be included as a category that is recognised for care work – e.g., we can currently get time off for taking care of family, but not friends.[50] Likewise, laws around child custody, around who can make medical decisions on behalf of someone else, about who can receive government support for caring, and so on, are currently designed with the nuclear family firmly in mind – but more expansive forms of caring collectives need to also be recognised. Government policies, in other words, need to be adjusted to better accommodate non-nuclear living arrangements and to ensure that these arrangements are not unfairly penalised. Cuba's recently passed Families Code is one possible model to emulate here. It offers an encouragingly expansive definition of 'family': 'a union of people linked by an affective, psychological and sentimental bond, who commit themselves to sharing life such that they support each other'; greater rights afforded to children (e.g., 'parental authority' is replaced by 'parental responsibility'); and demands for equality in domestic labour.[51] These kinds of reforms may have the potential to enable caregiving practices to flourish beyond the specific confines of the heteropatriarchal family and could therefore represent an initial move towards the more equitable and effective sharing of reproductive labour.

Another approach to initiating the seismic changes we have envisioned here would be to reconceptualise and re-invest in institutions of communal reproduction. Services and resources which are today viewed as depressing last resorts for those who are denied access to the conventional family might be made considerably more appealing to those who benefit from them. After all, as Barrett and McIntosh note, living outside the family *is* currently an option,

> but only under conditions considerably less attractive than those within it. Yet it need not be so. Old people's homes could be a lot more like residential hotels, or else like self-governing communities. A home for the handicapped can be considerably more stimulating for a teenager with Down's syndrome than living alone with her parents. A nursery or children's home can provide positive social experiences of cooperation, companionship and varied activities. It is the over-valuation of family life that devalues these other lives. The family sucks the juice out of everything around it, leaving other institutions stunted and distorted.[52]

A post-work world of social reproduction would aim to offer much more support for the caring functions currently assigned to the family. Take childcare, for example: in the kind of society we are picturing, much greater support for communal childcare would be available – in particular, in the form of high-quality, twenty-four-hour universal care (again, we must stress that post-work does not, and cannot, mean the complete eradication of all labour). This was a prominent and popular demand of feminist movements in the 1970s, though one that came to be sidelined in the ensuing decades.[53] Yet there are already demonstrable tendencies towards this that we could seek to capitalise on, with government support for childcare rising in recent decades. Germany and Denmark are the countries perhaps furthest down this path. In Denmark, for example, high-quality day care is guaranteed for children and heavily subsidised by the state; for the poorest, access is free.[54] Staff are mostly professionalised and well paid.[55] And a large portion of childcare provision is run by the voluntary non-profit sector (while being financed by the government).[56] Although problems undoubtedly remain – most notably, a lack of childcare workers leading to challenges in meeting universal access – such examples nevertheless point towards what it might mean to communalise childcare. Based on the distinction between public provision and public funding, we can also imagine support for more experimental models of early years care, such as co-production (actively involving parents and caregivers) and co-operative models (owned and operated by workers) – all of which could be resourced at more macro levels of government while being run locally. Such approaches might also offer some much-needed respite from the productivist bent of the contemporary welfare state.[57]

In a world of communal care, aimed at reducing the pressure to consolidate reproductive labour into the nuclear family, we would also hope to see greater respect for children's autonomy. Children, as we have seen, are too often conceived of as little bundles of human capital that need to be developed, trained, and primed for a world of relentless competition. In a post-work society, children would have more time to simply be kids – reversing the dwindling amount of play time seen in many countries in recent decades.[58] We might first imagine following the Welsh example by turning play into a right through legislation.[59] This means that Welsh cities must now ensure there are nearby spaces for children to play, local councils should offer activities to support children's free time, and housing developers must assess how new developments will impact children's opportunities for recreation. Greater autonomy would also grant children enhanced capacity to leave abusive situations and place limits on parents' power over them. In line with the principles of communal care, children would be far less beholden to and dependent on the handful of people they are tethered to via genetic coincidence, and there would be far greater opportunity for them to build their own support networks in safe and supported ways.

When it comes to elder care, proposals around communal provision require some delicacy. Certainly, many older people find the idea of institutional care unappealing. While we must recognise that the decades-long trend towards at-home care is absolutely a measure of government cost-cutting, it nevertheless tallies with the genuine preferences of many care recipients. A lot of older people understandably wish to retain their independence and continue living in the places they feel most comfortable. How, then, might one approach reform here? The first thing to note is that, with the home and family opened up beyond their current isolated forms, at-home elder care would *already* be transformed. It would be able to draw upon considerably more caring resources than are currently available. Furthermore, we could utilise digital platforms – shorn of their profit-making imperatives – to help coordinate the needs of care recipients with the provision of care suppliers.[60] These technologies remain useful for matching dispersed actors, for searching and finding resources, and for coordinating among providers.

We can also draw upon recent experimentation with place-based, self-organised and community-centred models of care and living.[61] Co-living models of housing, for example, are becoming an attractive solution for many people over sixty in the UK, with schemes arising to address particular needs, interests, and demographics.[62] These models often involve an explicit focus on community and on integrating services and resources beyond individual residences. Collectives of older women have turned to co-housing as a means of extending their independence, concentrating their resources, and circumventing the loneliness that can sometimes plague those who decide to age in place.[63] London Older Lesbian Co-housing, for example, started from the perspective that residential care homes or independent living schemes may not be ideally suited to those who have not lived much of their lives in heterosexual nuclear families, and therefore that older people (should they experience discomfort being out in these settings) could feel as if they were being pushed back into the closet as they aged.[64] Developing a tailored co-living community is seen as a key approach to addressing this.

To supplement such spaces, infrastructure for community-based long-term care could also be built – spaces that are distinct from both the home and the hospital but which can house the proper resources demanded by carers and the cared for.[65] This would help to de-medicalise the home (which, as we saw earlier, has become a major source of new domestic health work) by providing a local, communal space for medical equipment and technologies and for professional assistance and appropriate training in how to use them. These spaces could also allow for carers to have a break and a rest – something which today can prove all too rare, given the requirement of 24/7 work within the family. Amenities could be offered for exercise and recovery for elderly people and carers alike – 'free saunas, studios and gyms ... as well as regular classes and activities' – in a model of public luxury that emphatically foregrounds the consideration of reproductive labour.[66] All of this could be run in turn by co-operative care groups, perhaps following something like the influential nurse-led Buurtzorg model from the Netherlands, in which self-managed teams of nurses based in specific neighbourhoods cooperate with individuals and wider community networks (including relatives, friends, and neighbours) to help people age well in their communities.[67]

When it comes to cooking, meanwhile, it would appear that capitalism has already created an ideal form for efficient, collective production: restaurants. While there is no doubting the rapidity of a smoothly run McDonald's production process, however, it is important to remember that this is premised on a *reduction of freedom* for the workers performing it. Far from being work undertaken out of a sense of commitment and responsibility to a collective project, restaurant work is organised by and for the accumulation of value (a burger and fries being merely a derivative side effect of this).[68] There are better options – ones that might more truly embody a collective project of freedom. As a first stage, we might imagine universal free school meals and breakfast clubs being provided for primary and secondary schools. Finland, for example, has had a free school meal programme in place since the 1940s, with all pupils provided with a decent meal, from pre-kindergarten right through to the end of secondary school.[69] The UN has also recently set out universal school meals as an important part of the right to food.[70] Such steps would be significant for time saving, of course, but also – in a world still characterised by scarcity – an important response to the food poverty experienced by so many children.

More broadly, we could also build upon the organisation of communal kitchens and canteens, which for some has enabled a kitchenless lifestyle. In fact, this might be deemed a linchpin of the commune-form, as early utopian socialist communes of the 1800s often experimented with attempts at public kitchens, as did the urban communes of the Russian Revolution.[71] Such ideas have fed into designs for feminist technologies as well. In the late 1800s and early 1900s, for instance, designers pushed specialised kitchen cabinets for individual dwellings that were aimed to supplement the use of community kitchens. These were wardrobe-sized cabinets which contained a number of the basic tools needed for cooking, arranged in what was thought to be the most convenient manner. Indeed,

> if kitchen development had taken a different turn, if families had decided to pool their efforts in community kitchens instead of making individual homes more self-sufficient than they had ever been, such cabinets would have been all that was needed for the few occasions that cooking was carried on.[72]

To this day, many contemporary experiments in collective living continue to revolve around a shared kitchen,[73] and they are a routine feature of many occupation-based protest movements.[74] However, while we want to encourage a diversity of approaches, we think it likely that private kitchens will continue to have a place in a post-work world. After all, many of us are likely to continue to find personal cookery pleasurable and fulfilling – an activity that, under conditions of expanded free time, might be an end in itself. As we argued earlier, once the labour of cooking becomes untethered from necessity, it can start to be taken up more as an autonomous activity. Being able to determine our own access to food is also an important right. That being said, however, communal kitchens do offer alternatives for the many times when cooking meals is more of a burden than a passion. Given that cooking is an activity which can really benefit from high-spec equipment and economies of scale, this makes a lot of sense. There are already a number employer-based canteens, for instance, that serve this purpose – such as the subsidised canteens of IKEA and John Lewis (the former for consumers, the latter for employees). We might also look to how London's political elite currently dine. As Rebecca May Johnson notes, 'It is telling that while there are no public canteens in the city (what council could now afford to hang on to such a quantity of land after cuts?), the houses of parliament have ten canteens.'[75] Here, members of Parliament can select among subsidised offerings ranging from roast sirloin to pan-seared salmon to chargrilled chermoula spiced squash – all at about the same price as a sandwich and coffee from Pret.[76] In the face of images of decrepit public services, we must insist that 'the idea that mass catering must be devoid of pleasure is false'.[77]

There is also a telling example of public canteens from World War II that we might wish to draw upon. While mostly thought of as a period of ration books and household scarcity, the war was also a period when many of society's worst off ate their best. In response to the problems of feeding the population during wartime, the British government set up 'communal feeding centres' – a name which was eventually vetoed by Winston Churchill as sounding too communist and replaced with the more nationalistic 'British Restaurants'. These were public kitchens, heavily subsidised by the government and designed to provide healthy and nutritious meals (no small feat during the war).[78] The kitchens were stocked with industrial equipment subsidised by the government, and meals were oriented towards food that could be made efficiently at scale. Some of these canteens had table service, others were organised more like a cafeteria, and many had services by which people could order food to take home.[79] In rural areas, there were even mobile services that would travel around to offer food. At their peak, these communal feeding centres were producing around 4 million meals every week. Their walls were decorated with works of art taken from Buckingham Palace and the national galleries – perhaps as good an example of private versus public luxury as one is likely to find. Cooking as it is currently organised is wildly inefficient and wasteful – of food, of energy, of time – but there are plenty of alternatives to learn from.

What, then, of that other aspect of domestic labour, housework? How might this be organised in (or towards) a post-work world? Research on the potential automation of domestic work suggests that hours of unpaid work could be saved every week using existing technologies, but this estimate is more reflective of outer bounds rather than realistic possibilities.[80] More likely, housework will continue to be performed by humans for the foreseeable future. As an approach to better managing this, we might imagine (as thinkers such as Alexandra Kollontai and Angela Davis have) teams of professionalised, well-remunerated cleaners efficiently taking up the necessary labour.[81] More immediate improvements could be made to this work by ensuring decent wages and better conditions for domestic workers. For far too long, these workers have been – explicitly – regulated by the state as a highly exploitable workforce: brought over from other countries on precarious visas, lorded over by clients who have few if any limits on their power, and subject to low pay and no benefits. Rectifying this is a crucial first step. To help with the costs, states such as Belgium, France, and Sweden have also subsidised payments for housework. As things stand, these subsidies could perhaps be focused on those in need of long-term care (be they disabled and/or elderly) – as evidence suggests that these are the people most in need of such outsourcing and most amenable to taking it up when it is affordable.[82] We could also imagine greater support for launderettes, organising the laundering needs of a community in a way that is far more temporally efficient and ecologically sustainable than current domestic methods. Such reforms may only be stepping stones, but they are nonetheless useful moves towards a more thoroughgoing socialisation of housework.

When it comes to housing – the material infrastructure of domestic social reproduction – a better future would first entail massive investment into social housing. So long as we remain under capitalism, the aim would be to decommodify housing so that access to safe, reliable, and good quality shelter is not dependent on wages. Any new developments could be designed in architecturally adventurous ways. As with much in the way of housing, Vienna is a helpful example here, with its social housing expressing a real sense of public luxury and with its use of design competitions fostering an interest in more experimental domestic forms.

In designing these spaces, there are important lessons to be learned from earlier socialised models regarding the continued importance of privacy.[83] As we saw in previous chapters, in many cases, collectivised residential spaces were rejected because of people's existing experiences with these models. Many working-class families lived at close quarters largely because of poverty, rather than choice, and bristled at suggestions of collectivism from middle-class reformers. Likewise, experiences of life during wartime led many to reject communal living and pine for the isolation of the suburban home. And a common refrain from experiments with failed communes is that privacy was neglected. These desires can't simply be dismissed as ideological mystifications, false consciousness, or knee-jerk reactions; rather, they speak to genuine feelings, preferences, and needs. Not everybody would feel comfortable living in fully collectivised living spaces for any great length of time, and many will want more than a single bedroom to retreat to. As such, visions of spatial futures would do well to be as attentive to private sufficiency as they are to public luxury, and must acknowledge that collective living cannot be imposed from the top down (whatever the benefits in terms of domestic workload).

Another key design decision, based on the idea of public luxury, involves integrating domestic residences and communal services by bringing facilities, amenities, and support within arms' reach. This was the ambition at the heart of many apartment hotels, of Red Vienna, and of several other experiments, and the failure to make resources accessible was one key reason why the mid-century American suburbs proved to be generally labour intensive. Dolores Hayden pursues this line of thinking in her classic article 'What Would a Non-Sexist City Be Like?' In imagining a metropolitan co-operative made up of forty households, she demands the following collective spaces and activities:

> (1) a day-care center with landscaped outdoor space, providing day care for forty children and after-school activities for sixty-four children; (2) a laundromat providing laundry service; (3) a kitchen providing lunches for the day-care center, take-out evening meals, and 'meals-on-wheels' for elderly people in the neighborhood; (4) a grocery depot, connected to a local food cooperative; (5) a garage with two vans providing dial-a-ride service and meals-on-wheels; (6) a garden (or allotments) where some food can be grown; (7) a home help office providing helpers for the elderly, the sick, and employed parents whose children are sick. The use of all of these collective services should be voluntary; they would exist in addition to private dwelling units and private gardens.[84]

Here, we see the idea of private sufficiency and public luxury articulated from an avowedly feminist perspective. Hayden offers a vision in which the temporal burdens of social reproduction would be substantially mitigated by community-steered services and spaces, many of them operated by residents themselves. Simply reducing the travel time and forward planning required to access vital neighbourhood resources would have obvious post-work benefits for those currently performing reproductive labour.

There are several steps one could take to update Hayden's vision for the twenty-first century, too. A phone and computer repair shop, for example, with a mobile team of technology trouble-shooters might prove to be a useful resource for older residents (and anyone whose Wi-Fi router has ever inexplicably stopped working). Local medical centres could be combined with self-help health facilities for those who prefer them, extending the idea of long-term care centres discussed above. For parents and caregivers there could be an ecologically friendly reusable nappy laundry service, a baby clothing rental service, regular breastfeeding support groups (with peer counsellors available for home visits on request), pre- and post-natal mental health groups, specialist baby and child loss counselling, a home-work help centre, and so on. Guest bedrooms, typically rarely used in those houses fortunate enough to have them, could be reimagined as a shared resource for use across a number of households.[85] This would mean one fewer room to heat, furnish, and clean, while retaining the requisite degree of occasional spatial flexibility.

We can also imagine building free time infrastructures – environments in which people can congregate, socialise, play, and build, all without the pressure of having to buy something or pay an entrance fee. There could be free, expansive, networked spaces for collaboration, as well as high-spec, communally accessible makerspaces, including everything from screen printing facilities, sewing machines, and kilns to top-of-the-line 3D printers; regular classes could be offered to those who wish to learn how to use these technologies, and a team of technicians could be made available to support people in realising their projects. Something similar could be put in place for media suites (enabling residents to produce and disseminate their own content), for music practice rooms, gyms, studios, and clubs. For younger residents, there could be book and toy libraries, ensuring greater access to both education and entertainment.[86] And, again taking inspiration from existing Viennese housing, we could look at including rooftop pools for the masses.[87] In fact, even America once had a plethora of municipal swimming pools. Not simply small, crowded pools, but vast 'resort pools' surrounded by sandy beaches and luxurious parks that would attract thousands – or even tens of thousands – of people at a time. They were left to decay, however, after they were desegregated; racial prejudices kept white populations away and municipalities were unwilling to fund construction or maintenance.[88] This experience demonstrates that racist and classist prejudices are a barrier that has to be confronted to realise public luxury for all. Yet we can already get a sense of how different this world would be from much of our own. In this vision, the better integration of home and neighbourhood not only frees up time from some of the more onerous elements of unpaid domestic labour but presents a vision of social reproduction in which it's easy to imagine how this free time might be enjoyably spent.

On the basis of such communal infrastructure we might also imagine a radically different stance towards technological innovation and the process of creativity. Historically, the absence of 'control over what is produced and how, [entails] a kind of freedom of choice among options one had not created in the first place. For example, one could choose between Westinghouse or General Electric refrigerators, but not between individual refrigerators or communal kitchens.'[89] The goal for post-work feminism must be to move away from capitalism's myopic approach to the development of domestic technologies, towards conscious and collective control over what technologies are being developed and how they are being deployed, all in an effort to reduce the amount of labour time necessary to spend on domestic (and other kinds of) work.

Communities could be turned from passive recipients of technologies into networks of active creators.[90] In fact, many communal experiments have been significant sources of domestic labour-saving innovation – and often in ways that breach our current domestic realist expectations surrounding the individualised family home. As Hayden writes of one Christian sect with communalist ambitions,

> The Shakers have to their credit an improved washing machine; the common clothespin; a double rolling pin for faster pastry making; a conical stove to heat flatirons; the flat broom; removable window sash, for easy washing; a window-sash balance; a round oven for more even cooking; a rotating oven shelf for removing items more easily; a butter worker; a cheese press; a pea sheller; an apple peeler; and an apple parer which quartered and cored the fruit.[91]

Members of the perfectionist religious society the Oneida Community, meanwhile, 'produced a lazy-susan dining-table center, an improved mop wringer, an improved washing machine, and an institutional-scale potato peeler'.[92]

Perhaps the most thoroughgoing (if admittedly isolated) moment of domestic proletarian innovation, though, can be attributed to inventor Frances Gabe. Driven by an admirable distaste for housework, Gabe built and patented a self-cleaning house. The inventiveness and thoughtfulness of the design is worth commenting on at length:

In each room, Ms. Gabe, tucked safely under an umbrella, could press a button that activated a sprinkler in the ceiling. The first spray sent a mist of sudsy water over walls and floor. A second spray rinsed everything. Jets of warm air blew it all dry. The full cycle took less than an hour. Runoff escaped through drains in Ms. Gabe's almost imperceptibly sloping floors. It was channeled outside and straight through her doghouse, where the dog was washed in the bargain ... The house, whose patent consisted of 68 individual inventions, also included a cupboard in which dirty dishes, set on mesh shelves, were washed and dried in situ. To deal with laundry – in many ways her masterstroke – Ms. Gabe designed a tightly sealed cabinet. Soiled clothing was placed inside on hangers, washed and dried there with jets of water and air, and then, still on hangers, pulled neatly by a chain into the clothes closet. Her sink, toilet and bathtub were also self-cleaning. Naturally, no conventional home, with its drapes, upholstery and wood furniture, could withstand Ms. Gabe's restorative deluge. But she had anticipated that. Her floors were coated with multiple layers of marine varnish. Furniture was encased in clear acrylic resin. Bedclothes were kept dry by means of an awning pulled over the bed before the cascade began. Upholstery was made from a waterproof fabric of Ms. Gabe's invention, which looked, The *Boston Globe* said in 1985, 'like heavily textured Naugahyde'. Pictures were coated in plastic and knickknacks displayed behind glass. Papers could be sealed in watertight plastic boxes; books wore waterproof jackets invented by Ms. Gabe. Electrical outlets were, mercifully, covered.[93]

While the aesthetic and functionality of the house may have left something to be desired, there is no doubting the single-minded thoroughness of this effort at eliminating housework. Once given control over our own labour processes, and when the goals of these processes are no longer determined by capitalist accumulation, we can expect entirely new pathways of technological development to emerge.

We might, for instance, imagine that in a world where tool libraries were more prevalent and convenience devices more readily shared, the nature of these technologies themselves would change. Most devices that we currently own are fragile, difficult to repair (for both practical and legal reasons), and not designed to be sturdy enough for the burdens that sharing might put on them. There are of course good profit-oriented reasons for this: after all, 'durability is unprofitable' and having consumers buy new products every year is by far the better option from a capitalist perspective. Without these incentives, however, technology would evolve in unforeseen directions. If our tools 'were designed for sharing, rather than for individual use, we believe they would change structurally, mechanically and in material composition'.[94]

We might look to develop technologies which better enable the sharing of domestic work – rather than, as we saw with twentieth-century appliances, individualising previously shared work. For instance, breast pumps and bottle sterilisers can be framed as technologies which enable the work of breastfeeding to be shared among a plethora of different caregivers: 'Instead of mother and nanny, we have the collaboration of caregiver one (expresser) and caregiver two (feeder), where caregiver three might be changer, and caregiver four might be minder, and these tasks routinely interchanged in their collaboration.'[95] Night feeds need no longer be the sole responsibility of the sleep-deprived lactating parent. Technologies could also be designed to support care work and other reproductive labour, rather than the work being forced into a framework determined by machinery. The Buurtzorg model, for example, relies on the kind of good-quality tech that allows nurses to be connected while mobile in the community – things like specialist software for recording and analysing client data that works reliably while on the go.

The examples we have considered here also indicate that socialist technology does not necessarily mean bigger, more centralised technology. The goal is, rather, to develop and adopt those technologies which best expand our freedom and accord with our autonomously chosen goals. In some cases, those goals might entail deploying economies of scale and building big – but in other cases, that freedom might be better served by less flashy, more decentralised and smaller-scale interventions.

Conclusion

While all of the above provides a sketch of how social reproduction might be organised within a transitional or post-work society, it is nonetheless the case that post-work is only one desirable goal among many. As we have seen, adjudicating between competing values is a core element of a truly free society, given that the use of our time would no longer be determined by coercion, dominance, or market discipline. Instead, we would be faced with the immense question of our own desires. What do we want to do with our time and how do we want to normatively organise our lives?[96] We, the authors of this book, are not designers of institutions (or of spaces or technologies, for that matter), and in any case, such practices will be largely subject to determination by the members of future societies.[97] But we can at least note here some key values – ecological, aesthetic, ethical, and so on – that might complicate a post-work agenda, or exist in tension with its aim of minimising necessary labour time.

More free time is just one value in a postcapitalist world – an important one, to be sure, since free time provides the basis of self-determination, but not one without trade-offs. It might be clear that the mining of natural resources should take a minimum of human activity, for instance, but the same does not hold for the labour involved in raising a child. More broadly, the problem for many people today is a *deficit* of care; the idea of reducing care labour could thus be viewed as at odds with what an equitable society should be like. Such work may benefit precisely from 'slow caring' that takes time – meaning that an increase in productivity and efficiency would be antithetical to its goals. Much personal care work additionally requires treating people holistically, and attempts to break this down into discrete automatable tasks may threaten the benefits of that work. Thus, we must be sensitive to the subtleties of any given labour process, but also aware of the desires and needs of both receivers and providers of care and other reproductive work.

The world we are envisioning would also require balancing ecological impacts with post-work ambitions. If a machine made it newly possible to automate away all domestic drudgery, yet its ecological ramifications were significant, a decision would have to be made about whether or not such a technology should be adopted. At the moment, such decisions are largely left up to profit-seeking companies and their marketing wings – but a post-capitalist society would have to take on that responsibility itself. Similar considerations hold for the organisation of agriculture and the goal of food sovereignty.[98] After all, aiming to re-localise food in order to ensure access to means of subsistence could mean giving up some efficiencies of scale and global divisions of labour. It might also require more labour-intensive forms of agriculture. Urban farming, for example, is a useful way to secure access to food for expanding city populations – and evidence suggests that it can have higher yields and be more sustainable than more industrialised forms of agriculture. Yet it would also entail giving up on the efficiencies that can emerge from more monocultural and industrial forms of food growing. That may well be the sort of trade-off which a future society deems worth it, though.

Lastly, we can imagine an array of trade-offs arising around the quantity and organisation of necessary labour. For example, residents of a neighbourhood may decide that they want better free-time infrastructure – a proposal which may require at least a temporary *increase* in the quantity of time devoted to necessary labour (building and maintaining a park takes time, after all).[99] Or a community may have to face the question of whether more localised co-operative forms of care provision might be better suited to such a world than more scalable public forms of provision. The latter option will perhaps often be the more straightforwardly 'post-work' option, mobilising efficiencies of scale to reduce the labour required to a minimum. Yet issues of accountability, flexibility, and solidarity might mean that a future society would instead prefer co-operative forms which could rely upon labour-intensive, democratic modes of operation. We might also raise trade-offs around the division of labour. A more rigid division, for example, could enable more specialisation of work and the subsequent efficiencies that can arise from it. Yet this goal of reducing labour is in tension with the goal of ensuring freedom for people to move between roles much more flexibly than they can at present. As always, the choice between various options is not something we can seek to definitively answer here, but represents a real tension with which a post-work world would have to grapple.

A post-work society should not be mistaken for a utopian endpoint, then, but instead understood as part of an unending Promethean process of extending the realm of freedom.[100] The point of a post-work world – and the reason for its necessary connection to a postcapitalist world – would be precisely that such decisions can be made meaningfully. The goal of minimising necessary labour in order to expand the realm of freedom is a condition for being able to ask these questions in a substantial way. Ultimately, what matters is not the endless reduction of necessary labour per se, but instead the liberation of time and the creation of institutions through which we might consciously and collectively guide the development of humanity. We need the freedom to determine the necessary.

Acknowledgements

In a December 1917 postscript to *The State and Revolution*, Vladimir Lenin famously explained that he had to stop writing his pamphlet on revolution because, well, a revolution had broken out.[1] We experienced our own version of this while writing the present book. Initially conceived of in 2015, our writing about social reproduction was delayed by the *work* of social reproduction as we saw the arrival of three wonderful children (the youngest of which was born mere days after we submitted this manuscript). To echo Lenin, however, 'such "interference" can only be welcomed'.

In the process of writing this book, we've been fortunate enough to have had the support of numerous people. We have benefited from the ideas, insights, and intellectual generosity of such estimable comrades as Emma Dowling, Jeremy Gilbert, Alva Gotby, Jo Littler, James Muldoon, Rodrigo Nunes, Tom O'Shea, Benedict Singleton, Will Stronge, and Zöe Sutherland. Their feedback has strengthened the book no end, and we are hugely grateful to them.

We are grateful, too, to all of those who have engaged with us about our ideas over the course of the past eight years – to the various panels, audiences, and commenters who have drawn us into discussion and prompted us to refine our point of view. Special thanks are due to the PhD students (past and present) of the University of West London's 'Gender, Technology and Work' research cluster, who remain an ongoing source of inspiration.

We would also like to express our appreciation for some of our friends, colleagues, and influences – Diann Bauer, Ray Brassier, Benjamin Bratton, Laboria Cuboniks, Mark Fisher, Sophie Lewis, Suhail Malik, Reza Negarestani, Peter Wolfendale, the team at Autonomy, and many more – and also to our family (who, against the odds, we love very much). This book would not have been possible without them. Central to the safe delivery of this manuscript have been the workers at Verso, who have been endlessly patient as we continued to churn out babies faster than we churned out chapters. Rosie Warren has been particularly wonderful on this score, offering encouragement and exceptional insight without once complaining about toddlers gatecrashing her editorial meetings.

And finally, we would like to recognise the work of all those who have given us the time to write this book – the teachers, cleaners, childminders, babysitters, and nursery staff who have given us some much-needed respite from intrafamilial domestic reproductive labour; the midwives, doctors, and nurses who have kept us alive, in often very trying conditions. We dedicate *After Work* to them – and to each other.

Helen Hester and Nick Srnicek
February 2023

Notes

1. Introduction

1 There were some interesting exceptions to this rule, to be sure. See, for instance, Albert, *Parecon: Life After Capitalism*; Gibson-Graham, *A Postcapitalist Politics*.

2 Fisher, *Capitalist Realism: Is There No Alternative?*

3 Saito, *Karl Marx's Ecosocialism*; Schmelzer, Vetter, and Vansintjan, *The Future Is Degrowth*.

4 Huws, *Reinventing the Welfare State*; Muldoon, *Platform Socialism*; Scholz and Schneider, *Ours to Hack and to Own*; Tarnoff, *Internet for the People*.

5 Benanav, 'How to Make a Pencil'; Morozov, 'Digital Socialism: The Calculation Debate in the Age of Big Data'; Rozworski and Philips, *People's Republic of Walmart*.

6 Alongside the work of Cordelia Belton, we might include: Roberts, *Marx's Inferno*; Hägglund, *This Life: Secular Faith and Spiritual Freedom*; Bernes, 'The Test of Communism'; Clegg and Lucas, 'Three Agricultural Revolutions'.

7 Green et al., 'Working Still Harder'; Gimenez-Nadal, Molina, and Sevilla, 'Effort at Work and Worker Well-Being in the US'; Eurofound, 'Working Conditions and Workers' Health'.

8 Rodrik and Stantcheva, 'Fixing Capitalism's Good Jobs Problem'.

9 Anderson, *Private Government*; Gourevitch and Robin, 'Freedom Now'.

10 Bouie, 'This Is What Happens When Workers Don't Control Their Own Lives'.

11   Gourevitch, *From Slavery to the Cooperative Commonwealth*, Ch. 4.

12   Mau, 'The Mute Compulsion of Economic Relations'; Roberts, *Marx's Inferno*.

13   Cohen, 'The Structure of Proletarian Unfreedom'.

14   Weeks, *The Problem with Work*; Srnicek and Williams, *Inventing the Future*.

15   Frey and Osborne, 'The Future of Employment: How Susceptible Are Jobs to Computerisation?'; Brynjolfsson and McAfee, *The Second Machine Age: Work, Progress, and Prosperity in a Time of Brilliant Technologies*.

16   Benanav, *Automation and the Future of Work*.

17   More precisely, we can say that reproductive labour is performed in a variety of contexts – waged and unwaged, in the home and elsewhere – and that it encompasses similar categories like 'care work', 'domestic work', and 'housework', without being equivalent to them.

18   Gorz, *Farewell to the Working Class: An Essay on Post-Industrial Socialism*, 85.

19   Silvia Federici is likely the most prominent socialist feminist thinker to present this view. As Zöe Sutherland and Marina Vishmidt write, 'In Federici's recent work, and in much related thinking on the politics of care, there is often a conflation of necessity and desirability, particularity and universality, gendered drudgery in the austerity present and utopian horizons (also gendered). Indeed, Federici's valorisation of the reproductive commons carries no overt critique of existing gendered divisions of labour, in fact transvaluing them as anti-capitalist so long as they occur in subsistence economies'. Sutherland and Vishmidt, 'The Soft Disappointment of Prefiguration', 10. For examples from Federici, see in particular the essays collected in: Federici, *Re-Enchanting the World: Feminism and the Politics of the Commons*.

20   Vishmidt, 'Permanent Reproductive Crisis'.

21   To give one recent example, 'rather than seeking to abolish the work of care, [Kate Soper's alternative hedonism project] would accord it proper respect'. Soper, *Post-Growth Living*, 87.

22   *The Telegraph*, 'NHS Is Fifth Biggest Employer in World'; *Full Fact*, 'How Many NHS Employees Are There?'

23   These include personal care workers in health services, primary- and pre-school teachers, and attendants/personal assistants. See 'Employees 16–64 years by occupation (SSYK 2012), age and year', statistikdatabasen. scb.se.

24   Dwyer, 'The Care Economy?', 404.

25 For an illuminating investigation of this transformation, see Winant, *The Next Shift*. As part of this transition, there are factors such as the aging demographics of the advanced capitalist countries, the turn to 'human capital'-centric economies, and the general structural transition implications of phenomena like Baumol's cost disease.

26 Data drawn from Statistics Canada, France's National Institute of Statistics and Economic Studies, Germany's Statistisches Bundesamt, Italy's National Institute of Statistics, Japan's Statistics Bureau, the UK Office for National Statistics, and the US Bureau of Economic Analysis. Using the Standard Industrial Classification (SIC) system, the figures were calculated by including the categories of 'accommodation and food service activities', 'education', and 'human health and social work activities'. For alternative classifications systems, the nearest approximations were used. Future research could look to improve the accuracy by focusing on more fine-grained categories, but for our purposes what is crucially important is the universal trend. Note that the COVID-19 pandemic had a significant negative impact on hospitality workers, leading to slight declines in these trends for 2020–2021.

27 Wilson et al., 'Working Futures 2017–2027', 93.

28 Oh, 'The Future of Work Is the Low-Wage Health Care Job'.

29 Source: 'Fastest growing occupations', bls.gov.

30 Norway once included unpaid work in its national accounts but eventually gave up on it in order to standardise with the rest of the world.

31 Folbre, *The Invisible Heart: Economics and Family Values*, 67.

32 The earliest efforts to measure this sector range back to 1919 and were made in America, Britain, Sweden, Denmark, and Norway (Hawrylyshyn, 'The Value of Household Services'). Since the 1990s, time-use surveys have become a popular and increasingly standardised way to measure how much labour goes on in the home. These surveys ask people to record their activities in the previous day and have begun to give us unprecedented insight into how households distribute and organise unpaid social reproduction. On the basis of this information, a number of governments have begun to put together 'satellite accounts' which attempt to estimate the value of this work, while academic researchers have paid an increasing amount of attention to the assumptions and measures of this work. (For more on the methodology of satellite accounts, see: Holloway, Short, and Tamplin, 'Household Satellite Account (Experimental) Methodology'; Abraham and Mackie, *Beyond the Market*; Landefeld and

McCulla, 'Accounting for Nonmarket Household Production Within a National Accounts Framework'; Suh, 'Care Time in the US: Measures, Determinants, and Implications'; Folbre, 'Valuing Non-Market Work'.) However, it is worth noting that there remain significant constraints in the measurement of this activity, and relying upon new measures should not be the only approach. For some critiques, see: Bryson, 'Time-Use Studies: A Potentially Feminist Tool'; Cameron and Gibson-Graham, 'Feminising the Economy'; Folbre, 'Valuing Non-Market Work'.

33 Webber and Payne, 'Chapter 3: Home Produced "Adultcare" Services'.

34 Slaughter, 'The Work That Makes Work Possible'.

35 International Labour Organization, 'Care Work and Care Jobs for the Future of Decent Work', 43.

36 Chart is based off of authors' calculations using data from the latest available time-use studies, data from the World Bank, and is weighted by the proportion of men and women in a given country. The time-use data comes from: Charmes, 'The Unpaid Care Work and the Labour Market: An Analysis of Time Use Data Based on the Latest World Compilation of Time-Use Surveys', 45–6.

37 Rai, Hoskyns, and Thomas, 'Depletion: The Cost of Social Reproduction'; Ervin et al., 'Gender Differences in the Association Between Unpaid Labour and Mental Health in Employed Adults'.

38 Fox, 'Frances Gabe, Creator of the Only Self-Cleaning Home, Dies at 101'.

39 Davis, *Women, Race, & Class*, 223.

40 Engels, *The Origin of the Family, Private Property and the State*; Kollontai, 'In the Front Line of Fire'; Kollontai, 'Working Woman and Mother'; Kollontai, 'The Labour of Women in the Revolution of the Economy'; Friedan, *The Feminine Mystique*; Sandberg, *Lean In*.

41 Weeks, *The Problem with Work*.

42 Or what Emma Dowling has called a 'care fix'; see Dowling, *The Care Crisis*.

43 Many thanks to Benedict Singleton for help in formulating this point.

2. Technologies

1 Fortunati, 'Robotization and the Domestic Sphere', 9.

2 Hardyment, 'Rising Out of Dust'; Samsung, 'Samsung KX50: The Future in Focus'.

3   Taipale et al., 'Robot Shift from Industrial Production to Social Repro-
    duction', 18.
4   Parks, 'Lifting the Burden of Women's Care Work'.
5   One interesting exception here is Fortunati's work over the past decade,
    which has focused on social robots while emphasising both their capitalist
    nature and their potential for postcapitalist uses. Fortunati, 'Robotization
    and the Domestic Sphere'.
6   Vishmidt, 'Permanent Reproductive Crisis'.
7   Quote from James Butler: Bastani, Sarkar, and Butler, 'Fully Automated
    Luxury Communism'.
8   National Alliance for Caregiving and the AARP, 'Caregiving in the US',
    50–4.
9   Cowan, 'The "Industrial Revolution" in the Home'.
10 Charmes, 'A Review of Empirical Evidence on Time Use in Africa from
    UN-Sponsored Surveys', 49.
11 O'Toole, *We Don't Know Ourselves*, Ch. 3.
12 Greenwood, Seshadri, and Yorukoglu, 'Engines of Liberation', 112.
13 Hardyment, *From Mangle to Microwave*, 12.
14 Ibid., 10; Cowan, 'The "Industrial Revolution" in the Home', 5.
15 Thompson, 'The Value of Woman's Work', 516.
16 Seccombe, *Weathering the Storm*, 125–6.
17 Bereano, Bose, and Arnold, 'Kitchen Technology and the Liberation of
    Women from Housework', 172.
18 Seccombe, *Weathering the Storm*, 129.
19 Bereano, Bose, and Arnold, 'Kitchen Technology and the Liberation of
    Women from Housework', 172.
20 Hardyment, *From Mangle to Microwave*, 147.
21 Bose, Bereano, and Malloy, 'Household Technology and the Social Con-
    struction of Housework', 65.
22 Hardyment, *From Mangle to Microwave*, 5–6.
23 Cowan, 'The "Industrial Revolution" in the Home', 7.
24 Ibid., 7.
25 Veit, 'An Economic History of Leftovers'.
26 Cowan, *More Work for Mother*, 106.
27 Cowan, 'The "Industrial Revolution" in the Home', 5; Parr, 'What Makes
    Washday Less Blue?'
28 Pursell, 'Domesticating Modernity'.
29 Cowan, *More Work for Mother*, 46–52.

30   Cowan, 'The "Industrial Revolution" in the Home', 8.

31   Gordon, *The Rise and Fall of American Growth*, 74.

32   Hardyment, *From Mangle to Microwave*, 144.

33   Dalla Costa, *Family, Welfare, and the State: Between Progressivism and the New Deal*, 15.

34   Ehrenreich and English, *Witches, Midwives, and Nurses: A History of Women Healers*.

35   Cowan, *More Work for Mother*, 76.

36   Schor extended Vanek's figures for two more decades and found the same trend continued. Vanek, 'Time Spent in Housework', 116; Schor, *The Overworked American*, 87.

37   The phrasing in terms of a 'paradox' comes from Joel Mokyr: Mokyr, 'Why "More Work for Mother?"'

38   The Cowan thesis was briefly rejected in the late 1980s, after research from Gershuny and Robinson cast doubt on it, but more recent research has again demonstrated the general point. Cowan, *More Work for Mother*; Gershuny and Robinson, 'Historical Changes in the Household Division of Labor'; Bittman, Rice, and Wajcman, 'Appliances and Their Impact'.

39   Staikov, 'Time-Budgets and Technological Progress', 470.

40   Gershuny finds that the rise in housework is particularly significant for middle-class housewives, who had lost domestic servants during this period. Gershuny, 'Are We Running Out of Time?', 17.

41   Dalla Costa and James, *The Power of Women and the Subversion of the Community*, 29.

42   A Westinghouse ad from 1922, for example, lauded domestic appliances as 'invisible servants'. On the actual relationship between the adoption of domestic technologies and the decline of servants, there is an interesting question about causality. Cowan plausibly suggests that the two processes were symbiotic, facilitated by capitalist firms seeking to drive new product lines for household technologies. Cowan, 'The "Industrial Revolution" in the Home', 22.

43   Cowan, *More Work for Mother*, 98.

44   Hardyment, *From Mangle to Microwave*, 56.

45   Ibid., 188.

46   Mohun, *Steam Laundries*, Ch. 11.

47   Mokyr, 'Why "More Work for Mother?"'

48   Ehrenreich and English, *For Her Own Good*, 197.

49   Cowan, *More Work for Mother*, Ch. 3.

50   Bittman, Rice, and Wajcman, 'Appliances and Their Impact', 412.

51   Bose, Bereano, and Malloy, 'Household Technology and the Social Construction of Housework', 74.

52   Glazer, *Women's Paid and Unpaid Labor*, 83.

53   Cowan, *More Work for Mother*, 79–80.

54   Wajcman, *Pressed for Time*, 201n7.

55   Glazer, *Women's Paid and Unpaid Labor*, 53–63.

56   Gordon, *The Rise and Fall of American Growth*, 524–5.

57   Ibid., 362.

58   Ormrod, '"Let's Nuke the Dinner": Discursive Practices of Gender in the Creation of a New Cooking Process'.

59   It is worth noting that not all technologies spread rapidly. The poor quality and varied requirements of dishwashers meant that even by the 1990s, only around 20 per cent of British households had a dishwasher. Silva, 'Transforming Housewifery: Dispositions, Practices and Technologies', 62.

60   Gomez, 'Bodies, Machines, and Male Power'.

61   Federici, 'The Restructuring of Housework and Reproduction in the United States in the 1970s', 47.

62   Krafchik, 'History of Diapers and Diapering'.

63   Thaman and Eichenfield, 'Diapering Habits', 16.

64   Boyer and Boswell-Penc, 'Breast Pumps', 124.

65   Lepore, 'Baby Food'.

66   This shift of work from waged to unwaged has been an important, if little noticed, element of feminist thinking about work – from the 'work transfer' discussed by Glazer to the 'abject' discussed by Gonzalez and Neton. See: Glazer, *Women's Paid and Unpaid Labor*; Giménez, *Marx, Women, and Capitalist Social Reproduction*; Gonzalez and Neton, 'The Logic of Gender'.

67   Glenn, *Forced to Care*, 154.

68   Mosebach, 'Commercializing German Hospital Care?', 81; Glazer, *Women's Paid and Unpaid Labor*, 110–12; Gordon, *The Rise and Fall of American Growth*, 489–90.

69   Mathauer and Wittenbecher, 'Hospital Payment Systems Based on Diagnosis-Related Groups: Experiences in Low- and Middle-Income Countries', 746; Freeman and Rothgang, 'Health', 375.

70   Gordon, *The Rise and Fall of American Growth*, 481.

71   Evans, 'Fellow Travelers on a Contested Path', 287–8.

72   Gordon, *The Rise and Fall of American Growth*, 490–1.

73   Glazer, *Women's Paid and Unpaid Labor*, 111.

74   Freeman and Rothgang, 'Health', 373; Stark, 'Warm Hands in Cold Age – On the Need of a New World Order of Care', 21, 24; Kirk and Glendinning, 'Trends in Community Care and Patient Participation', 371.

75   Mauldin, 'Support Mechanism'; Reinhard, Levine, and Samis, 'Home Alone'.

76   Guberman et al., 'How the Trivialization of the Demands of High-Tech Care in the Home Is Turning Family Members Into Para-Medical Personnel'.

77   Glazer, *Women's Paid and Unpaid Labor*, 188–91; Glenn, *Forced to Care*, 155–7.

78   Mauldin, 'Support Mechanism'; Ginsburg and Rapp, 'Disability/Anthropology'.

79   Thanks to Zöe Sutherland for pointing this out to us.

80   Sadler and McKevitt, '"Expert Carers"'.

81   Folbre, *The Invisible Heart*, 59.

82   McDonald et al., 'Complex Home Care', 249.

83   Glazer, *Women's Paid and Unpaid Labor*, 188–91.

84   On such a transfer of work, Martha Giménez notes that the 'effect of unwaged consumption work is to allow capital to lower the overall level of wages and increase the rate of exploitation, as the reduction in the costs of consumer goods made possible by self-service in fact cheapens labour power'. Giménez, *Marx, Women, and Capitalist Social Reproduction*, 237.

85   Gershuny, *After Industrial Society?*

86   Lambert, *Shadow Work*.

87   At their most intense, 'these household sustainability efforts cause people committed to what one informant called "a less eco-hostile existence" to sacrifice their own mental health, and even their desire to have children in the first place, to get day-to-day things done in a way that feels consistent with their environmental values'. Munro, 'Unwaged Work and the Production of Sustainability in Eco-Conscious Households', 677.

88   Gordon, *The Rise and Fall of American Growth*; Gordon, 'Interpreting the "One Big Wave" in US Long-Term Productivity Growth'.

89   Gordon and Sayed, 'Transatlantic Technologies'.

90   Some progress continues to be made though, e.g. Clegg et al., 'Learning to Navigate Cloth Using Haptics'.

91 Notably, Wages for Housework argued that if housewives were paid a wage, then there would be an incentive to introduce new technologies. Sweeney, 'Wages for Housework: The Strategy for Women's Liberation', 105.

92 Krenz and Strulik, 'Automation and the Fall and Rise of the Servant Economy'.

93 Samuel, 'Happy Mother's Day'.

94 Chen and Adler, 'Assessment of Screen Exposure in Young Children, 1997 to 2014'.

95 Madrigal, 'Raised by YouTube'.

96 'Whilst that which is more similar to material labor still tends to resist the process of machinization, it is the less tangible part (thinking, learning, communicating, amusing, educating, and so on) that has been machinized.' Fortunati, 'Immaterial Labor and Its Machinization', 140.

97 Huws, 'The Hassle of Housework', 19.

98 We would be remiss in not mentioning the ways in which digital platforms have facilitated the pandemic-driven shift of waged work from the workplace to the home. The rise of such 'remote work' has certainly added complications to the performance of unwaged domestic work, but crucially it has not shifted the imperatives that dominate waged work. Whether performed in the home or elsewhere, waged work still demands productivity, discipline, and the surveillance and control that guarantee the performance of the work for capitalists. By contrast, what we are interested in in this section is the shift of *unwaged* work into a *waged* form, along with the shifts that inaugurates.

99 Huws et al., 'Work in the European Gig Economy', 16.

100 Landefeld, Fraumeni, and Vojtech, 'Accounting for Household Production', 216.

101 The one exception here is France, which spends one more minute eating at home than it did in 1974. Warde et al., 'Changes in the Practice of Eating', 368.

102 Mokyr, 'Why "More Work for Mother?"', 30. It is notable that the work being taken up by low-wage restaurant workers is not mentioned.

103 Smith, Ng, and Popkin, 'Trends in US Home Food Preparation and Consumption'.

104 Kim and Leigh, 'Are Meals at Full-Service and Fast-Food Restaurants "Normal" or "Inferior"?'

105 Bureau of Labor Statistics, 'Consumer Expenditures in 2016', 10;

Smith, Ng, and Popkin, 'Trends in US Home Food Preparation and Consumption'.

106 Calculations from USDA data – note a measurement change means there is a slight shift in calculations in 1997: 'Food Expenditure Series', ers.usda. gov.

107 Marino-Nachison, 'GrubHub: Here's Why People Order Delivery'; Smith, 'Food Delivery Is a Window Into Our Busy, Overworked Lives'.

108 Garlick, 'Dark Kitchens'; Wiener, 'Our Ghost-Kitchen Future'; Hancock and Bradshaw, 'Can Food Delivery Services Save UK Restaurants?'; Lee and Pooler, 'Travis Kalanick Expands "Dark Kitchens" Venture Across Latin America'.

109 Yeo, 'Which Company Is Winning the Restaurant Food Delivery War?'

110 Marino-Nachison, 'Food & Dining'.

111 Warde, 'Convenience Food', 521.

112 Bonke, 'Choice of Foods: Allocation of Time and Money, Household Production and Market Services, Part II'.

113 Warde et al., 'Changes in the Practice of Eating', 368; Bianchi et al., 'Is Anyone Doing the Housework?', 208.

114 Bram and Gorton, 'How Is Online Shopping Affecting Retail Employment?'

115 Mims, 'How Our Online Shopping Obsession Choked the Supply Chain'.

116 UNCTAD, 'Estimates of Global E-Commerce 2019 and Preliminary Assessment of Covid-19 Impact on Online Retail 2020', 6.

117 Sources: 'Internet sales as a percentage of total retail sales (ratio) (%)', ons.gov.uk and 'E-Commerce Retail Sales as a Percent of Total Sales', fred.stlouisfed.org.

118 Satariano and Bubola, 'Pasta, Wine and Inflatable Pools'.

119 Evans, 'Step Changes in Ecommerce'.

120 'Aldi Meets Amazon – Digitalisation & Discount Retailers: Disruption in Grocery Retail'; Retail Feedback Group, 'Retail Feedback Group Study Finds Online Supermarket Shoppers Register Improved Overall Satisfaction and Higher First-Time Use'.

121 Evans, 'The Ecommerce Surge'.

122 Bradshaw and Lee, 'Catch Them If You Can'; Bradshaw, 'Why Tech Investors Want to Pay for Your Groceries'.

123 Ehrenreich, 'Maid to Order', 96.

124 Berg, 'A Gendered Socio-Technical Construction: The Smart House', 169.

125 Miles, *Home Informatics*; Berg, 'A Gendered Socio-Technical Construction: The Smart House', 171.

126 Wajcman, *Pressed for Time*, 130.

127 Gardiner, *Gender, Care and Economics*, 177.

128 Hardyment, 'Rising Out of Dust'; Strengers and Nicholls, 'Aesthetic Pleasures and Gendered Tech-Work in the 21st-Century Smart Home', 73; Darby, 'Smart Technology in the Home'.

129 Berg, 'A Gendered Socio-Technical Construction: The Smart House', 170; Strengers and Nicholls, 'Aesthetic Pleasures and Gendered Tech-Work in the 21st-Century Smart Home', 74.

130 Strengers and Nicholls, 'Aesthetic Pleasures and Gendered Tech-Work in the 21st-Century Smart Home', 73-4.

131 Evans, 'Smart Homes and Vegetable Peelers'.

132 Woyke, 'The Octogenarians Who Love Amazon's Alexa'.

133 Mattern, 'Maintenance and Care'; Mattu and Hill, 'The House That Spied on Me'.

134 Strengers and Nicholls, 'Aesthetic Pleasures and Gendered Tech-Work in the 21st-Century Smart Home', 76, 78.

135 Ibid., 78.

136 Wajcman, *Pressed for Time*, 127.

137 Strengers and Nicholls, 'Aesthetic Pleasures and Gendered Tech-Work in the 21st-Century Smart Home', 76.

138 Wajcman, *Feminism Confronts Technology*, 100.

139 Evans, 'Smart Homes and Vegetable Peelers'.

140 Mattu and Hill, 'The House That Spied on Me'.

141 Wolfe, 'Roomba Vacuum Maker iRobot Betting Big on the "Smart" Home'.

142 Webb, 'Amazon's Roomba Deal Is Really About Mapping Your Home'.

143 Phrase borrowed from a talk by Murray Goulden.

144 Waters, 'Amazon Wants to Be in the Centre of Every Home'.

145 Mims, 'Amazon's Plan to Move In to Your Next Apartment Before You Do'; Matsakis, 'Cops Are Offering Ring Doorbell Cameras in Exchange for Info'; Bradshaw, 'Google Signs $750m Deal with ADT to Sell Its Nest Devices'.

146 Greenwood, Seshadri, and Yorukoglu, 'Engines of Liberation'; de V. Cavalcanti and Tavares, 'Assessing the "Engines of Liberation"';

Coen-Pirani, León, and Lugauer, 'The Effect of Household Appliances on Female Labor Force Participation'; Dinkelman, 'The Effects of Rural Electrification on Employment'.

147 For clarity, the activities included here are: 'Planning, purchasing goods and services (except medical and personal care services), care of children and adults (both in the household and outside the household), general cleaning, care and repair of the house and grounds (including yard work, but excluding gardening), preparing and clearing food, making, mending, and laundering of clothing and other household textiles'. Ramey and Francis, 'A Century of Work and Leisure', 202–4.

148 Goodin et al., *Discretionary Time*, 75.

149 Bittman, Rice, and Wajcman, 'Appliances and Their Impact', 412.

150 Bereano, Bose, and Arnold, 'Kitchen Technology and the Liberation of Women from Housework', 180; Papanek and Hennessey, *How Things Don't Work*, 23.

151 Spigel, 'Designing the Smart House'.

3. Standards

1   Krisis Group, 'Manifesto against Labour'.

2   Gorz, *Farewell to the Working Class: An Essay on Post-Industrial Socialism*, 82.

3   Soper, *Post-Growth Living*, 87.

4   Morris, *News from Nowhere and Other Writings*, 54.

5   Pfannebecker and Smith, *Work Want Work*, Ch. 1.

6   Johnson, 'I Dream of Canteens'.

7   Shove, *Comfort, Cleanliness and Convenience*, 3.

8   Ferree, 'The Gender Division of Labor in Two-Earner Marriages', 178.

9   The management of standards is rarely discussed explicitly, but one notable exception is Ruth Schwartz Cowan's work. See Cowan, *More Work for Mother*, 214.

10 When Jordan Peterson demands that young men clean their rooms and invokes metaphysical battles between chaos and order, he is therefore following a long discursive line on these boundary distinctions.

11 Cited in Cowan, *More Work for Mother*, 167.

12 McClintock, 'Soft-Soaping Empire: Commodity Racism and Imperial Advertising', 129.

13   Davin, 'Imperialism and Motherhood', 19.
14   Willimott, *Living the Revolution*, 56–7.
15   Kelley, '"The Virtues of a Drop of Cleansing Water"'.
16   Vishwanath, 'The Politics of Housework in Contemporary India'.
17   Davis, *Women, Race, & Class*, Ch. 5.
18   Shove, *Comfort, Cleanliness and Convenience*, 86–7.
19   Shove, *Comfort, Cleanliness and Convenience*, 99.
20   Zhang, 'How "Clean" Was Sold to America with Fake Science'.
21   Everts, 'How Advertisers Convinced Americans They Smelled Bad'.
22   Zhang, 'How "Clean" Was Sold to America with Fake Science'.
23   Schor, *The Overworked American*, 89.
24   Shove, *Comfort, Cleanliness and Convenience*, 131.
25   Gordenker, 'Laundry Logic'.
26   Strasser, *Never Done*, 268.
27   Cowan, *More Work for Mother*, 177.
28   Mohun, *Steam Laundries*, 264.
29   Cowan, *More Work for Mother*, 167; 216–19.
30   Gordenker, 'Laundry Logic'.
31   Grand View Research, 'Dry-Cleaning & Laundry Services Market Size Report, 2020–2027'.
32   Neff, 'The Dirt on Laundry Trends Around the World'.
33   Shorter, *The Making of the Modern Family*, 69.
34   Hardyment, *From Mangle to Microwave*, 14.
35   Seccombe, *Weathering the Storm*, 47–8.
36   Arnold and Burr, 'Housework and the Application of Science', 156–9; Hoy, *Chasing Dirt*, 113–17; Woersdorfer, *The Evolution of Household Technology and Consumer Behaviour, 1800–2000*, Ch. 3.
37   Cowan, *More Work for Mother*, 187–8; Mokyr, 'Why "More Work for Mother?"', 17, 33.
38   Hoy, *Chasing Dirt*, 140–9.
39   Ehrenreich and English, *For Her Own Good*, 175.
40   Bereano, Bose, and Arnold, 'Kitchen Technology and the Liberation of Women from Housework', 166–7.
41   Mokyr, 'Why "More Work for Mother?"', 29.
42   Cowan, *More Work for Mother*, 177.
43   Tronto, *Moral Boundaries*, 118.
44   Bianchi et al., 'Housework: Who Did, Does or Will Do It, and How Much Does it Matter?', 57.

45 Robinson and Milkie, 'Back to the Basics', 216.

46 Sayer, Cohen, and Casper, 'Women, Men, and Work', 26.

47 Greaves, 'A Causal Mechanism for Childhood Acute Lymphoblastic Leukaemia'.

48 Ehrenreich and English, *For Her Own Good*, 176.

49 Casey and Littler, 'Mrs Hinch, the Rise of the Cleanfluencer and the Neoliberal Refashioning of Housework'.

50 Evans, 'Lockdowns Lower Personal Grooming Standards, Says Unilever'; 'Monthly Briefing from WFH Research'.

51 Schor, *The Overworked American*, 91.

52 Rowbotham, *Dreamers of a New Day*, 142.

53 Ehrenreich and English, *For Her Own Good*, 178.

54 Mokyr, 'Why "More Work for Mother?"', 19.

55 Ehrenreich and English, *For Her Own Good*, 180.

56 Rowbotham, *Dreamers of a New Day*, 129.

57 Hayden, *Grand Domestic Revolution*, 159.

58 Neuhaus, 'The Way to a Man's Heart', 532.

59 Ibid., 533.

60 Silva, 'Transforming Housewifery: Dispositions, Practices and Technologies', 59.

61 Freeman, *The Making of the Modern Kitchen*, 45.

62 Strasser, *Never Done*, 276–7; Neuhaus, 'The Way to a Man's Heart', 533; Shapiro, *Something from the Oven*.

63 Barthes, *Mythologies*, 78.

64 Neuhaus, 'The Way to a Man's Heart', 533.

65 OECD, 'Society at a Glance 2011 – OECD Social Indicators', 23.

66 Strasser, 'What's in Your Microwave Oven?'

67 Yates and Warde, 'The Evolving Content of Meals in Great Britain', 303–5.

68 Bowen, Brenton, and Elliott, *Pressure Cooker*, 113; Greene et al., 'Economic Issues in the Coexistence of Organic, Genetically Engineered (GE), and Non-GE Crops', 8–9.

69 Fielding-Singh, 'A Taste of Inequality: Food's Symbolic Value across the Socioeconomic Spectrum'.

70 Cited in Bowen, Brenton, and Elliott, *Pressure Cooker*, 4.

71 Daly and Ferragina, 'Family Policy in High-Income Countries'; Lutz, 'Care as a Fictitious Commodity', 4; Daly, 'Families versus State and Market', 143; Gauthier, *The State and the Family*, 173.

72 Ferragina, 'The Political Economy of Family Policy Expansion', 12.
73 Huber and Stephens, 'Postindustrial Social Policy', 269.
74 Source: Chart PF3.2.A and Chart PF3.2.D in the OECD Family Database.
75 OECD, 'Doing Better for Families', 15.
76 Gauthier, Smeeding, and Furstenberg, 'Are Parents Investing Less Time in Children?', 648.
77 Samman, Presler-Marshall, and Jones, 'Women's Work', 30.
78 Esping-Andersen, *Incomplete Revolution*.
79 Ferragina, 'The Political Economy of Family Policy Expansion', 7.
80 Vaalavuo, 'Women and Unpaid Work'.
81 Source: 'Children aged less than 3 years in formal childcare', ec.europa. eu. Note that directly comparable US data for this and the next chart was not available, but evidence suggests similar processes have occurred there. See Cascio, 'Early Childhood Education in the United States', 70.
82 Source: 'Children in formal childcare or education by age group and duration - % over the population of each age group - EU-SILC survey', ec.europa.eun
83 Bianchi, 'Family Change and Time Allocation in American Families', 25; Aguiar and Hurst, 'Measuring Trends in Leisure', 981; Gauthier, Smeeding, and Furstenberg, 'Are Parents Investing Less Time in Children?', 654–5; Bittman, Craig, and Folbre, 'Packaging Care', 134; Sani and Treas, 'Educational Gradients in Parents' Child-Care Time Across Countries, 1965–2012'.
84 Importantly, this study focused on white two-parent households: Bittman, Craig, and Folbre, 'Packaging Care', 134.
85 Bittman and Wajcman, 'The Rush Hour: The Quality of Leisure Time and Gender Equity'; Bittman, Craig, and Folbre, 'Packaging Care', 147.
86 Gauthier, Smeeding, and Furstenberg, 'Are Parents Investing Less Time in Children?'; Sayer, 'Trends in Housework', 22.
87 Schor, *The Overworked American*, 92.
88 Senior, *All Joy and No Fun*, 126.
89 Whittle and Hailwood, 'The Gender Division of Labour in Early Modern England', 21.
90 Schor, *The Overworked American*, 92.
91 Boswell, *The Kindness of Strangers*.
92 Schor, *The Overworked American*, 93; Hulbert, *Raising America*, Ch. 1.
93 Park, *Mothering Queerly, Queering Motherhood*, 63.

94 Seccombe, *Weathering the Storm*, 108, 129–31.

95 Gardiner, *Gender, Care and Economics*, 191.

96 Schor, *The Overworked American*, 93; Cowan, *More Work for Mother*, 179.

97 Gardiner, *Gender, Care and Economics*, 193.

98 Senior, *All Joy and No Fun*, 152.

99 Bernstein and Triger, 'Over-Parenting', 1225; Hays, *The Cultural Contradictions of Motherhood*. This mode of parenting takes a variety of similar forms, such as 'helicopter parenting', 'concerted cultivation', 'curling parents' (in Nordic countries), or simply 'overparenting'.

100 Senior, *All Joy and No Fun*, 154.

101 Bernstein and Triger, 'Over-Parenting', 1227.

102 Senior, *All Joy and No Fun*, 123; Ramey and Ramey, 'The Rug Rat Race'; Doepke and Zilibotti, *Love, Money, and Parenting: How Economics Explains the Way We Raise Kids*.

103 Schaefer, 'Disposable Mothers', 337–8.

104 Ramey and Ramey, 'The Rug Rat Race'.

105 Doepke and Zilibotti, *Love, Money, and Parenting: How Economics Explains the Way We Raise Kids*.

106 Mose, *Playdate*.

107 Bianchi et al., 'Housework: Who Did, Does or Will Do It, and How Much Does It Matter?', 60.

108 Folbre, *The Invisible Heart*, 33.

109 Kornrich and Furstenberg, 'Investing in Children', 11.

110 Coontz, *The Way We Never Were*, 389.

111 Ramey and Ramey, 'The Rug Rat Race'.

112 Ishizuka, 'Social Class, Gender, and Contemporary Parenting Standards in the United States'; Sani and Treas, 'Educational Gradients in Parents' Child-Care Time Across Countries, 1965–2012'.

113 Lareau, *Unequal Childhoods: Class, Race, and Family Life*, 238–9.

114 Harris, *Kids These Days*, 35–6.

115 Bernstein and Triger, 'Over-Parenting', 1228–9.

116 Roberts, 71-2.

117 Cruz, 'Utah Passes "Free-Range" Parenting Law'.

118 There are some growing movements against this intensive parenting – so-called 'free range' parenting, for instance, or older discourses around de-schooling – but given the structural pressures set against such movements, it is difficult to imagine them as more than niche parenting models

so long as we remain within capitalism. Thanks to Zöe Sutherland for emphasising these examples to us.

119 Veblen, *The Theory of the Leisure Class*, 24.

120 Ibid., 26.

121 The phrase 'conspicuous busyness' comes from Shir-Wise, 'Disciplined Freedom'.

122 Gershuny, 'Busyness as the Badge of Honor for the New Superordinate Working Class', 303–9.

123 Jacobs and Gerson, *The Time Divide*, 35; Kuhn and Lozano, 'The Expanding Workweek?'

124 Weeks, *The Problem with Work*, 70–1; Jacobs and Gerson, *The Time Divide*, 164; Cha and Weeden, 'Overwork and the Slow Convergence in the Gender Gap in Wages'.

125 Most work on gig platforms is done to supplement other income; see, for instance: Forde et al., 'The Social Protection of Workers in the Platform Economy'; Gray and Suri, *Ghost Work*; Pesole et al., 'Platform Workers in Europe: Evidence from the COLLEEM Survey'; Fabo, Karanovic, and Dukova, 'In Search of an Adequate European Policy Response to the Platform Economy'; Schmid-Drüner, 'The Situation of Workers in the Collaborative Economy'; Vallas and Schor, 'What Do Platforms Do?'; Huws et al., 'The Platformisation of Work in Europe: Results from Research in 13 European Countries'.

126 Kesvani, 'Rise, Grind and Ruin'; Sprat, 'Why The Rise Of "Work Porn" Is Making Us Miserable'.

127 Jones and Muldoon, 'Rise and Grind'.

128 Wajcman, *Pressed for Time*, Ch. 4.

129 Sullivan, 'Busyness, Status Distinction and Consumption Strategies of the Income Rich, Time Poor', 20.

130 Ibid.

131 Shir-Wise, 'Disciplined Freedom'.

132 Gershuny, 'Busyness as the Badge of Honor for the New Superordinate Working Class', 295.

133 This is an argument that Jonathan Gershuny derives from Gary Becker's neoclassical framework, but one need not believe consumption is a 'production of final satisfactions' in order to take the point that the nature of an occupation strongly determines one's interests and incentives. The latter, of course, is a basic Marxist principle.

134 Weeks, *The Problem with Work*, 60.

135 Friedan, *The Feminine Mystique*, Ch. 10; Fortunati, *The Arcane of Repro-duction: Housework, Prostitution, Labor and Capital*, 40; Gonzalez and Neton, 'The Logic of Gender', 65.

136 Taken from a Bendix advertisement in *Life* magazine.

137 Vanek, 'Time Spent in Housework', 120.

138 Hofferth and Sandberg, 'Changes in American Children's Time, 1981–1997'; Harris, *Kids These Days*, 26–7.

139 Ibid., 13–14.

140 Bernstein and Triger, 'Over-Parenting', 1231.

141 Munro, 'The Welfare State and the Bourgeois Family-Household', 202.

142 King, 'School Bans Parents from Wearing Pyjamas While Dropping Kids Off'.

143 Roberts and Evans, 'The "Benevolent Terror" of the Child Welfare System'.

144 Ibid., 22, 163.

145 Munro, 'Unproductive Workers and State Repression', 624.

4. Families

1   As Göran Therborn notes in his overview of worldwide trends, 'despite significant regional variations, and in spite of informal experimentation among the younger generations, mainly of Europe, the Americas and some parts of Africa, marriage remains the dominant institution of the global socio-sexual order. Any opposite argument would be provincial, at most'. Indeed, only 'in the Caribbean, the Andes, countries of Southern Africa, and possibly Scandinavia is marriage seriously challenged by informal sexual unions' (Therborn, *Between Sex and Power*, 186).

2   Gershuny, *Changing Times*, 132–4.

3   It is important to note that the majority of studies exploring this territory tend to concentrate upon the dynamics between heterosexual (presumably cis) co-parents, and the framing of gendered work within these discus-sions inevitably reflects that. As Michelle O'Brien remarks, the 'national surveys that provide statisticians with representative data don't include means of identifying trans people. Queer researchers generally lack the resources for rigorous empirical investigations' (O'Brien, 'Trans Work: Employment Trajectories, Labour Discipline and Gender Freedom', 49). As such, there are some notable gaps in terms of accounting for the

organisation of working time within different kinds of families and units of social reproduction; these limitations unfortunately find expression within this chapter, too, as there is little data available to produce a more inclusive analysis of gender, reproductive labour, and free time. Research on same-sex couples does seem to suggest that the division of labour is much fairer, with domestic labour often explicitly being recognised as work and as a valuable contribution to the household. Oerton, '"Queer Housewives?"'; Weeks, Donovan, and Heaphy, 'Everyday Experiments: Narratives of Non-Heterosexual Relationships'.

4   Charmes, 'The Unpaid Care Work and the Labour Market: An Analysis of Time Use Data Based on the Latest World Compilation of Time-Use Surveys', 47.

5   National Alliance for Caregiving and the AARP, 'Caregiving in the US', 6.

6   Landefeld, Fraumeni, and Vojtech, 'Accounting for Household Production', 216.

7   Office for National Statistics, 'Women Shoulder the Responsibility of "Unpaid Work"'.

8   Samman, Presler-Marshall, and Jones, 'Women's Work', 19.

9   Note that these time-use surveys across countries are not all performed in the same years. Therefore, for simplicity, we have rounded survey dates to their nearest five-year period. Adapted from: Sayer, 'Trends in Housework', 28.

10   Adapted from ibid., 28.

11   Wajcman, *Pressed for Time*, 117.

12   Senior, *All Joy and No Fun*, 55.

13   Wajcman, *Pressed for Time*, 127; Senior, *All Joy and No Fun*, 57.

14   Wajcman, *Pressed for Time*, 127.

15   Charmes, 'Time Use Across the World: Findings of a World Compilation of Time Use Surveys'; Charmes, 'Variety and Change of Patterns in the Gender Balance Between Unpaid Care-Work, Paid Work and Free Time Across the World and Over Time', 5.

16   Office for National Statistics, 'Men Enjoy Five Hours More Leisure Time Per Week Than Women'.

17   Bittman and Wajcman, 'The Rush Hour: The Quality of Leisure Time and Gender Equity', 176.

18   For an early argument about the important of the quality of leisure, see Linder, *The Harried Leisure Class*.

19   Bittman and Wajcman, 'The Rush Hour: The Quality of Leisure Time and Gender Equity', 185.

20   Willis, 'The Family'.

21   Cowan, 'From Virginia Dare to Virginia Slims', 59.

22   Cited in Thomson, 'Domestic Drudgery Will Be a Thing of the Past: Co-operative Women and the Reform of Housework', 118.

23   Whittle and Hailwood, 'The Gender Division of Labour in Early Modern England', 20–5.

24   Gillis, *A World of Their Own Making*, 9; Tilly and Scott, *Women, Work, and Family*, 13.

25   Tilly and Scott, *Women, Work, and Family*, 124; Cowan, *More Work for Mother*, 18; Marglin, 'What Do Bosses Do? The Origins and Functions of Hierarchy in Capitalist Production'; Landes, 'What Do Bosses Really Do?'

26   Fraser, 'Contradictions of Capital and Care', 105.

27   O'Brien, 'To Abolish the Family', 365.

28   Tilly and Scott, *Women, Work, and Family*, 144.

29   Ehrenreich and English, *For Her Own Good*, 13.

30   Positions Politics, 'Abjection and Abstraction'.

31   Census data from the period tend to underemphasize 'the home-based component, since enumerators did not ask – or were unable to detect – every woman who took in a boarder, did some homework for a piece rate, and so on'. Seccombe, *Weathering the Storm*, 34; Humphries, 'Enclosures, Common Rights, and Women', 37–8.

32   Tilly and Scott, *Women, Work, and Family*, 126.

33   Seccombe, *Weathering the Storm*, 146; Humphries, 'Enclosures, Common Rights, and Women'.

34   Seccombe, *Weathering the Storm*, 146.

35   Tilly and Scott, *Women, Work, and Family*, 196.

36   Seccombe, *Weathering the Storm*, 111.

37   O'Brien, 'To Abolish the Family', 378.

38   Marx and Engels, 'The Communist Manifesto', 226.

39   Hartman, *Wayward Lives, Beautiful Experiments*, 90.

40   O'Brien, 'To Abolish the Family', 377.

41   Ibid., 381.

42   Therborn, *Between Sex and Power*, 24.

43   Seccombe, *Weathering the Storm*, 1.

44   Coontz, *The Social Origins of Private Life*, 352.

45 Whittle and Hailwood, 'The Gender Division of Labour in Early Modern England', 21; Thompson, 'Time, Work-Discipline, and Industrial Capitalism', 60.

46 Gillis, *A World of Their Own Making*, 87.

47 Seccombe, *Weathering the Storm*, 205, 48–9, 49.

48 Forty, *Objects of Desire: Design and Society, 1750-1980*, 99–104.

49 Gillis, *A World of Their Own Making*, 87.

50 Thompson, 'Time, Work-Discipline, and Industrial Capitalism', 85.

51 Seccombe, *Weathering the Storm*, 49.

52 Gillis, *A World of Their Own Making*, 76.

53 Of course, among wealthier families, 'the real toil of housework was being assumed by domestic servants, but where the woman of the house did most of the domestic tasks, convention demanded that she represent it as a labour of love. To the beneficiaries of female domestic labour, ironed shirts and elaborate dinners appeared as if by magic.' Gillis, *A World of Their Own Making*, 76.

54 Thomson, 'Domestic Drudgery Will Be a Thing of the Past: Co-operative Women and the Reform of Housework', 120.

55 Luxton, 'Time for Myself: Women's Work and the "Fight for Shorter Hours"', 173–4.

56 Coontz, *The Way We Never Were*, 208.

57 Ibid., 208–9.

58 Stoltzfus, *Citizen, Mother, Worker*, 36.

59 Gauthier, *The State and the Family*, 76.

60 Coontz, *The Way We Never Were*, 210.

61 Stoltzfus, *Citizen, Mother, Worker*.

62 Coontz, *The Way We Never Were*, 210.

63 Landry, *Black Working Wives*, 110.

64 Coontz, *The Way We Never Were*, 210.

65 Beveridge, 'Social Insurance and Allied Services', 49.

66 See, for instance, Abramovitz, *Regulating the Lives of Women: Social Welfare Policy from Colonial Times to the Present*.

67 Gordon, 'What Does Welfare Regulate?', 612–13.

68 Fraser, *Fortunes of Feminism*, 98.

69 Fraser, 'Contradictions of Capital and Care', 111.

70 Lewis, 'Gender and Welfare Regimes', 164.

71 Lewis, 'Gender and the Development of Welfare Regimes', 161.

72 Groot, 'Part-Time Employment in the Breadwinner Era', 23.

73 Olivetti and Petrongolo, 'The Economic Consequences of Family Policies', 207.

74 Munro, 'The Welfare State and the Bourgeois Family-Household', 202–4.

75 Griffiths, 'The Only Way Out Is Through'.

76 Cooper, *Family Values*, 36.

77 Ibid., 36.

78 Coontz, *The Way We Never Were*, 349; Therborn, *Between Sex and Power*, 314.

79 Lewis, 'The Decline of the Male Breadwinner Model', 153.

80 Coontz, *The Way We Never Were*, 210.

81 Tilly and Scott, *Women, Work, and Family*, 214.

82 Therborn, *Between Sex and Power*, 287.

83 Race is a significant differentiating factor here, however. Landry makes the case that, for middle-class Black women at the turn of the twentieth century, paid work was seen not merely as 'a response to economic circumstance, but fulfilment of women's right to self-actualization'. His argument is that a rejection of expectations surrounding domesticity and femininity – expectations from which Black women, along with many other women of colour, were excluded to begin with – persisted in the US until the middle of the century and continues to exert a shaping influence on race and gender today: 'we might say that because of their different ideology of womanhood, black wives possessed a greater preference for employment than white wives with similar nonmarket (husband's) income, educational levels, and motherhood status. For black wives, employment seems to have been desirable regardless of these other factors'. This account downplays the role of material need, however; elsewhere in his argument, Landry does indeed acknowledge that economic considerations, rather than simple hostility to domestic ideology, was a major factor in Black women's labour force participation at this time. See Landry, *Black Working Wives*, 79, 111.

84 O'Brien, 'To Abolish the Family', 407.

85 Hartmann, 'The Unhappy Marriage of Marxism and Feminism', 19.

86 Landry, *Black Working Wives*, 137.

87 From the mainstream side, this shifted has consisted of discussions of labour activation (e.g., Kenworthy, 'Labour Market Activation'; Bonoli, *Origins of Active Social Policy*) and dual breadwinner models (e.g., Lewis, 'The Decline of the Male Breadwinner Model'; Kowalewska and Vitali, 'Work/Family Arrangements Across the OECD'), while more critical

studies have emphasised workfare states (e.g., Peck, *Workfare States*; Jessop, 'Towards a Schumpeterian Workfare State?').

88 Esping-Andersen, *The Three Worlds of Welfare Capitalism.*

89 Gingrich and Ansell, 'The Dynamics of Social Investment: Human Capital, Activation, and Care', 283.

90 For one influential origin of activation policy, see the Tony Blair-approved report: Commission on Social Justice, 'Social Justice'.

91 Southern Europe is an exception, since they started from a low level. Huber and Stephens, 'Partisan Governance, Women's Employment, and the Social Democratic Service State', 268; Hemerijck, *Changing Welfare States*, 132.

92 Although, of course, this transition has also been driven by certain strands of feminism looking to escape the confines of the house and dependence on a man's wage, as well as the enabling function of various domestic and medical technologies. Albanesi and Olivetti, 'Gender Roles and Technological Progress'; Goldin and Katz, 'The Power of the Pill'.

93 Morgan, *Working Mothers and the Welfare State*, Ch. 4.

94 Goodin et al., *Discretionary Time*, 168.

95 Federici, 'The Restructuring of Housework and Reproduction in the United States in the 1970s', 44.

96 Blank, 'Evaluating Welfare Reform in the United States'.

97 Thus, the name of the programme was changed from Aid to Families with Dependent Children to the *Temporary* Assistance for Needy Families.

98 Office for National Statistics, 'Families in the Labour Market, 2014', 7–8.

99 Pew Research Center, 'Raising Kids and Running a Household', 2.

100 Canon, Fessenden, and Kudlyak, 'Why Are Women Leaving the Labor Force?', 2; Bianchi, 'Family Change and Time Allocation in American Families', 24.

101 Orloff, 'Farewell to Maternalism'.

102 Source: OECD.

103 Seccombe, *Weathering the Storm*, 195.

104 For the ways in which informal norms can continue to structure social hierarchies even after legislative and material changes, see Coffee, 'Mary Wollstonecraft, Freedom and the Enduring Power of Social Domination'.

105 Ciccia and Bleijenbergh, 'After the Male Breadwinner Model?'

106 Kowalewska and Vitali, 'Work/Family Arrangements Across the OECD', 7–8.

107 Lewis, 'The Decline of the Male Breadwinner Model', 156; Kowalewska and Vitali, 'Work/Family Arrangements Across the OECD', 4.

108 Ciccia and Bleijenbergh, 'After the Male Breadwinner Model?', 73.

109 Kenny and Yang, 'The Global Childcare Workload from School and Preschool Closures During the COVID-19 Pandemic'; Hozić and Sun, 'Gender and the Great Resignation'.

110 Schor, *The Overworked American*, 79; Zuzanek, 'What Happened to the Society of Leisure?', 30. Two notable exceptions are France and Germany where government policies have been implemented in an effort to reduce time spent in paid work. See Alesina, Glaeser, and Sacerdote, 'Work and Leisure in the US and Europe'.

111 Schor, *The Overworked American*; Hochschild and Machung, *The Second Shift*.

112 Gershuny, 'Gender Symmetry, Gender Convergence and Historical Work-Time Invariance in 24 Countries', 12.

113 Wajcman, *Pressed for Time*, 65.

114 At least one recent survey has suggested that the level of time pressure remains about the same, or even decreasing according to some questions, but it is worth noting that this research took place during the post-2008 economic downturn, with its high levels of under- and unemployment. Robinson, 'Americans Less Rushed But No Happier', 1094.

115 Bittman, 'Parenting and Employment: What Time-Use Surveys Show', 152–4; Zuzanek, 'Time Use, Time Pressure, Personal Stress, Mental Health, and Life Satisfaction from a Life Cycle Perspective'; Garhammer, 'Pace of Life and Enjoyment of Life'; Robinson and Godbey, 'Busyness as Usual', 418, 420.

116 Southerton and Tomlinson, '"Pressed for Time"– The Differential Impacts of a "Time Squeeze"', 217–18.

117 Wajcman, *Pressed for Time*, 75–8.

118 Jacobs and Gerson, *The Time Divide*, 45.

119 Bittman, 'Parenting and Employment: What Time-Use Surveys Show', 161, 165.

120 Pew Research Center, 'Raising Kids and Running a Household', 7.

121 Goodin et al., *Discretionary Time*, 89–90; Sayer, 'Gender, Time and Inequality', 296; Zuzanek, 'What Happened to the Society of Leisure?', 30.

122 Bianchi, 'Family Change and Time Allocation in American Families', 27–9.

123 Goodin et al., *Discretionary Time*, 91.

124 O'Hara, 'Household Labor, the Family, and Macroeconomic Instability in the United States', 108–9.
125 OECD, 'Doing Better for Families', 23.
126 Blau and Winkler, 'Women, Work, and Family', 3.
127 Autor, Dorn, and Hanson, 'When Work Disappears', 1; Martin et al., 'Births: Final Data for 2015', 8; OECD, 'Doing Better for Families', 25.
128 85 per cent of single parents in America are single mothers. Authors' calculations from data: 'Household Relationship And Living Arrangements Of Children Under 18 Years, By Age And Sex: 2016', census.gov.
129 Blau and Winkler, 'Women, Work, and Family', 4; Alexander, *The New Jim Crow*, 179.
130 The one exception here is Germany, which will see less single-parent households because of its declining fertility rate. OECD, 'Doing Better for Families', 29.
131 United Nations, Department of Economic and Social Affairs, Population Division, 'Database on Household Size and Composition 2022'.
132 Seccombe, *Weathering the Storm*, 196.
133 United Nations, Department of Economic and Social Affairs, Population Division, 'Database on Household Size and Composition 2022'.
134 Ivanova and Büchs, 'Implications of Shrinking Household Sizes for Meeting the 1.5°C Climate Targets'.
135 The exclusion from the family that many trans people experience, for instance, leads to innumerable challenges both economically and in terms of social reproduction. See Belinsky, 'Transgender and Disabled Bodies', 193.

5. Spaces

1 Hayden, *Grand Domestic Revolution*, 294.
2 Hester, 'Promethean Labours and Domestic Realism'.
3 Hayden, *Grand Domestic Revolution*, 10.
4 Attwood, *Gender and Housing in Soviet Russia*, 1–3.
5 Stites, *Revolutionary Dreams: Utopian Vision and Experimental Life in the Russian Revolution*, 208–9.
6 Attwood, *Gender and Housing in Soviet Russia*, 28.
7 Ibid., 79.
8 Stites, *Revolutionary Dreams: Utopian Vision and Experimental Life in the Russian Revolution*, 200.

9   Ibid., 64–6.

10   Attwood, *Gender and Housing in Soviet Russia*, 96.

11   Attwood, 93.

12   There were smaller scale attempts to embrace communal living and new forms of relationship, too. One commune established in the Kitai-Gorod region of Moscow in 1924, for example, started out as a concerted attempt by a group of ten university friends to realise a vision of the new *byt*. The group agreed that 'the commune had to live in total equality, and, just as importantly, it had to be composed of both men and women. Only then did they stand a chance of offering a genuine alternative to the old family'. Willimott, *Living the Revolution*, 90.

13   Attwood, *Gender and Housing in Soviet Russia*, 68.

14   Ibid., 4.

15   Ibid., 131.

16   Buchli, *An Archaeology of Socialism*, 74, 68.

17   Ibid., 65.

18   Ibid., 121.

19   Ibid., 26.

20   Ibid., 28.

21   Attwood, *Gender and Housing in Soviet Russia*, 109.

22   Buchli, *An Archaeology of Socialism*, 65, 76.

23   Ibid., 105.

24   Stites, *Revolutionary Dreams: Utopian Vision and Experimental Life in the Russian Revolution*, 204, 208.

25   Buchli, *An Archaeology of Socialism*, 78.

26   Adams, *Architecture in the Family Way*, 40.

27   Lauster, *The Death and Life of the Single-Family House*, 17.

28   Adams, *Architecture in the Family Way*, 40.

29   Gilman, *The Home: Its Work and Influence*, 151.

30   Puigjaner, 'Bootleg Hotels', 33.

31   Allen, *Building Domestic Liberty*, 151.

32   Hardyment, *From Mangle to Microwave*, 183.

33   The Ansonia has gained recent notoriety as a key inspiration for the 'Anconia', the titular setting for the television show *Only Murders in the Building*. See Counter, 'The Apartments That Inspired "Only Murders in the Building" Have Their Own Bloody History'.

34   Rowbotham, *Dreamers of a New Day*, 136.

35   Foster, 'The Finnish Women's Co-Operative Home', 11. Interestingly,

and in further evidence of the appeal of co-operative housekeeping at this time, the report also includes an inset advert for the Tribune Institute Co-operative Club which invites members to leverage 'neighbourly co-operation' to buy milk and eggs at wholesale prices. These prices are designed to cover the cost of delivery and the 'jobbers' commission' while 'eliminating the retailer's profit and expensive overhead'.

36   Freeman, *The Making of the Modern Kitchen*, 29.

37   Ibid., 31.

38   As Ehrenreich and English note, the housewife-cum-domestic scientist was faced with the 'massive clerical work of maintaining a family filing system for household accounts, financial records, medical records, "house-hints," birthdays of friends and relatives … not to mention the recipe files and an inventory file giving the location and condition of each item of clothing possessed by the family'. Ehrenreich and English, *For Her Own Good*, 179.

39   Rowbotham, *Dreamers of a New Day*, 143.

40   Freeman, *The Making of the Modern Kitchen*, 31.

41   Ibid., 32.

42   Hayden, *Grand Domestic Revolution*, 200.

43   Though, as Hayden notes, many reformers 'grew up in households marked by real financial need', and Gilman watched her mother 'suffer from attempting to get by economically, and failing in health and spirits'. Hayden, *Grand Domestic Revolution*, 300.

44   Hartman, *Wayward Lives, Beautiful Experiments*, 250.

45   Rowbotham, *Dreamers of a New Day*, 129.

46   Ehrenreich and English, *For Her Own Good*, 190.

47   Hartman, *Wayward Lives, Beautiful Experiments*, 250.

48   Allen, *Building Domestic Liberty*, 79.

49   Hayden, *Grand Domestic Revolution*, 167.

50   Puigjaner, 'Bootleg Hotels', 37.

51   Glendinning, *Mass Housing*, 11.

52   Archer, 'The Frankfurt Kitchen Changed How We Cook – and Live'.

53   Stavrides, *Common Space*, 111.

54   Blau, *The Architecture of Red Vienna, 1919–1934*, 387.

55   Heynen, 'Taylor's Housewife', 42.

56   Blau, *The Architecture of Red Vienna, 1919–1934*, 183. Both May and Schutte-Lihotzky would go on to play key roles in the development of the new Soviet city of Magnitogorsk in the early 1930s.

57   Archer, 'The Frankfurt Kitchen Changed How We Cook – and Live'.

58   Freeman, *The Making of the Modern Kitchen*, 39.

59   Heynen, 'Taylor's Housewife', 43–4.

60   Heynen, 'Taylor's Housewife', 45.

61   Ibid., 46.

62   Freeman, *The Making of the Modern Kitchen*, 42.

63   Blau, *The Architecture of Red Vienna, 1919–1934*, 79.

64   Boughton, *Municipal Dreams*, 43.

65   Duma and Lichtenberger, 'Remembering Red Vienna'.

66   Blau, *The Architecture of Red Vienna, 1919–1934*, 157.

67   Ibid., 205.

68   Ibid.

69   Ibid., 212.

70   Ibid., *The Architecture of Red Vienna, 1919–1934*, 212.

71   Duma and Lichtenberger, 'Remembering Red Vienna'.

72   Stavrides, *Common Space*, 115.

73   Blau, *The Architecture of Red Vienna, 1919–1934*, 215.

74   Hester, 'Promethean Labours and Domestic Realism'.

75   Duma and Lichtenberger, 'Remembering Red Vienna'.

76   Heindl, 'Alternatives to the Housing Crisis: Case Study Vienna'.

77   Fitzpatrick, 'What Could Vienna's Low-Cost Housing Policy Teach the UK?'; Förster, 'Social Housing Policies in Vienna, Austria', 1.

78   Fahey and Norris, 'Housing', 479.

79   Andrews and Sánchez, 'The Evolution of Homeownership Rates in Selected OECD Countries: Demographic and Public Policy Influences'.

80   Adkins, Cooper, and Konings, *The Asset Economy*; Harvey, *The Limits to Capital*; Bryant, Spies-Butcher, and Stebbing, 'Comparing Asset-Based Welfare Capitalism'.

81   Lacayo, 'Suburban Legend: William Levitt'.

82   Hayden, *Grand Domestic Revolution*, 23.

83   Ibid.

84   Gordon, *The Rise and Fall of American Growth*, 341.

85   Ibid., 161.

86   Su, 'The Rising Value of Time and the Origin of Urban Gentrification'.

87   Hayden, *Redesigning the American Dream*, 55.

88   Gilman, *The Home: Its Work and Influence*, 18.

89   Gordon, *The Rise and Fall of American Growth*, 357.

90   Nixon and Khrushchev 'The Kitchen Debate [Online Transcript]'.

91 Cowan, *More Work for Mother*; Potter, 'Debunking the "Housing Variety as a Barrier to Mass Production" Hypothesis'.

92 Faichney, 'Advertising Housework'.

93 Kwak, *A World of Homeowners*, 53–4.

94 Ibid., 58.

95 Ibid., 51.

96 Ibid., 60.

97 Glendinning, *Mass Housing*, 94.

98 Fogelson, *Bourgeois Nightmares*.

99 Colomina, *Domesticity at War*, 91.

100 Oliveri, 'Single-Family Zoning, Intimate Association, and the Right to Choose Household Companions', 1408. Oliveri also notes that this ongoing tendency is in tension with associational rights.

101 Colomina, 'Unbreathed Air 1956'; Spigel, 'Yesterday's Future, Tomorrow's Home'; Preciado, *Pornotopia*; Hester, 'Anti-Work Architecture'.

102 Murphy, *Last Futures*, 115.

103 Ibid., 115.

104 Bob Fitch Photography Archive, 'Rural Communes in Northern California, 1969–1970'.

105 Murphy, *Last Futures*, 118.

106 Williams, *Sex and Buildings*, 83.

107 Sadler, 'Drop City Revisited', 5.

108 Williams, *Sex and Buildings*, 79.

109 Sadler, 'Drop City Revisited', 7.

110 Virno, 'The Ambivalence of Disenchantment', 33.

111 *Drop City* [documentary].

112 Fisher, 'K-Punk, or the Glampunk Art Pop Discontinuum', 274.

113 Scott, *Architecture or Techno-Utopia*, 44.

114 Mackay, *Radical Feminism*, 40.

115 Anahita, 'Nestled into Niches', 724.

116 Ibid., 724.

117 Sandilands, 'Lesbian Separatist Communities and the Experience of Nature', 143.

118 Ibid., 143.

119 Ibid., 138.

120 Ibid., 149.

121 Luis, *Herlands*, 95.

122 Ibid., 96.

123 This is by no means necessarily the case, and separatism's histories tend to be more complex and diverse than they are made out to be. See Mackay, *Female Masculinities and the Gender Wars*. Thank you to Jo Littler for pointing us towards this reference.

124 McCandless, 'Some Thoughts About Racism, Classism, and Separatism', 107.

125 This is in contrast to Hartman's more favourable assessment of different forms of exodus in Black women's lives in the opening decades of the twentieth century. Here, the search for 'something else' – the 'resolute, stubborn desire for an elsewhere and an otherwise that had yet to emerge clearly' – is positioned as one of the only possible bases for the pursuit of freedom in a world of curtailed possibilities. The idea of its strategic utility for a collective politics is subordinated to its real potential to initiate the kind of lived experiments in personal liberation that she explores in the book. See Hartman, *Wayward Lives, Beautiful Experiments*, 46.

126 Combahee River Collective, 'The Combahee River Collective Statement', 21.

127 Ibid., 19.

128 McCandless, 'Some Thoughts About Racism, Classism, and Separatism', 108.

129 Srnicek and Williams, *Inventing the Future*, 35.

130 Davis, 'Who Will Build the Ark?', 220.

131 Luis, *Herlands*, 25.

132 Gerrity, 'Residential Co-Living Trend Accelerates in Asia'; Harrad, 'This New Co-Living Space Is the Dystopian Symptom of a London Failing Young People'; Kusisto, 'Tiny Rooms, Shared Kitchens'.

133 Yuile, 'Ungating Community: Opening the Enclosures of Financialised Housing', 97.

134 Kusisto, 'Tiny Rooms, Shared Kitchens'.

135 As is typical of capitalism's formal primacy of exchange-value over use-value. Grima, 'Home Is the Answer, but What Is the Question?', 16–17.

136 Lee, Kemp, and Reina, 'Drivers of Housing (Un)Affordability in the Advanced Economies'; Florida and Schneider, 'The Global Housing Crisis'.

137 Florida and Schneider, 'The Global Housing Crisis'; Meek, 'Where Will We Live?'

138 Williams, *Sex and Buildings*, 26.

139 Arundel and Doling, 'The End of Mass Homeownership?', 650; Macfarlane, 'Is It Time to End Our Obsession with Home Ownership?'
140 Weisman, *Discrimination by Design*, 132.
141 Ibid., 131.

6. After Work

1 Cohen, *Karl Marx's Theory of History: A Defence*, 307.
2 This formulation, and much of the discussion in this section is indebted to: Hägglund, *This Life: Secular Faith and Spiritual Freedom*. Thanks as well to Tom O'Shea for his incisive comments on earlier drafts of this section.
3 Benanav, *Automation and the Future of Work*, 89. There are echoes here as well of Theodor Adorno's well-known aphorism, 'There is tenderness only in the coarsest demand: that no-one shall go hungry anymore.'
4 Gourevitch, *From Slavery to the Cooperative Commonwealth*; Roberts, *Marx's Inferno*; Anderson, *Private Government*; O'Shea, 'Socialist Republicanism'; Muldoon, 'A Socialist Republican Theory of Freedom and Government'. For a critical review of these positions, see Kandiyali, 'Should Socialists Be Republicans?'
5 The idea that market relations constitute a form of domination remains contentious, but for our purposes we can avoid taking a strong commitment either way and therefore leave aside the debates on the issue.
6 Roberts, *Marx's Inferno*, Ch. 3.
7 Hägglund, *This Life: Secular Faith and Spiritual Freedom*, 299.
8 Marx, *Grundrisse*, 611.
9 As Aaron Benanav points out, this dualist position – a realm of freedom and a realm of necessity – can usefully be contrasted with those of 'Charles Fourier, William Morris, and Herbert Marcuse, who essentially suggested that the collapse of spheres could be achieved by turning all work into play'. Benanav, *Automation and the Future of Work*, 132n7.
10 On the specifically *ineradicable* nature of the realm of necessity and the mutual interdependence between the realm of necessity and the realm of freedom, see Hägglund, *This Life: Secular Faith and Spiritual Freedom*, 222.
11 One of the few pieces to have directly addressed reproductive labour in the context of the realm of freedom and realm of necessity is: Browne, 'Disposable Time, Freedom, and Care'.

12   Care Collective, *The Care Manifesto: The Politics of Interdependence*, 33.

13   Dowling, *The Care Crisis*.

14   Marx and Engels, 'The Communist Manifesto', 226; Weikart, 'Marx, Engels, and the Abolition of the Family', 657.

15   Firestone, *The Dialectic of Sex: The Case for Feminist Revolution*; Piercy, *Woman on the Edge of Time*; Lewis, *Full Surrogacy Now*; Lewis, *Abolish the Family*; King, 'Black "Feminisms" and Pessimism'; O'Brien, 'To Abolish the Family'; O'Brien and Abdelhadi, *Everything for Everyone*; Weeks, 'Abolition of the Family'; Hester, *Xenofeminism*.

16   Lewis, *Abolish the Family*, 1.

17   Voce, Cecco, and Michael, '"Cultural Genocide"'.

18   Sophie Lewis (one of the foremost theorists of family abolition working today and a key influence on this book) does not shy away from engaging with these facts in their work. As they note, the term 'family abolitionism' might prove a rather easier rhetorical weapon to wield if we specify from the start 'that we mean the white, cisheteropatriarchal, nuclear, colonial family'. But while this move might feel safer, it nevertheless overlooks the fact that the family – as an institution for the privatisation of care – may be a problem regardless of its whiteness, its cisnormativity, its coloniality, and so on. As such, it might 'actually pose more dangers in its invitation to excuse or romanticize the political character of all nonwhite, mixed, gay, and/or indigenous homes, while neglecting most people's family-abolitionist needs and excluding them from family abolitionist politics!' See Lewis, *Abolish the Family*, 30.

19   Plato, *The Republic*; Marx and Engels, 'The Communist Manifesto'; Brooks, 'The Nuclear Family Was a Mistake'.

20   Marx and Engels, 'The Communist Manifesto', 230; Rawls, *A Theory of Justice*, 64.

21   World Health Organization, 'Violence Against Women Prevalence Estimates, 2018', 20.

22   Sooryanarayana, Choo, and Hairi, 'A Review on the Prevalence and Measurement of Elder Abuse in the Community'.

23   Malatino, *Trans Care*, 6.

24   Grossman et al., 'Parental Responses to Transgender and Gender Nonconforming Youth'; McCarthy and Parr, 'Is LGBT Homelessness Different?'; Tierney and Ward, 'Coming Out and Leaving Home'.

25   This includes 10 per cent of people who are estranged from a parent or child and an additional 8 per cent who are estranged from a sibling. A

further 9 per cent are estranged from extended family members. Pillemer, *Fault Lines*, Ch. 1.

26 Usher et al., 'Family Violence and Covid-19'; Ivandic, Kirchmaier, and Linton, 'Changing Patterns of Domestic Abuse During Covid-19 Lockdown'.

27 Lewis, *Abolish the Family*, 85–6.

28 Seymour, 'Abolition'.

29 As Barrett and McIntosh argue, we should 'work for immediate changes that will increase the possibilities of *choice* so that alternatives to the existing favoured patterns of family life become realistically available and desirable'. Barrett and McIntosh, *The Anti-Social Family*, 134.

30 Ibid., 159.

31 Rosenberg, 'Afterword', 281.

32 The phrase comes from Big Bill Haywood, a founder and former leader of the Industrial Workers of the World, in response to a journalist who asked how Haywood could be smoking an expensive cigar.

33 Davis, 'Who Will Build the Ark?', 43.

34 Gorz, *Paths to Paradise: On the Liberation from Work*, 103.

35 Cohen, 'Capitalism, Freedom, and the Proletariat', 155.

36 Hägglund, *This Life: Secular Faith and Spiritual Freedom*, 261.

37 Hägglund, *This Life: Secular Faith and Spiritual Freedom*, 11–12.

38 'Value, Capitalism, and Communism' [YouTube].

39 Keynes, 'Economic Possibilities for Our Grandchildren', 22.

40 Hägglund, 'What Is Democratic Socialism? Part I: Reclaiming Freedom'.

41 Coffee, 'Mary Wollstonecraft, Freedom and the Enduring Power of Social Domination'; Coffee, 'Two Spheres of Domination'.

42 O'Shea, 'Radical Republicanism and the Future of Work', 1059–61.

43 There is a vast body of literature which shows that comparative advantage does not explain the gendered division of labour in the home, but for two recent pieces, see: Siminski and Yetsenga, 'Specialization, Comparative Advantage, and the Sexual Division of Labor'; Syrda, 'Gendered Housework'.

44 Hägglund raises this concept in the context of critiquing Fredric Jameson and Moishe Postone for their lack of any determinate idea of what might be done with freedom. Hägglund, *This Life: Secular Faith and Spiritual Freedom*, 274.

45 Roberts, 'Free Time and Free People'.

46 While it came too late to our attention to be fully integrated, Paul

Gomberg's work offers a fascinating argument about how and why necessary labour should be shared. Gomberg, *How to Make Opportunity Equal*.

47   Fraser, *Fortunes of Feminism*, Ch. 2.

48   Gomberg sets out an example of how this might work within a hospital – a difficult, but suggestive case, given the wide disparities in skills and routinisation required to make a hospital operational. Gomberg, *How to Make Opportunity Equal*, 76–7.

49   Barrett and McIntosh, *The Anti-Social Family*, 148.

50   Folbre, *The Invisible Heart: Economics and Family Values*, 229.

51   Rosa, 'Did Cuba Just Abolish the Family?'; Herrera, 'Families, Plural'. A copy of the legislation can be found here: 'Proyecto Codigo de las Familias', parlamentocubano.gob.cu.

52   Barrett and McIntosh, *The Anti-Social Family*, 78.

53   Covert, 'Child Care'.

54   Esping-Andersen, *Incomplete Revolution*, 138.

55   Topping, 'How Do UK Childcare Costs Stack up Against the Best?'

56   Cameron and Moss, *Care Work in Europe: Current Understandings and Future Directions*, 18.

57   'Existing welfare states are all essentially "productivist". They are all centrally concerned to ensure a smooth supply of labour to the productive sectors of the formal economy, and they are all anxious that the welfare state not get too badly in the way of that'. Goodin, 'Work and Welfare', 13.

58   Baines and Blatchford, 'School Break and Lunch Times and Young People's Social Lives: A Follow-up National Study', 33–5; Dodd et al., 'Children's Play and Independent Mobility in 2020'; Jarrett, 'A Research-Based Case for Recess', 1.

59   Chakrabortty, 'Which Is the Only Country to Protect in Law the Child's Right to Play?'

60   For more on how digital platforms could be used, see Huws, *Reinventing the Welfare State*, Ch. 8.

61   Stronge et al., 'The Future of Work and Employment Policies in the Comunitat Valenciana'; Bottema, 'Housing and Care Cooperatives in the Netherlands: Spatial Diagrams of Cluster Living'; Hester, 'Households Beyond Thresholds'; Leask and Gilmartin, 'Implementation of a Neighbourhood Care Model in a Scottish Integrated Context – Views from Patients'; Leask, Bell, and Murray, 'Acceptability of Delivering an Adapted Buurtzorg Model in the Scottish Care Context'.

62 Scanlon and Arrigoitia, 'Development of New Cohousing'; Arrigoitia and Scanlon, 'Collaborative Design of Senior Co-Housing'; Hudson, 'Senior Co-Housing'.

63 Iecovich, 'Aging in Place'; Sixsmith and Sixsmith, 'Ageing in Place in the United Kingdom'.

64 Mackay, 'Pioneering Cohousing for London's Lesbians'; Shelley, 'Building Safe Choices'.

65 Much of what follows in this section builds off of the pioneering report by Autonomy: Farruggia, Oikonomidis, and Siravo, 'Long Term Care Centres: Making Space for Ageing'.

66 Farruggia, Oikonomidis, and Siravo, 'Long Term Care Centres', 12.

67 Monsen and Blok, 'Buurtzorg'; Drennan et al., 'Learning from an Early Pilot of the Dutch Buurtzorg Model of District Nursing in England'; Leask, Bell, and Murray, 'Acceptability of Delivering an Adapted Buurtzorg Model in the Scottish Care Context'.

68 Prole.info, 'Abolish Restaurants: A Worker's Critique of the Food Service Industry'.

69 Pellikka, Manninen, and Taivalmaa, 'School Feeding', 13.

70 Fakhri, 'Interim Report of the Special Rapporteur on the Right to Food', 22.

71 Hayden, *Grand Domestic Revolution*, Chs. 8, 10; Willimott, *Living the Revolution*, 16.

72 Hardyment, *From Mangle to Microwave*, 175.

73 See, for example, the Intersectional Townhouse in Vienna, which was designed by Gabu Heindl with and for an association of accessibility activists. The architect describes the project as a 'one-kitchen-house'. GABU Heindl Architektur, 'Intersectional City House, Vienna'.

74 Zaidi, 'The Gift of Food'.

75 Johnson, 'I Dream of Canteens'.

76 UK Parliament, 'Catering Services'; Walker, 'The MPs' Menu'.

77 Johnson, 'I Dream of Canteens'.

78 Atkins, 'Communal Feeding in War Time: British Restaurants, 1940–1947', 149–50.

79 Ryan, 'The Curious History of Government-Funded British Restaurants in World War 2'.

80 Hertog et al., 'The Future of Unpaid Work', 16–17.

81 Kollontai, 'Communism and the Family', 255; Davis, *Women, Race, & Class*, 232.

82 Devetter, 'Can Public Policies Bring about the Democratization of the Outsourcing of Household Tasks?', 382.

83 Something Ruth Cowan Schwarz also argues was a crucial factor in the rejection of these approaches.

84 Hayden, 'What Would a Non-Sexist City Be Like?', 182.

85 Weisman, *Discrimination by Design*, 155.

86 For accounts of experiments with libraries of things, see Robison and Shedd, *Audio Recorders to Zucchini Seeds*.

87 Hatherley, 'Rooftop Pools for Everyone'.

88 Wiltse, *Contested Waters*, Chs. 4, 6.

89 Bridenthal, 'The Dialectics of Production and Reproduction in History', 9.

90 Graziano and Trogal, 'On Domestic Fantasies and Anti-Work Politics', 1144.

91 Hayden, *Grand Domestic Revolution*, 48.

92 Ibid., 48.

93 Fox, 'Frances Gabe, Creator of the Only Self-Cleaning Home, Dies at 101'.

94 Papanek and Hennessey, *How Things Don't Work*, 77, 27.

95 Best, 'Wages for Housework Redux', 916.

96 For one interesting answer to this question, Belton makes a suggestive, if brief, case for understanding the goal of communism to be a sort of 'communist welfare' aimed at maximising aggregate subjective well-being, which she deems to align with the idea of 'production for need'. See 'Value, Capitalism, and Communism' [YouTube].

97 For one detailed plan of how this might work in practice, see Bohmer, Chowdhury, and Hahnel, 'Reproductive Labor in a Participatory Socialist Society'.

98 On the importance of food sovereignty to a postcapitalist world, see Clegg and Lucas, 'Three Agricultural Revolutions', 104–8.

99 Gourevitch, 'Post-Work Socialism?', 27–32.

100 Brassier, 'Prometheanism and Its Critics'.

Acknowledgments

1 Thanks to Rodrigo Nunes for reminding us of this story. See Lenin, *The State and Revolution*.

References

Abraham, Katharine, and Christopher Mackie, eds, *Beyond the Market: Designing Nonmarket Accounts for the United States*, Washington, DC: National Research Council, 2005, nap.edu.

Abramovitz, Mimi, *Regulating the Lives of Women: Social Welfare Policy from Colonial Times to the Present*, Boston: South End Press, 1996.

Adams, Annmarie, *Architecture in the Family Way: Doctors, Houses and Women, 1870–1900*, Montreal: McGill-Queen's University Press, 2001.

Adkins, Lisa, Melinda Cooper, and Martijn Konings, *The Asset Economy*, Cambridge: Polity, 2020.

Aguiar, Mark, and Erik Hurst. 'Measuring Trends in Leisure: The Allocation of Time Over Five Decades', *Quarterly Journal of Economics* 122: 3, 2007.

Albanesi, Stefania, and Claudia Olivetti, 'Gender Roles and Technological Progress', Working Paper, National Bureau of Economic Research, 2007.

Albert, Michael, *Parecon: Life After Capitalism*, London: Verso, 2004.

'Aldi Meets Amazon – Digitalisation & Discount Retailers: Disruption in Grocery Retail', London: YouGov, 2017.

Alesina, Alberto, Edward L. Glaeser, and Bruce Sacerdote, 'Work and Leisure in the US and Europe: Why So Different?' Working Paper, National Bureau of Economic Research, 2005.

Alexander, Michelle, *The New Jim Crow*, New York: The New Press, 2012.

Allen, Polly Wynn, *Building Domestic Liberty: Charlotte Perkins Gilman's Architectural Feminism*, Amherst: University of Massachusetts Press, 1988.

Anahita, Sine, 'Nestled into Niches: Prefigurative Communities on Lesbian Land', *Journal of Homosexuality* 56: 6, 2009.

Anderson, Elizabeth, *Private Government: How Employers Rule Our Lives*, Oxford: Princeton University Press, 2019.

Andrews, Dan, and Aida Caldera Sánchez, 'The Evolution of Homeownership Rates in Selected OECD Countries: Demographic and Public Policy Influences', *OECD Journal: Economic Studies* 2011: 1.

Archer, Sarah, 'The Frankfurt Kitchen Changed How We Cook — and Live', *Bloomberg*, 8 May 2019, bloomberg.com.

Arnold, Erik, and Lesley Burr, 'Housework and the Application of Science', in *Smothered by Invention: Technology in Women's Lives*, eds Wendy Faulkner and Erik Arnold, London: Pluto Press, 1985.

Arrigoitia, Melissa Fernández, and Kathleen Scanlon, 'Collaborative Design of Senior Co-Housing: The Case of Featherstone Lodge', in *Ways of Residing in Transformation*, eds Sten Gromark, Mervi Ilmonen, Katrin Paadam, and Eli Støa, London: Routledge, 2016.

Arundel, Rowan, and John Doling, 'The End of Mass Homeownership? Changes in Labour Markets and Housing Tenure Opportunities Across Europe', *Journal of Housing and the Built Environment* 32: 4, 2017.

Atkins, Peter J., 'Communal Feeding in War Time: British Restaurants, 1940–1947', in *Food and War in Twentieth Century Europe*, eds Ina Zweiniger-Bargielowska, Rachel Duffett, and Alain Drouard, Farnham: Ashgate, 2011.

Attwood, Lynne, *Gender and Housing in Soviet Russia: Private Life in a Public Space*, Manchester: Manchester University Press, 2017.

Autor, David, David Dorn, and Gordon Hanson, 'When Work Disappears: Manufacturing Decline and the Falling Marriage-Market Value of Men', Working Paper, National Bureau of Economic Research, 2017.

Baines, Ed, and Peter Blatchford, 'School Break and Lunch Times and Young People's Social Lives: A Follow-up National Study', London: UCL Institute of Education, 2019, nuffieldfoundation. org.

Barrett, Michèle, and Mary McIntosh, *The Anti-Social Family*, London: Verso, 2015.

Barthes, Roland, *Mythologies*, trans. Annette Lavers, New York: The Noonday Press, 1972.

Bastani, Aaron, Ash Sarkar, and James Butler, 'Fully Automated Luxury Communism', NovaraFM, 2015, novaramedia.com.

Belinsky, Zoe, 'Transgender and Disabled Bodies: Between Pain and the Imaginary', in *Transgender Marxism*, eds Jules Joanne Gleeson and Elle O'Rourke, London: Pluto Press, 2021.

Benanav, Aaron, *Automation and the Future of Work*, London: Verso, 2020.

———, 'How to Make a Pencil', *Logic Magazine*, 2020, logicmag. io.

Bereano, Philip, Christine Bose, and Erik Arnold, 'Kitchen Technology and the Liberation of Women from Housework', in *Smothered by Invention: Technology in Women's Lives*, eds Wendy Faulkner and Erik Arnold, London: Pluto Press, 1985.

Berg, Anne-Jorunn, 'A Gendered Socio-Technical Construction: The Smart House', in *Bringing Technology Home: Gender and Technology in a Changing Europe*, eds Cynthia Cockburn and Ruza Furst Dilic, Buckingham: Open University Press, 1994.

Bernes, Jasper, 'The Test of Communism', *Nilpotencies* (blog), 7 March 2021, jasperbernesdotnet.files.wordpress.com.

Bernstein, Gaia, and Zvi Triger, 'Over-Parenting', *UC Davis Law Review* 44: 4, 2011.

Best, Beverley, 'Wages for Housework Redux: Social Reproduction and the Utopian Dialectic of the Value-Form', *Theory & Event* 24: 4, 2021.

Beveridge, William, 'Social Insurance and Allied Services', London, 1942, ia801604.us.archive.org.

Bianchi, Suzanne, 'Family Change and Time Allocation in American Families', *Annals of the American Academy of Political and Social Science* 638: 1, 2011.

Bianchi, Suzanne, Melissa Milkie, Liana Sayer, and John Robinson, 'Is Anyone Doing the Housework? Trends in the Gender Division of Household Labor', *Social Forces* 79: 1, 2000.

———, 'Housework: Who Did, Does or Will Do It, and How Much Does It Matter?' *Social Forces* 91: 1, 2012.

Bittman, Michael, 'Parenting and Employment: What Time-Use Surveys Show', in *Family Time: The Social Organization of Care*, eds Nancy Folbre and Michael Bittman, London: Routledge, 2004.

Bittman, Michael, Lyn Craig, and Nancy Folbre, 'Packaging Care: What Happens When Children Receive Nonparental Care?' in *Family Time: The Social Organization of Care*, eds Nancy Folbre and Michael Bittman, London: Routledge, 2004.

Bittman, Michael, James Mahmud Rice, and Judy Wajcman, 'Appliances and Their Impact: The Ownership of Domestic Technology and Time Spent on Household Work', *British Journal of Sociology* 55: 3, 2004.

Bittman, Michael, and Judy Wajcman, 'The Rush Hour: The Quality of Leisure Time and Gender Equity', in *Family Time:*

The Social Organization of Care, eds Nancy Folbre and Michael Bittman, London: Routledge, 2004.

Blank, Rebecca, 'Evaluating Welfare Reform in the United States', *Journal of Economic Literature* 40: 4, 2002.

Blau, Eve, *The Architecture of Red Vienna, 1919–1934*, Cambridge: MIT Press, 2018.

Blau, Francine, and Anne Winkler, 'Women, Work, and Family', Working Paper, National Bureau of Economic Research, 2017.

Bob Fitch Photography Archive, 'Rural Communes in Northern California, 1969–1970', 25 July 2016, exhibits.stanford.edu.

Bohmer, Peter, Savvina Chowdhury, and Robin Hahnel, 'Reproductive Labor in a Participatory Socialist Society', *Review of Radical Political Economics* 52: 4, 2020.

Bonke, Jens, 'Choice of Foods: Allocation of Time and Money, Household Production and Market Services, Part II', MAPP Working Paper, 1993.

Bonoli, Giuliano, *Origins of Active Social Policy: Labour Market and Childcare Policies in a Comparative Perspective*, Oxford: Oxford University Press, 2013.

Bose, Christine E., Philip L. Bereano, and Mary Malloy, 'Household Technology and the Social Construction of Housework', *Technology and Culture* 25: 1, 1984.

Boswell, John, *The Kindness of Strangers: The Abandonment of Children in Western Europe from Late Antiquity to the Renaissance*, Chicago: Vintage Books, 1990.

Bottema, Gianna, 'Housing and Care Cooperatives in the Netherlands: Spatial Diagrams of Cluster Living', MPhil Projective Cities, London: Architectural Association, 2019, issuu.com.

Boughton, John, *Municipal Dreams: The Rise and Fall of Council Housing*, London: Verso, 2018.

Bouie, Jamelle, 'This Is What Happens When Workers Don't Control Their Own Lives', *New York Times*, 14 December 2021, nytimes.com.

Bowen, Sarah, Joslyn Brenton, and Sinikka Elliott, *Pressure Cooker: Why Home Cooking Won't Solve Our Problems and What We Can Do About It*, Oxford: Oxford University Press, 2019.

Boyer, Kate, and Maia Boswell-Penc, 'Breast Pumps: A Feminist Technology, or (Yet) "More Work for Mother"?' in *Feminist Technology*, eds Linda Layne, Sharra Vostral, and Kate Boyer, Chicago: University of Illinois Press, 2010.

Bradshaw, Tim, 'Google Signs $750m Deal with ADT to Sell Its Nest Devices', *Financial Times*, 3 August 2020, ft.com.

———, 'Why Tech Investors Want to Pay for Your Groceries', *Financial Times*, 4 May 2021, ft.com.

Bradshaw, Tim, and Dave Lee, 'Catch Them If You Can: The $14bn Rise of Rapid Grocery Delivery Services', *Financial Times*, 12 April 2021, ft.com.

Bram, Jason, and Nicole Gorton, 'How Is Online Shopping Affecting Retail Employment?' *Liberty Street Economics* (blog), 5 October 2017, libertystreeteconomics.newyorkfed.org.

Brassier, Ray, 'Prometheanism and Its Critics', in *#Accelerate: The Accelerationist Reader*, eds Robin Mackay and Armen Avanessian, Falmouth: Urbanomic, 2014.

Bridenthal, Renate, 'The Dialectics of Production and Reproduction in History', *Radical America* 10: 2, 1976.

Brooks, David, 'The Nuclear Family Was a Mistake', *The Atlantic*, 2020, theatlantic.com.

Browne, Paul Leduc, 'Disposable Time, Freedom, and Care', *Science & Society* 75: 3, 2011.

Bryant, Gareth, Ben Spies-Butcher, and Adam Stebbing, 'Comparing Asset-Based Welfare Capitalism: Wealth Inequality, Housing Finance and Household Risk', *Housing Studies* 2022.

Brynjolfsson, Erik, and Andrew McAfee, *The Second Machine Age: Work, Progress, and Prosperity in a Time of Brilliant Technologies*, New York: W.W. Norton & Company, 2014.

Bryson, Valerie. 'Time-Use Studies: A Potentially Feminist Tool'.

International Feminist Journal of Politics 10: 2, 2008, 135–53.

Buchli, Victor, *An Archaeology of Socialism*, Oxford: Routledge, 2000.

Bureau of Labor Statistics, 'Consumer Expenditures in 2016', 2018.

Cameron, Claire, and Peter Moss, *Care Work in Europe: Current Understandings and Future Directions*, New York: Routledge, 2007.

Cameron, Jenny, and J. K. Gibson-Graham, 'Feminising the Economy: Metaphors, Strategies, Politics', *Gender, Place & Culture* 10: 2, 2003.

Canon, Maria, Helen Fessenden, and Marianna Kudlyak, 'Why Are Women Leaving the Labor Force?' Richmond: Federal Reserve Bank of Richmond, 2015.

Care Collective, *The Care Manifesto: The Politics of Interdependence*, London: Verso, 2020.

Cascio, Elizabeth U. 'Early Childhood Education in the United States: What, When, Where, Who, How, and Why', Working Paper, National Bureau of Economic Research, 2021.

Casey, Emma, and Jo Littler, 'Mrs Hinch, the Rise of the Cleanfluencer and the Neoliberal Refashioning of Housework: Scouring Away the Crisis?' *Sociological Review* 70: 3, May 2022.

Cavalcanti, Tiago V. de V., and José Tavares, 'Assessing the "Engines of Liberation": Home Appliances and Female Labor Force Participation', *Review of Economics and Statistics* 90: 1, 2008.

Cha, Youngjoo, and Kim A. Weeden, 'Overwork and the Slow Convergence in the Gender Gap in Wages', *American Sociological Review* 79: 3, 2014.

Chakrabortty, Aditya, 'Which Is the Only Country to Protect in Law the Child's Right to Play?' *Guardian*, 22 August 2018, theguardian.com.

Chang, Grace, *Disposable Domestics: Immigrant Women Workers in the Global Economy*, Chicago: Haymarket Books, 2016.

Charmes, Jacques, 'A Review of Empirical Evidence on Time Use in Africa from UN-Sponsored Surveys', in *Gender, Time Use, and Poverty in Sub-Saharan Africa*, eds C. Mark Blackden and Quentin Wodon, World Bank Working Paper No. 73, Washington, DC: World Bank, 2006.

———, 'The Unpaid Care Work and the Labour Market: An Analysis of Time Use Data Based on the Latest World Compilation of Time-Use Surveys', Working Paper, Geneva: International Labour Organization, 2019, ilo.org.

———, 'Time Use Across the World: Findings of a World Compilation of Time Use Surveys', UN Human Development, 2015.

———, 'Variety and Change of Patterns in the Gender Balance Between Unpaid Care-Work, Paid Work and Free Time Across the World and Over Time: A Measure of Wellbeing?' *Wellbeing, Space and Society* 3, 2022.

Chen, Weiwei, and Jessica L. Adler, 'Assessment of Screen Exposure in Young Children, 1997 to 2014', *JAMA Pediatrics* 173: 4, 2019.

Ciccia, Rossella, and Inge Bleijenbergh, 'After the Male Breadwinner Model? Childcare Services and the Division of Labor in European Countries', *Social Politics: International Studies in Gender, State & Society* 21: 1, 2014.

Clegg, Alexander, Wenhao Yu, Zackory Erickson, Jie Tan, C. Karen Liu, and Greg Turk, 'Learning to Navigate Cloth Using Haptics', *ArXiv*, 20 March 2017, arxiv.org.

Clegg, John, and Rob Lucas, 'Three Agricultural Revolutions', *South Atlantic Quarterly* 119: 1, 2020.

Coen-Pirani, Daniele, Alexis León, and Steven Lugauer, 'The Effect of Household Appliances on Female Labor Force Participation: Evidence from Microdata', *Labour Economics* 17: 3, 2010.

Coffee, Alan M.S.J. 'Mary Wollstonecraft, Freedom and the Enduring Power of Social Domination', *European Journal of Political Theory* 12: 2, 2013.

————, 'Two Spheres of Domination: Republican Theory, Social Norms and the Insufficiency of Negative Freedom', *Contemporary Political Theory* 14: 1, 2015.

Cohen, G.A., 'Capitalism, Freedom, and the Proletariat', in *On the Currency of Egalitarian Justice, and Other Essays in Political Philosophy*, Princeton: Princeton University Press, 2011.

————, *Karl Marx's Theory of History: A Defence*, Princeton: Princeton University Press, 2001.

————, 'The Structure of Proletarian Unfreedom', *Philosophy & Public Affairs* 12: 1, 1983.

Colomina, Beatriz, *Domesticity at War*, Cambridge: MIT Press, 2007.

————, 'Unbreathed Air 1956', *Grey Room* 15, 2004.

Combahee River Collective. 'The Combahee River Collective Statement', in *How We Get Free: Black Feminism and the Combahee River Collective*, ed. Keeanga-Yamahtta Taylor, Chicago: Haymarket Books, 2017.

Commission on Social Justice, 'Social Justice: Strategies for National Renewal', 1994, ippr.org.

Coontz, Stephanie, *The Social Origins of Private Life: A History of American Families, 1600–1900*, London: Verso, 1988.

————, *The Way We Never Were: American Families and the Nostalgia Trap*, New York: Basic Books, 2016.

Cooper, Melinda, *Family Values: Between Neoliberalism and the New Social Conservatism*, New York: Zone Books, 2017.

Counter, Rosemary, 'The Apartments That Inspired "Only Murders in the Building" Have Their Own Bloody History'. *Vanity Fair*, 6 July 2022, vanityfair.com.

Covert, Bryce. 'Child Care: The Radical Is Popular', *Lux Magazine*, 2021, lux-magazine.com.

Cowan, Ruth Schwartz, 'From Virginia Dare to Virginia Slims: Women and Technology in American Life', *Technology and Culture* 20: 1, 1979.

————, *More Work for Mother: The Ironies of Household Technology from the Open Hearth to the Microwave*, London: Free Association Books, 1989.

————, 'The "Industrial Revolution" in the Home: Household Technology and Social Change in the 20th Century', *Technology and Culture* 17: 1, 1976.

Cruz, Donna De La, 'Utah Passes "Free-Range" Parenting Law', *New York Times*, 29 March 2018, nytimes.com.

Dalla Costa, Mariarosa, *Family, Welfare, and the State: Between Progressivism and the New Deal*, trans. Rafaella Capanna, Brooklyn: Common Notions, 2015.

Dalla Costa, Mariarosa, and Selma James, *The Power of Women and the Subversion of the Community*, Bristol: Falling Wall Press, 1975.

Daly, Mary, 'Families versus State and Market', in *The Oxford Handbook of the Welfare State*, eds Francis G. Castles, Stephan Leibfried, Jane Lewis, Herbert Obinger, and Christopher Pierson, Oxford: Oxford University Press, 2012.

Daly, Mary, and Emanuele Ferragina, 'Family Policy in High-Income Countries: Five Decades of Development', *Journal of European Social Policy* 28: 3, 2018.

Darby, Sarah J., 'Smart Technology in the Home: Time for More Clarity', *Building Research & Information* 46: 1, 2018.

Davin, Anna, 'Imperialism and Motherhood', *History Workshop*, 5, 1978.

Davis, Angela Y., *Women, Race, & Class*, New York: Ballantine Books Inc., 2011.

Davis, Mike, 'Who Will Build the Ark?' *New Left Review* 61, 2010.

Devetter, François-Xavier, 'Can Public Policies Bring about the Democratization of the Outsourcing of Household Tasks?' *Review of Radical Political Economics* 48: 3, 2016.

Dinkelman, Taryn, 'The Effects of Rural Electrification on Employment: New Evidence from South Africa', *American Economic Review* 101: 7, 2011.

Dodd, Helen F., Lily FitzGibbon, Brooke E. Watson, and Rachel J. Nesbit, 'Children's Play and Independent Mobility in 2020: Results from the British Children's Play Survey', *International Journal of Environmental Research and Public Health* 18: 8, 2021.

Doepke, Matthias, and Fabrizio Zilibotti, *Love, Money, and Parenting: How Economics Explains the Way We Raise Kids*, Princeton: Princeton University Press, 2019.

Dowling, Emma, *The Care Crisis: What Caused It and How Can We End It?* London: Verso, 2021.

Drennan, Vari, Fiona Ross, Melania Calestani, Mary Saunders, and Peter West, 'Learning from an Early Pilot of the Dutch Buurtzorg Model of District Nursing in England', *Primary Health Care* 28: 6, 2018.

Drop City. Documentary, 2012.

Duma, Veronika, and Hanna Lichtenberger, 'Remembering Red Vienna', *Jacobin*, 10 February 2017, jacobin.com.

Dwyer, Rachel E., 'The Care Economy? Gender, Economic Restructuring, and Job Polarization in the US Labor Market', *American Sociological Review* 78: 3, 2013.

Ehrenreich, Barbara, 'Maid to Order', in *Global Woman: Nannies, Maids and Sex Workers in the New Economy*, eds Barbara Ehrenreich and Arlie Hochschild, London: Granta Books, 2003.

Ehrenreich, Barbara, and Deirdre English, *For Her Own Good: Two Centuries of the Experts Advice to Women*, New York: Random House Inc, 2005.

———, *Witches, Midwives, and Nurses: A History of Women Healers*, New York: The Feminist Press CUNY, 2010.

Engels, Friedrich, *The Origin of the Family, Private Property and the State*, London: Penguin Classics, 2010.

Ervin, Jennifer, Yamna Taouk, Ludmila Fleitas Alfonzo, Belinda Hewitt, and Tania King. 'Gender Differences in the Association Between Unpaid Labour and Mental Health in Employed Adults: A Systematic Review'. *The Lancet Public Health* 7: 9, 2022.

Esping-Andersen, Gøsta, *Incomplete Revolution: Adapting Welfare States to Women's New Roles*, Cambridge: Polity Press, 2009.

———, *The Three Worlds of Welfare Capitalism*, Cambridge: Polity Press, 1989.

Eurofound, 'Working Conditions and Workers' Health', Luxembourg: Publications Office of the European Union, 2019.

Evans, Benedict, 'Smart Homes and Vegetable Peelers', *Benedict Evans* (blog), 3 February 2018, ben-evans.com.

———, 'Step Changes in Ecommerce', *Benedict Evans* (blog), 25 April 2021, ben-evans.com.

———, 'The Ecommerce Surge', *Benedict Evans* (blog), 18 August 2020, ben-evans.com.

Evans, Judith, 'Lockdowns Lower Personal Grooming Standards, Says Unilever', *Financial Times*, 23 April 2020, ft.com.

Evans, Robert, 'Fellow Travelers on a Contested Path: Power, Purpose, and the Evolution of European Health Care Systems', *Journal of Health Politics, Policy and Law* 30: 1–2, 2005.

Everts, Sarah, 'How Advertisers Convinced Americans They Smelled Bad', *Smithsonian*, 2 August 2012, smithsonianmag.com.

Fabo, Brian, Jovana Karanovic, and Katerina Dukova, 'In Search of an Adequate European Policy Response to the Platform Economy', *Transfer: European Review of Labour and Research* 23: 2, 2017.

Fahey, Tony, and Michelle Norris, 'Housing', in *The Oxford Handbook of the Welfare State*, eds Francis G. Castles, Stephan Leibfried, Jane Lewis, Herbert Obinger, and Christopher Pierson, Oxford: Oxford University Press, 2012.

Faichney, Sylvia, 'Advertising Housework: Labor and the Promotion of Pleasure in 1970s Domestic Interiors', *Blind Field: A Journal of Cultural Inquiry*, 22 September 2017, blindfieldjournal. com.

Fakhri, Michael, 'Interim Report of the Special Rapporteur on the Right to Food', New York: United Nations Office for the

Coordination of Humanitarian Affairs, 2022, ohchr.org.

Farruggia, Francesca, Stavros Oikonomidis, and Julian Siravo, 'Long Term Care Centres: Making Space for Ageing', Cranbourne: Autonomy, 2020, autonomy.work.

Federici, Silvia, *Re-Enchanting the World: Feminism and the Politics of the Commons*, Oakland: PM Press, 2018.

———, 'The Restructuring of Housework and Reproduction in the United States in the 1970s', in *Revolution at Point Zero: Housework, Reproduction, and Feminist Struggle*, Oakland: PM Press, 2012.

Ferragina, Emanuele, 'The Political Economy of Family Policy Expansion', *Review of International Political Economy* 26: 6, 2019.

Ferree, Myra Marx, 'The Gender Division of Labor in Two-Earner Marriages: Dimensions of Variability and Change', *Journal of Family Issues* 12: 2, 1991.

Fielding-Singh, Priya, 'A Taste of Inequality: Food's Symbolic Value across the Socioeconomic Spectrum', *Sociological Science* 4, 2017.

Firestone, Shulamith, *The Dialectic of Sex: The Case for Feminist Revolution*, New York: Farrar, Straus and Giroux, 2003.

Fisher, Mark, *Capitalist Realism: Is There No Alternative?* Winchester: Zero Books, 2009.

———, 'K-Punk, or the Glampunk Art Pop Discontinuum', in *K-Punk: The Collected and Unpublished Writings of Mark Fisher (2004–2016)*, ed. Darren Ambrose, London: Repeater, 2018.

Fitzpatrick, Michael, 'What Could Vienna's Low-Cost Housing Policy Teach the UK?' *Guardian*, 12 December 2017, theguardian.com.

Florida, Richard, and Benjamin Schneider, 'The Global Housing Crisis', *Bloomberg*, 11 April 2018, bloomberg.com.

Fogelson, Robert M., *Bourgeois Nightmares: Suburbia, 1870–1930*, New Haven: Yale University Press, 2005.

Folbre, Nancy, *The Invisible Heart: Economics and Family Values*, New York: The New Press, 2001.

———, 'Valuing Non-Market Work', New York: UN Human Development, 2015.

Forde, Chris, Mark Stuart, Simon Joyce, Liz Oliver, Danat Valizade, Gabrielle Alberti, Kate Hardy, Vera Trappmann, Charles Umney, and Calum Carson, 'The Social Protection of Workers in the Platform Economy', Brussels: European Parliament Policy Department A: Economic and Scientific Policy, 2017, europarl. europa.eu.

Förster, Wolfgang, 'Social Housing Policies in Vienna, Austria: A Contribution to Social Cohesion', Glasgow: Glasgow School of Art, 10 May 2013, sites.eca.ed.ac.uk/.

Fortunati, Leopoldina, 'Immaterial Labor and Its Machinization', *Ephemera* 7: 1, 2007.

———, 'Robotization and the Domestic Sphere', *New Media & Society*, 2018.

———, *The Arcane of Reproduction: Housework, Prostitution, Labor and Capital*, Brooklyn: Autonomedia, 1995.

Forty, Adrian, *Objects of Desire: Design and Society, 1750-1980*, London: Thames and Hudson, Ltd, 1986.

Foster, Elene, 'The Finnish Women's Co-Operative Home', *New York Tribune*, 3 November 1918.

Fox, Margalit, 'Frances Gabe, Creator of the Only Self-Cleaning Home, Dies at 101', *New York Times*, 18 July 2017, nytimes.com.

Fraser, Nancy, 'Contradictions of Capital and Care', *New Left Review* II: 100, 2016.

———, *Fortunes of Feminism: From State-Managed Capitalism to Neoliberal Crisis*, London: Verso, 2013.

Freeman, June, *The Making of the Modern Kitchen*, Oxford: Berg, 2004.

Freeman, Richard, and Heinz Rothgang, 'Health', in *The Oxford Handbook of The Welfare State*, eds Francis G. Castles, Stephan

Leibfried, Jane Lewis, Herbert Obinger, and Christopher Pierson, Oxford: Oxford University Press, 2012.

Frey, Carl Benedikt, and Michael Osborne, 'The Future of Employment: How Susceptible Are Jobs to Computerisation?', 2013, oxfordmartin.ox.ac.uk.

Friedan, Betty, *The Feminine Mystique*, London: Penguin Classics, 2010.

Full Fact, 'How Many NHS Employees Are There?', 1 June 2017, fullfact.org.

Furstenberg, Frank F., 'On a New Schedule: Transitions to Adulthood and Family Change', *Future of Children* 20: 1, 2010.

Fussell, Elizabeth, 'The Transition to Adulthood in Aging Societies', *Annals of the American Academy of Political and Social Science* 580, 2002.

GABU Heindl Architektur, 'Intersectional City House, Vienna', 2016, gabuheindl.at/.

Gardiner, Jean, *Gender, Care and Economics*, Houndmills: Macmillan, 1997.

Garhammer, Manfred, 'Pace of Life and Enjoyment of Life', *Journal of Happiness Studies* 3: 3, 2002.

Garlick, Hattie, 'Dark Kitchens: Is This the Future of Takeaway?' *Financial Times*, 8 June 2017, ft.com.

Gauthier, Anne H., *The State and the Family: A Comparative Analysis of Family Policies in Industrialized Countries*, Oxford: Oxford University Press, 1999.

Gauthier, Anne H., Timothy M. Smeeding, and Frank F. Furstenberg, 'Are Parents Investing Less Time in Children? Trends in Selected Industrialized Countries', *Population and Development Review* 30: 4, 2004.

Gerrity, Michael, 'Residential Co-Living Trend Accelerates in Asia', 2 February 2018, worldpropertyjournal.com.

Gershuny, Jonathan, *After Industrial Society? The Emerging Self-Service Economy*, London: Palgrave, 1978.

————, 'Are We Running Out of Time?' *Futures* 24: 1, 1992.

————, 'Busyness as the Badge of Honor for the New Superordinate Working Class', *Social Research* 72: 2, 2005.

————, *Changing Times: Work and Leisure in Postindustrial Society*, Oxford: Oxford University Press, 2003.

————, 'Gender Symmetry, Gender Convergence and Historical Work-Time Invariance in 24 Countries', Oxford: Centre for Time Use Research, 2018.

Gershuny, Jonathan, and John P. Robinson, 'Historical Changes in the Household Division of Labor', *Demography* 25: 4, 1988.

Gibson-Graham, J.K., *A Postcapitalist Politics*, Minneapolis: University of Minnesota Press, 2006.

Gillis, John R., *A World of Their Own Making: Myth, Ritual, and the Quest for Family Values*, Cambridge: Harvard University Press, 1997.

Gilman, Charlotte Perkins, *The Home: Its Work and Influence*, CreateSpace Independent Publishing Platform, 2016.

Giménez, Martha E., *Marx, Women, and Capitalist Social Reproduction: Marxist Feminist Essays*, Chicago: Haymarket Books, 2019.

Gimenez-Nadal, J. Ignacio, José Alberto Molina, and Almudena Sevilla, 'Effort at Work and Worker Well-Being in the US', Bonn: IZA Institute of Labor Economics, 2022, iza.org.

Gingrich, Jane, and Ben Ansell, 'The Dynamics of Social Investment: Human Capital, Activation, and Care', in *The Politics of Advanced Capitalism*, eds Pablo Beramendi, Silja Häusermann, Herbert Kitschelt, and Hanspeter Kriesi, Cambridge: Cambridge University Press, 2015.

Ginsburg, Faye, and Rayna Rapp, 'Disability/Anthropology: Rethinking the Parameters of the Human', *Current Anthropology* 61: S21, 2020.

Glazer, Nona Y., *Women's Paid and Unpaid Labor: The Work Transfer in Health Care and Retailing*, Philadelphia: Temple University Press, 1993.

Glendinning, Miles, *Mass Housing: Modern Architecture and State Power – A Global History*, London: Bloomsbury Visual Arts, 2021.

Glenn, Evelyn Nakano, *Forced to Care*, Cambridge: Harvard University Press, 2012.

Goldin, Claudia, and Lawrence Katz, 'The Power of the Pill: Oral Contraceptives and Women's Career and Marriage Decisions', *Journal of Political Economy* 110: 4, 2002.

Gomberg, Paul, *How to Make Opportunity Equal: Race and Contributive Justice*, Malden: Wiley-Blackwell, 2007.

Gomez, M. Carme Alemany, 'Bodies, Machines, and Male Power', in *Bringing Technology Home: Gender and Technology in a Changing Europe*, eds Cynthia Cockburn and Ruza Furst Dilic, Buckingham: Open University Press, 1994.

Gonzalez, Maya, and Jeanne Neton, 'The Logic of Gender', in *Endnotes 3: Gender, Race, Class and Other Misfortunes*, Brighton, 2013.

Goodin, Robert, 'Work and Welfare: Towards a Post-Productivist Welfare Regime', *British Journal of Political Science* 31: 1, 2001.

Goodin, Robert E., James Mahmud Rice, Antti Parpo, and Lina Eriksson, *Discretionary Time: A New Measure of Freedom*, Cambridge: Cambridge University Press, 2008.

Gordenker, Alice, 'Laundry Logic', *Japan Times*, 16 September 2010, japantimes.co.jp.

Gordon, Linda, 'What Does Welfare Regulate?' *Social Research* 55: 4, 1988.

Gordon, Robert, 'Interpreting the "One Big Wave" in US Long-Term Productivity Growth', Working Paper, National Bureau of Economic Research, 2000, nber.org.

———, *The Rise and Fall of American Growth: The US Standard of Living since the Civil War*, Princeton: Princeton University Press, 2016.

Gordon, Robert J., and Hassan Sayed, 'Transatlantic Technologies: The Role of ICT in the Evolution of US and European

Productivity Growth', *International Productivity Monitor* 38, 2020.

Gorz, André, *Farewell to the Working Class: An Essay on Post-Industrial Socialism*, trans. Michael Sonenscher, London: Pluto Press, 1997.

———, *Paths to Paradise: On the Liberation from Work*, trans. Malcolm Imrie, Boston: South End Press, 1985.

Gourevitch, Alex, *From Slavery to the Cooperative Commonwealth: Labor and Republican Liberty in the Nineteenth Century*, New York: Cambridge University Press, 2015.

———, 'Post-Work Socialism?' *Catalyst* 6: 2, 2022.

Gourevitch, Alex, and Corey Robin, 'Freedom Now', *Polity* 52: 3, 2020.

Grand View Research, 'Dry-Cleaning & Laundry Services Market Size Report, 2020–2027', 2020, grandviewresearch.com.

Gray, Mary L., and Siddharth Suri, *Ghost Work: How to Stop Silicon Valley from Building a New Global Underclass*, Boston: Houghton Mifflin Harcourt, 2019.

Graziano, Valeria, and Kim Trogal, 'On Domestic Fantasies and Anti-Work Politics: A Feminist History of Complicating Automation', *Theory & Event* 24: 4, 2021.

Greaves, Mel, 'A Causal Mechanism for Childhood Acute Lymphoblastic Leukaemia', *Nature Reviews Cancer*, 2018.

Green, Francis, Alan Felstead, Duncan Gallie, and Golo Henseke, 'Working Still Harder', *ILR Review* 75: 2, 2022.

Greene, Catherine, Seth J. Wechsler, Aaron Adalja, and James Hanson, 'Economic Issues in the Coexistence of Organic, Genetically Engineered (GE), and Non-GE Crops', Economic Information Bulletin, United States Department of Agriculture, 2016, ers.usda.gov.

Greenwood, Jeremy, Ananth Seshadri, and Mehmet Yorukoglu, 'Engines of Liberation', *The Review of Economic Studies* 72: 1, 2005.

Griffiths, Kate Doyle, 'The Only Way Out Is Through: A Reply to Melinda Cooper', Verso, 26 March 2018, versobooks.com.

Grima, Joseph, 'Home Is the Answer, but What Is the Question?' in *SQM: The Quantified Home*, ed. Space Caviar, Zürich: Lars Müller Publishers, 2014.

Groot, T. J. (Timon) de. 'Part-Time Employment in the Bread-winner Era: Dutch Employers' Initiatives to Control Female Labor Force Participation, 1945–1970'. *Enterprise & Society*, 2022, 1–27.

Grossman, Arnold H., Jung Yeon Park, John A. Frank, and Stephen T. Russell, 'Parental Responses to Transgender and Gender Nonconforming Youth: Associations with Parent Support, Parental Abuse, and Youths' Psychological Adjustment', *Journal of Homosexuality* 68: 8, 2021.

Guberman, Nancy, Éric Gagnon, Denyse Côté, Claude Gilbert, Nicole Thivièrge, and Marielle Tremblay, 'How the Trivialization of the Demands of High-Tech Care in the Home Is Turning Family Members Into Para-Medical Personnel', *Journal of Family Issues* 26: 2, 2005.

Hägglund, Martin, *This Life: Secular Faith and Spiritual Freedom*, New York: Pantheon Books, 2019.

———, 'What Is Democratic Socialism? Part I: Reclaiming Freedom', *Los Angeles Review of Books*, 15 July 2020, lareviewofbooks.org.

Hancock, Alice, and Tim Bradshaw, 'Can Food Delivery Services Save UK Restaurants?' *Financial Times*, 28 November 2020, ft.com.

Hardyment, Christina, *From Mangle to Microwave: Mechanization of the Household*, Cambridge: Polity Press, 1988.

———, 'Rising Out of Dust', *The Guardian*, 11 August 1990.

Harrad, Tom, 'This New Co-Living Space Is the Dystopian Symptom of a London Failing Young People', *i-D*, 20 June 2017, i-d.vice.com.

Harris, Malcolm, *Kids These Days: The Making of Millennials*, New York: Back Bay Books, 2018.

Hartman, Saidiya, *Wayward Lives, Beautiful Experiments: Intimate Histories of Riotous Black Girls, Troublesome Women and Queer Radicals*, London: Serpent's Tail, 2019.

Hartmann, Heidi, 'The Unhappy Marriage of Marxism and Feminism: Towards a More Progressive Union', *Capital & Class* 3: 2, 1979.

Harvey, David, *The Limits to Capital*, London: Verso Books, 2006.

Hatherley, Owen, 'Rooftop Pools for Everyone', *Tribune*, 7 June 2021, tribunemag.co.uk/.

Hawrylyshyn, Oli, 'The Value of Household Services: A Survey of Empirical Estimates', *Review of Income and Wealth* 22: 2, 1976.

Hayashi, Mayumi, 'The Care of Older People in Japan: Myths and Realities of Family "Care"', *History & Policy*, 2011, history andpolicy.org.

Hayden, Dolores, *Grand Domestic Revolution: History of Feminist Designs for American Homes, Neighbourhoods and Cities*, Cambridge: MIT Press, 1996.

————, *Redesigning the American Dream: Gender, Housing and Family Life*, 2nd Edition. New York: W.W. Norton & Company, 2002.

————, 'What Would a Non-Sexist City Be Like? Speculations on Housing, Urban Design, and Human Work', *Signs* 5: 3, 1980.

Hays, Sharon, *The Cultural Contradictions of Motherhood*, London: Yale University Press, 1996.

Heindl, Gabu, 'Alternatives to the Housing Crisis: Case Study Vienna', Simon Fraser University, 19 May 2017, youtube.com/watch?v=hLhDItRvBVY.

Hemerijck, Anton, *Changing Welfare States*, Oxford: Oxford University Press, 2013.

Herrera, Leidys Maria Labrador, 'Families, Plural', *Granma*, 19 May 2022, en.granma.cu/.

Hertog, Ekaterina, Setsuya Fukuda, Rikiya Matsukura, Nobuko Nagase, and Vili Lehdonvirta, 'The Future of Unpaid Work: Estimating the Effects of Automation on Time Spent on Housework and Care Work in Japan and the UK', n.d., 28.

Hester, Helen, 'Anti-Work Architecture: Domestic Labour, Speculative Design, and Automated Plenty', *Open Philosophy* 6:1, 2023, degruyter.com.

———— 'Households Beyond Thresholds: Care, Collectivity, and Covid-19', *Architectural Review*, 2021, architectural-review.com.

————, 'Promethean Labours and Domestic Realism', *e-flux*, 2017, e-flux.com.

————, *Xenofeminism*, Cambridge: Polity, 2018.

Heynen, Hilde, 'Taylor's Housewife: On the Frankfurt Kitchen', in *SQM: The Quantified Home*, ed. Space Caviar, Zurich: Lars Müller Publishers, 2014.

Hochschild, Arlie, and Anne Machung, *The Second Shift: Working Families and the Revolution at Home*, New York: Penguin Books, 2012.

Hofferth, Sandra L., and John F. Sandberg, 'Changes in American Children's Time, 1981–1997', *Advances in Life Course Research* 6, 2001.

Holloway, Sue, Sandra Short, and Sarah Tamplin, 'Household Satellite Account (Experimental) Methodology', London: Office for National Statistics, 2002.

Hoy, Suellen, *Chasing Dirt: The American Pursuit of Cleanliness*, New York: Oxford University Press, 1997.

Hozić, Aida, and Xiao Sun. 'Gender and the Great Resignation'. *Phenomenal World* (blog), 28 January 2023, phenomenalworld. org.

Huber, Evelyne, and John D. Stephens, 'Partisan Governance, Women's Employment, and the Social Democratic Service State', *American Sociological Review* 65: 3, 2000.

————, 'Postindustrial Social Policy', in *The Politics of Advanced*

Capitalism, eds Pablo Beramendi, Silja Häusermann, Herbert Kitschelt, and Hanspeter Kriesi, Cambridge: Cambridge University Press, 2015.

Hudson, Jim, 'Senior Co-Housing: Restoring Sociable Community in Later Life', in *Self-Build Homes*, eds Michaela Benson and Iqbal Hamiduddin, *Social Discourse, Experiences and Directions*, UCL Press, 2017.

Hulbert, Ann, *Raising America: Experts, Parents, and a Century of Advice About Children*, New York: Vintage Books, 2004.

Humphries, Jane, 'Enclosures, Common Rights, and Women: The Proletarianization of Families in the Late Eighteenth and Early Nineteenth Centuries', *Journal of Economic History* 50: 1, 1990.

Huws, Ursula, *Reinventing the Welfare State: Digital Platforms and Public Policies*, London: Pluto Press, 2020.

———, 'The Hassle of Housework: Digitalisation and the Commodification of Domestic Labour', *Feminist Review* 123: 1, 2019.

Huws, Ursula, Neil Spencer, Matthew Coates, and Kaire Holts, 'The Platformisation of Work in Europe: Results from Research in 13 European Countries', Brussels: Foundation for European Progressive Studies, UNI Europa, and University of Hertfordshire, 2019.

Huws, Ursula, Neil Spencer, Dag Syrdal, and Kaire Holts, 'Work in the European Gig Economy: Research Results from the UK, Sweden, Germany, Austria, the Netherlands, Switzerland and Italy', Brussels: Foundation for European Progressive Studies, 2017.

Iecovich, Esther, 'Aging in Place: From Theory to Practice', *Anthropological Notebooks* 20: 1, 2014.

International Labour Organization, 'Care Work and Care Jobs for the Future of Decent Work', Geneva: ILO, 2018.

Ishizuka, Patrick, 'Social Class, Gender, and Contemporary Parenting Standards in the United States: Evidence from a National Survey Experiment', *Social Forces* 98: 1, 2019.

Ivandic, Ria, Thomas Kirchmaier, and Ben Linton, 'Changing Patterns of Domestic Abuse During Covid-19 Lockdown', London: Centre for Economic Performance, London School of Economics and Political Science, 2020, cep.lse.ac.uk.

Ivanova, Diana, and Milena Büchs, 'Implications of Shrinking Household Sizes for Meeting the 1.5°C Climate Targets', *Ecological Economics* 202, 2022.

Jacobs, Jerry, and Kathleen Gerson, *The Time Divide: Work, Family, and Gender Inequality*, Cambridge: Harvard University Press, 2006.

Jarrett, Olga S, 'A Research-Based Case for Recess', Clemson: US Play Coalition, Clemson University, 2013, playworks.org.

Jessop, Bob, 'Towards a Schumpeterian Workfare State? Preliminary Remarks on Post-Fordist Political Economy', *Studies in Political Economy* 40: 1, 1993.

Johnson, Rebecca May, 'I Dream of Canteens', *Dinner Document* (blog), 30 April 2019, dinnerdocument.com.

Jones, Philip, and James Muldoon, 'Rise and Grind: Microwork and Hustle Culture in the UK', Cranbourne: Autonomy, 2022, autonomy.work.

Kandiyali, Jan, 'Should Socialists Be Republicans?' *Critical Review of International Social and Political Philosophy*, 2022, 1–18.

Kelley, Victoria, '"The Virtues of a Drop of Cleansing Water": Domestic Work and Cleanliness in the British Working Classes, 1880–1914', *Women's History Review* 18: 5, 2009.

Kenny, Charles, and George Yang, 'The Global Childcare Workload from School and Preschool Closures During the COVID-19 Pandemic', Washington, DC: Center for Global Development, 2021, cgdev.org.

Kenworthy, Lane, 'Labour Market Activation', in *The Oxford Handbook of the Welfare State*, eds Francis G. Castles, Stephan Leibfried, Jane Lewis, Herbert Obinger, and Christopher Pierson, Oxford: Oxford University Press, 2012.

Kesvani, Hussein, 'Rise, Grind and Ruin: The Dangerous Fetishization of "Hustle Porn"', *MEL Magazine* (blog), 12 November 2018, melmagazine.com.

Keynes, John Maynard, 'Economic Possibilities for Our Grandchildren', in *Revisiting Keynes: Economic Possibilities for Our Grandchildren*, eds Lorenzo Pecchi and Gustavo Piga, London: MIT Press, 2008.

Khazan, Olga, 'How Often People in Various Countries Shower', *The Atlantic*, 17 February 2015, theatlantic.com.

Kim, DaeHwan, and J. Paul Leigh, 'Are Meals at Full-Service and Fast-Food Restaurants "Normal" or "Inferior"?' *Population Health Management* 14: 6, 2011.

King, Jordan, 'School Bans Parents from Wearing Pyjamas While Dropping Kids Off', *Metro*, 4 October 2021, metro.co.uk/.

King, Tiffany Lethabo, 'Black "Feminisms" and Pessimism: Abolishing Moynihan's Negro Family', *Theory & Event* 21: 1, 2018.

Kirk, Susan, and Caroline Glendinning, 'Trends in Community Care and Patient Participation: Implications for the Roles of Informal Carers and Community Nurses in the United Kingdom', *Journal of Advanced Nursing* 28: 2, 1998.

Kirkham, Chris, 'Percentage of Young Americans Living with Parents Rises to 75-Year High', *Wall Street Journal*, 21 December 2016, wsj.com.

Kollontai, Alexandra, 'Communism and the Family', in *Selected Writings*, London: Allison & Busby, 1977.

———, 'In the Front Line of Fire', in *Selected Writings*, London: Allison & Busby, 1977.

———, 'The Labour of Women in the Revolution of the Economy', in *Selected Writings*, London: Allison & Busby, 1977.

———, 'Working Woman and Mother', in *Selected Writings*, London: Allison & Busby, 1977.

Kornrich, Sabino, and Frank Furstenberg, 'Investing in Children:

Changes in Parental Spending on Children, 1972–2007', *Demography* 50: 1, 2013.

Kowalewska, Helen, and Agnese Vitali, 'Work/Family Arrangements Across the OECD: Incorporating the Female-Breadwinner Model', LIS Working Paper Series, 2019, econstor.eu/.

Krafchik, Bernice, 'History of Diapers and Diapering', *International Journal of Dermatology* 55: S1, 2016.

Krenz, Astrid, and Holger Strulik, 'Automation and the Fall and Rise of the Servant Economy', University of Göttingen Working Papers in Economics, University of Goettingen, 2022, ideas. repec.org.

Krisis Group, 'Manifesto against Labour', 1999, krisis.org/.

Kuhn, Peter, and Fernando Lozano, 'The Expanding Workweek? Understanding Trends in Long Work Hours among US Men, 1979–2006', *Journal of Labor Economics* 26: 2, 2008.

Kusisto, Laura, 'Tiny Rooms, Shared Kitchens: Co-Living on the Rise in Big Cities', *Wall Street Journal*, 16 October 2018, wsj. com.

Kwak, Nancy H, *A World of Homeowners: American Power and the Politics of Housing Aid*, Chicago London: University of Chicago Press, 2018.

Lacayo, Richard, 'Suburban Legend: William Levitt', *Time*, 3 July 1950, content.time.com.

Lambert, Craig, *Shadow Work: The Unpaid, Unseen Jobs That Fill Your Day*, Berkeley: Counterpoint, 2015.

Landefeld, J. Steven, Barbara M. Fraumeni, and Cindy M. Vojtech, 'Accounting for Household Production: A Prototype Satellite Account Using the American Time Use Survey', *Review of Income and Wealth* 55: 2, 2009.

Landefeld, J. Steven, and Stephanie McCulla, 'Accounting for Nonmarket Household Production Within a National Accounts Framework', *Review of Income and Wealth* 46: 3, 2000.

Landes, David S., 'What Do Bosses Really Do?' *Journal of Economic History* 46: 3, 1986.

Landry, Bart, *Black Working Wives: Pioneers of the American Family Revolution*, Berkeley: University of California Press, 2000.

Lareau, Annette, *Unequal Childhoods: Class, Race, and Family Life*, 2nd Edition, Berkeley: University of California Press, 2011.

Lauster, Nathanael, *The Death and Life of the Single-Family House: Lessons from Vancouver on Building a Livable City*, Philadelphia: Temple University Press, 2016.

Leask, Calum F., Jacqueline Bell, and Fiona Murray, 'Acceptability of Delivering an Adapted Buurtzorg Model in the Scottish Care Context', *Public Health* 179, 2020.

Leask, Calum F., and Andrea Gilmartin, 'Implementation of a Neighbourhood Care Model in a Scottish Integrated Context – Views from Patients', *AIMS Public Health* 6: 2, 2019.

Lee, Dave, and Michael Pooler, 'Travis Kalanick Expands "Dark Kitchens" Venture Across Latin America', *Financial Times*, 6 September 2022, ft.com.

Lee, Yeonhwa, Peter A. Kemp, and Vincent J. Reina, 'Drivers of Housing (Un)Affordability in the Advanced Economies: A Review and New Evidence', *Housing Studies* 37: 10, 2022.

Lenin, Vladimir, *The State and Revolution*, Martino Fine Books, 2011, marxists.org.

Lepore, Jill, 'Baby Food', *The New Yorker*, 12 January 2009, newyorker.com.

Lewis, Jane, 'Gender and the Development of Welfare Regimes', *Journal of European Social Policy* 2: 3, 1992.

——, 'Gender and Welfare Regimes: Further Thoughts', *Social Politics: International Studies in Gender, State & Society* 4: 2, 1997.

——, 'The Decline of the Male Breadwinner Model: Implications for Work and Care', *Social Politics: International Studies in Gender, State & Society* 8: 2, 2001.

Lewis, Sophie, *Abolish the Family: A Manifesto for Care and Liberation*, Verso, 2022.

———, *Full Surrogacy Now: Feminism Against Family*, London: Verso Books, 2019.

Linder, Steffan, *The Harried Leisure Class*, New York: Columbia University Press, 1970.

Luis, Keridwen N., *Herlands: Exploring the Women's Land Movement in the United States*, Minneapolis: University of Minnesota Press, 2018.

Lutz, Helma, 'Care as a Fictitious Commodity: Reflections on the Intersections of Migration, Gender and Care Regimes', *Migration Studies*, 2017.

Luxton, Meg, 'Time for Myself: Women's Work and the "Fight for Shorter Hours"', in *Feminism and Political Economy: Women's Work, Women's Struggles*, eds Heather Jon Maroney and Meg Luxton, Toronto: Methuen, 1987.

Macfarlane, Laurie, 'Is It Time to End Our Obsession with Home Ownership?' *UCL IIPP Blog* (blog), 13 July 2021, medium.com.

Mackay, 'Pioneering Cohousing for London's Lesbians', *Community-Led Housing London* (blog), 14 July 2020, communityledhousing.london.

Mackay, Finn, *Female Masculinities and the Gender Wars: The Politics of Sex*, London: I.B. Tauris, 2021.

———, *Radical Feminism: Feminist Activism in Movement*, Houndmills: Palgrave Macmillan, 2015.

Madrigal, Alexis C., 'Raised by YouTube', *The Atlantic*, November 2018, theatlantic.com.

Malatino, Hil, *Trans Care*, Minneapolis: University of Minnesota Press, 2020.

Marglin, Stephen, 'What Do Bosses Do? The Origins and Functions of Hierarchy in Capitalist Production', *Review of Radical Political Economics* 6: 2, 1974.

Marino-Nachison, David, 'Food & Dining: Predicting the "Death of the Kitchen"', *Barron's*, 20 June 2018, barrons.com.

———, 'GrubHub: Here's Why People Order Delivery', *Barron's*, 13 March 2018, barrons.com.

Martin, Joyce, Brady Hamilton, Michelle Osterman, Anne Driscoll, and T.J. Mathews, 'Births: Final Data for 2015', *National Vital Statistics Report* 66: 1, 2017.

Marx, Karl, *Grundrisse: Foundations of the Critique of Political Economy*, trans. Martin Nicolaus, London: Penguin Books, 1993.

Marx, Karl, and Friedrich Engels, 'The Communist Manifesto', in *Economic and Philosophical Manuscripts of 1844, and the Communist Manifesto*, Amherst: Prometheus Books, 1988.

Mathauer, Inke, and Friedrich Wittenbecher, 'Hospital Payment Systems Based on Diagnosis-Related Groups: Experiences in Low- and Middle-Income Countries', *Bulletin of the World Health Organization* 91, 2013.

Matsakis, Louise, 'Cops Are Offering Ring Doorbell Cameras in Exchange for Info', *Wired*, 8 February 2019, wired.com.

Mattern, Shannon, 'Maintenance and Care', *Places Journal*, 2018, placesjournal.org.

Mattu, Surya, and Kashmir Hill, 'The House That Spied on Me', *Gizmodo*, 7 February 2018, gizmodo.com.

Mau, Søren, '"The Mute Compulsion of Economic Relations": Towards a Marxist Theory of the Abstract and Impersonal Power of Capital', *Historical Materialism* 29: 3, 2021.

Mauldin, Laura, 'Support Mechanism', *Real Life*, 22 October 2020, reallifemag.com.

McCandless, Cathy, 'Some Thoughts About Racism, Classism, and Separatism', in *Top Ranking: A Collection of Articles on Racism and Classism in the Lesbian Community*, eds Joan P. Gibbs and Sara Bennett, New York: Come!Unity Press, 1980.

McCarthy, Lindsey, and Sadie Parr, 'Is LGBT Homelessness

Different? Reviewing the Relationship Between LGBT Identity and Homelessness', *Housing Studies* 2022.

McClintock, Anne, 'Soft-Soaping Empire: Commodity Racism and Imperial Advertising', in *Travellers' Tales: Narratives of Home and Displacement*, ed. George Robertson, London: Routledge, 1994.

McDonald, Janet, Eileen McKinlay, Sally Keeling, and William Levack, 'Complex Home Care: Challenges Arising from the Blurring of Boundaries Between Family and Professional Care', *Kōtuitui: New Zealand Journal of Social Sciences Online* 12: 2, 2017.

Meek, James, 'Where Will We Live?' *London Review of Books*, 9 January 2014, lrb.co.uk.

Miles, Ian, *Home Informatics: Information Technology and the Transformation of Everyday Life*, London: Continuum International Publishing, 1988.

Mims, Christopher, 'Amazon's Plan to Move In to Your Next Apartment Before You Do', *Wall Street Journal*, 1 June 2019, wsj.com.

——, 'How Our Online Shopping Obsession Choked the Supply Chain. Interview by Cam Wofl', *GQ*, 11 November 2021, gq.com.

Mohun, Arwen P., *Steam Laundries: Gender, Technology and Work in the United States and Great Britain, 1880–1940*, Baltimore: Johns Hopkins University Press, 1999.

Mokyr, Joel, 'Why "More Work for Mother?" Knowledge and Household Behavior, 1870–1945', *Journal of Economic History* 60: 1, 2000.

Monsen, Karen A., and Jos de Blok, 'Buurtzorg: Nurse-Led Community Care', *Creative Nursing* 19: 3, 2013.

'Monthly Briefing from WFH Research', February 2022, mailchi.mp.

Morgan, Kimberly J., *Working Mothers and the Welfare State: Religion and the Politics of Work-Family Policies in Western Europe and the United States*, Stanford: Stanford University Press, 2006.

Morozov, Evgeny, 'Digital Socialism: The Calculation Debate in the Age of Big Data', *New Left Review* 116/117, 2019.

Morris, William, *News from Nowhere and Other Writings*, London: Penguin, 1993.

Mose, Tamara R., *Playdate: Parents, Children, and the New Expectations of Play*, New York: NYU Press, 2016.

Mosebach, Kai, 'Commercializing German Hospital Care? Effects of New Public Management and Managed Care under Neoliberal Conditions', *German Policy Studies* 5: 1, 2009.

Muldoon, James, 'A Socialist Republican Theory of Freedom and Government', *European Journal of Political Theory*, 2019.

——, *Platform Socialism: How to Reclaim Our Digital Future from Big Tech*, London: Pluto Press, 2022.

Munro, Kirstin, 'The Welfare State and the Bourgeois Family-Household', *Science & Society* 85: 2, 2021.

——, 'Unproductive Workers and State Repression', *Review of Radical Political Economics* 53: 4, 2021.

——, 'Unwaged Work and the Production of Sustainability in Eco-Conscious Households', *Review of Radical Political Economics* 50: 4, 2018.

Murphy, Douglas, *Last Futures: Nature, Technology and the End of Architecture*, London: Verso, 2016.

National Alliance for Caregiving and the AARP, 'Caregiving in the US', 2015, caregiving.org.

Neff, Jack, 'The Dirt on Laundry Trends Around the World', *AdAge*, 14 June 2010, adage.com.

Neuhaus, Jessamyn, 'The Way to a Man's Heart: Gender Roles, Domestic Ideology, and Cookbooks in the 1950s', *Journal of Social History* 32: 3, 1999.

Nixon, Richard, and Nikita Khrushchev, 'The Kitchen Debate [Online Transcript]', Moscow, Russia, 24 July 1959, cia.gov.

O'Brien, M.E., 'To Abolish the Family: The Working Class Family and Gender Liberation in Capitalist Development', *Endnotes* 5, 2019.

O'Brien, M.E., and Eman Abdelhadi, *Everything for Everyone: An Oral History of the New York Commune, 2052–2072*, Brooklyn: Common Notions, 2022.

O'Brien, Michelle, 'Trans Work: Employment Trajectories, Labour Discipline and Gender Freedom', in *Transgender Marxism*, eds Jules Joanne Gleeson and Elle O'Rourke, London: Pluto Press, 2021.

OECD, 'Doing Better for Families', Paris, 2011, oecd.org.

————, 'Society at a Glance 2011 – OECD Social Indicators', Paris: OECD Publishing, 2011, oecd.org.

Oerton, Sarah, '"Queer Housewives?": Some Problems in Theorising the Division of Domestic Labour in Lesbian and Gay Households', *Women's Studies International Forum* 20: 3, 1997.

Office for National Statistics, 'Families in the Labour Market, 2014', London, 2014, webarchive.nationalarchives.gov.uk.

Office for National Statistics, 'Men Enjoy Five Hours More Leisure Time Per Week Than Women', 9 January 2018, ons.gov.uk.

Office for National Statistics, 'Women Shoulder the Responsibility of "Unpaid Work"', 10 November 2016, visual.ons.gov.uk.

Oh, Soo, 'The Future of Work Is the Low-Wage Health Care Job', *Vox*, 3 July 2017, vox.com.

O'Hara, Phillip Anthony, 'Household Labor, the Family, and Macroeconomic Instability in the United States: 1940s—1990s', *Review of Social Economy* 53: 1, 1995.

Oliveri, Rigel C., 'Single-Family Zoning, Intimate Association, and the Right to Choose Household Companions', *Florida Law Review* 67: 4, 2016.

Olivetti, Claudia, and Barbara Petrongolo, 'The Economic Consequences of Family Policies: Lessons from a Century of Legislation in High-Income Countries', *Journal of Economic Perspectives* 31: 1, 2017.

Orloff, Ann Shola, 'Farewell to Maternalism: Welfare Reform, Liberalism, and the End of Mothers' Right to Choose Between Employment and Full-Time Care', IPR Working Paper, Institute for Policy Research at Northwestern University, 2005.

Ormrod, Susan, '"Let's Nuke the Dinner": Discursive Practices of Gender in the Creation of a New Cooking Process', in *Bringing Technology Home: Gender and Technology in a Changing Europe*, eds Cynthia Cockburn and Ruza Furst Dilic, Buckingham: Open University Press, 1994.

O'Shea, Tom, 'Radical Republicanism and the Future of Work', *Theory & Event* 24: 4, 2021.

———, 'Socialist Republicanism', *Political Theory*, 2019.

O'Toole, Fintan, *We Don't Know Ourselves: A Personal History of Ireland Since 1958*, London: Apollo, 2021.

Papanek, Victor, and James Hennessey, *How Things Don't Work*, New York: Pantheon Books, 1977.

Park, Shelley, *Mothering Queerly, Queering Motherhood: Resisting Monomaternalism in Adoptive, Lesbian, Blended, and Polygamous Families*, Albany: SUNY Press, 2013.

Parks, Jennifer A., 'Lifting the Burden of Women's Care Work: Should Robots Replace the "Human Touch"?' *Hypatia* 25: 1, 2010.

Parr, Joy, 'What Makes Washday Less Blue? Gender, Nation, and Technology Choice in Postwar Canada', *Technology and Culture* 38: 1, 1997.

Peck, Jamie, *Workfare States*, New York: Guilford Press, 2001.

Pellikka, Katri, Marjaana Manninen, and Sanna-Liisa Taivalmaa, 'School Feeding: Investment in Effective Learning – Case Finland', Ministry for Foreign Affairs of Finland and Finnish National Agency for Education, 2019, oph.fi.

Pesole, Annarosa, Cesira Urzi Brancati Maria, Enrique Fernandez Macias, Federico Biagi, and Ignacio Gonzalez Vazquez, 'Platform Workers in Europe: Evidence from the COLLEEM Survey', EUR – Scientific and Technical Research Reports,

Publications Office of the European Union, 2018, JRC112157, publications.jrc.ec.europa.eu.

Pew Research Centre, 'Raising Kids and Running a Household: How Working Parents Share the Load', 2015, pewsocialtrends. org.

Pfannebecker, Mareile, and J.A. Smith, *Work Want Work: Labour and Desire at the End of Capitalism*, London: Zed Books, 2020.

Piercy, Marge, *Woman on the Edge of Time*, New York: Random House, 2020.

Pillemer, Karl, *Fault Lines: Fractured Families and How to Mend Them*, New York: Avery, 2020.

Plato, *The Republic*, trans. H.D.P. Lee and Desmond Lee, 3rd edition, London: Penguin Classics, 2007.

Positions Politics, 'Abjection and Abstraction: An Interview with Maya Gonzalez and Jeanne Neton', *Episteme* 7, 2021, positions politics.org.

Potter, Brian, 'Debunking the "Housing Variety as a Barrier to Mass Production" Hypothesis', Substack newsletter, *Construction Physics* (blog), 7 October 2022, constructionphysics.substack. com.

Preciado, Paul B., *Pornotopia: An Essay on Playboy's Architecture and Biopolitics*, New York: Zone Books, 2014.

Prole.info, 'Abolish Restaurants: A Worker's Critique of the Food Service Industry', in *Abolish Work*, Oakland: PM Press, 2014.

Puigjaner, Anna, 'Bootleg Hotels: On Kitchenless Apartments', in *SQM: The Quantified Home*, ed. Space Caviar, Zurich: Lars Müller Publishers, 2014.

Pursell, Carroll, 'Domesticating Modernity: The Electrical Association for Women, 1924–86', *British Journal for the History of Science* 32: 1, 1999.

Rai, Shirin M., Catherine Hoskyns, and Dania Thomas, 'Depletion: The Cost of Social Reproduction', *International Feminist Journal of Politics* 16: 1, 2014.

Ramey, Garey, and Valerie Ramey, 'The Rug Rat Race', Washington, DC: Brookings Institution, 2010.

Ramey, Valerie A., and Neville Francis, 'A Century of Work and Leisure', *American Economic Journal: Macroeconomics* 1: 2, 2009.

Rawls, John, *A Theory of Justice: Revised Edition*, Cambridge: Harvard University Press, 1999.

Reinhard, Susan, Carol Levine, and Sarah Samis, 'Home Alone: Family Caregivers Providing Complex Chronic Care', Washington, DC: AARP, 2012, aarp.org.

Retail Feedback Group, 'Retail Feedback Group Study Finds Online Supermarket Shoppers Register Improved Overall Satisfaction and Higher First-Time Use', New York, 11 December 2019, retailfeedback.com.

Roberts, Dorothy, *Torn Apart: How the Child Welfare System Destroys Black Families – And How Abolition Can Build a Safer World*, New York: Basic Books, 2022.

Roberts, Dorothy, and Nia T. Evans, 'The "Benevolent Terror" of the Child Welfare System', *Boston Review*, 31 March 2022, bostonreview.net.

Roberts, William Clare, 'Free Time and Free People', *Los Angeles Review of Books*, 15 July 2020, lareviewofbooks.org.

———, *Marx's Inferno: The Political Theory of Capital*, Princeton University Press, 2018.

Robison, Mark, and Lindley Shedd, eds, *Audio Recorders to Zucchini Seeds: Building a Library of Things*, Santa Barbara: Libraries Unlimited, 2017.

Robinson, John, and Geoffrey Godbey, 'Busyness as Usual', *Social Research* 72: 2, 2005.

Robinson, John P., 'Americans Less Rushed But No Happier: 1965–2010 Trends in Subjective Time and Happiness', *Social Indicators Research* 113: 3, 2013.

Robinson, John P., and Melissa A. Milkie, 'Back to the Basics: Trends in and Role Determinants of Women's Attitudes toward

Housework', *Journal of Marriage and Family* 60: 1, 1998.

Rodrik, Dani, and Stefanie Stantcheva, 'Fixing Capitalism's Good Jobs Problem', *Oxford Review of Economic Policy* 37: 4, 2021.

Rosa, Sophie, 'Did Cuba Just Abolish the Family?' *Novara Media*, 13 October 2022, novaramedia.com.

Rosenberg, Jordy. 'Afterword: One Utopia, One Dystopia', in *Transgender Marxism*, eds Jules Joanne Gleeson and Elle O'Rourke, London: Pluto Press, 2021.

Rowbotham, Sheila, *Dreamers of a New Day: Women Who Invented the Twentieth Century*, London: Verso, 2011.

Rozworski, Michal, and Leigh Philips, *People's Republic of Walmart: How the World's Biggest Corporations Are Laying the Foundation for Socialism*, London: Verso, 2019.

Ryan, Deborah Sugg, 'The Curious History of Government-Funded British Restaurants in World War 2', *Find My Past*, 22 June 2020, findmypast.co.uk.

Sadler, Euan, and Christopher McKevitt, '"Expert Carers": An Emergent Normative Model of the Caregiver', *Social Theory & Health* 11: 1, 2013.

Sadler, Simon, 'Drop City Revisited', *Journal of Architectural Education* 59: 3, 2006.

Saito, Kohei, *Karl Marx's Ecosocialism: Capital, Nature, and the Unfinished Critique of Political Economy*, New York: Monthly Review Press, 2017.

Samman, Emma, Elizabeth Presler-Marshall, and Nicola Jones, 'Women's Work: Mothers, Children and the Global Childcare Crisis', London: Overseas Development Institute, 2016, odi.org.

Samsung, 'Samsung KX50: The Future in Focus', 29 August 2019, news.samsung.com.

Samuel, Alexandra, 'Happy Mother's Day: Kids' Screen Time Is a Feminist Issue', JSTOR Daily, 3 May 2016, daily.jstor.org.

Sandberg, Sheryl, *Lean In: Women, Work, and the Will to Lead*, London: W.H. Allen, 2015.

Sandilands, Catriona, 'Lesbian Separatist Communities and the Experience of Nature: Toward a Queer Ecology', *Organization & Environment* 15: 2, 2002.

Sani, Giulia M. Dotti, and Judith Treas, 'Educational Gradients in Parents' Child-Care Time Across Countries, 1965–2012', *Journal of Marriage and Family* 78: 4, 2016.

Satariano, Adam, and Emma Bubola, 'Pasta, Wine and Inflatable Pools: How Amazon Conquered Italy in the Pandemic', *New York Times*, 26 September 2020, nytimes.com.

Sayer, Liana, 'Gender, Time and Inequality: Trends in Women's and Men's Paid Work, Unpaid Work and Free Time', *Social Forces* 84: 1, 2005.

———, 'Trends in Housework', in *Dividing the Domestic: Men, Women, and Household Work in Cross-National Perspective*, eds Judith Treas and Sonja Drobnič, Stanford: Stanford University Press, 2010.

Sayer, Liana, Philip Cohen, and Lynne Casper, *Women, Men, and Work*, New York: Russell Sage Foundation, 2004.

Scanlon, Kath, and Melissa Fernández Arrigoitia, 'Development of New Cohousing: Lessons from a London Scheme for the Over-50s', *Urban Research & Practice* 8: 1, 2015.

Schaefer, Tali, 'Disposable Mothers: Paid In-Home Caretaking and the Regulation of Parenthood', *Yale Journal of Law & Feminism* 19: 2, 2008.

Schmelzer, Matthias, Andrea Vetter, and Aaron Vansintjan, *The Future Is Degrowth: A Guide to a World Beyond Capitalism*, London: Verso, 2022.

Schmid-Drüner, Marion, 'The Situation of Workers in the Collaborative Economy', Brussels: European Parliament, 2016, op.europa.eu.

Scholz, Trebor, and Nathan Schneider, eds, *Ours to Hack and to Own: The Rise of Platform Cooperativism, a New Vision for the Future of Work and a Fairer Internet*, New York: OR Books, 2017.

Schor, Juliet, *The Overworked American: The Unexpected Decline of Leisure*, New York: Basic Books, 1993.

Scott, Felicity D., *Architecture or Techno-Utopia: Politics After Modernism*, Cambridge: MIT Press, 2007.

Seccombe, Wally, *Weathering the Storm: Working-Class Families from the Industrial Revolution to the Fertility Decline*, London: Verso, 1995.

Senior, Jennifer, *All Joy and No Fun: The Paradox of Modern Parenthood*, New York: Ecco, 2014.

Seymour, Richard, 'Abolition: Notes on a Normie Shitstorm by Richard Seymour', *Salvage* (blog), 27 January 2022, salvage.zone.

Shapiro, Laura, *Something from the Oven: Reinventing Dinner in 1950s America*, London: Penguin Books, 2004.

Shelley, Julia, 'Building Safe Choices – LGBT Housing Futures: A Feasibility Study', London: Stonewall Housing, 2016, building safechoices.org.uk.

Shir-Wise, Michelle, 'Disciplined Freedom: The Productive Self and Conspicuous Busyness in "Free" Time', *Time & Society* 28: 4, 2019.

Shorter, Edward, *The Making of the Modern Family*, New York: Basic Books, 1975.

Shove, Elizabeth, *Comfort, Cleanliness and Convenience: The Social Organization of Normality*, Oxford: Berg Publishers, 2003.

Silva, Elizabeth, 'Transforming Housewifery: Dispositions, Practices and Technologies', in *The New Family?*, eds Elizabeth Silva and Carol Smart, London: Sage Publications Ltd., 1999.

Siminski, Peter, and Rhiannon Yetsenga, 'Specialization, Comparative Advantage, and the Sexual Division of Labor', *Journal of Labor Economics* 40: 4, 2022.

Sixsmith, Andrew, and Judith Sixsmith, 'Ageing in Place in the United Kingdom', *Ageing International* 32: 3, 2008.

Slaughter, Anne-Marie, 'The Work That Makes Work Possible', *The Atlantic*, 23 March 2016, theatlantic.com.

Smith, Lindsey P., Shu Wen Ng, and Barry M. Popkin, 'Trends in US Home Food Preparation and Consumption: Analysis of National Nutrition Surveys and Time Use Studies from 1965–1966 to 2007–2008', *Nutrition Journal* 12, 2013.

Smith, Thomas, 'Food Delivery Is a Window Into Our Busy, Overworked Lives', *OneZero*, 31 July 2020, onezero.medium.com.

Sooryanarayana, Rajini, Wan-Yuen Choo, and Noran N. Hairi, 'A Review on the Prevalence and Measurement of Elder Abuse in the Community', *Trauma, Violence, & Abuse* 14: 4, 2013.

Soper, Kate, *Post-Growth Living: For an Alternative Hedonism*, London: Verso, 2020.

Southerton, Dale, and Mark Tomlinson, '"Pressed for Time" – The Differential Impacts of a "Time Squeeze"', *Sociological Review* 53: 2, 2005.

Spigel, Lynn, 'Designing the Smart House: Posthuman Domesticity and Conspicuous Production', *European Journal of Cultural Studies* 8: 4, 2005.

———, 'Yesterday's Future, Tomorrow's Home', *Emergences: Journal for the Study of Media & Composite Cultures* 11: 1, 2001.

Sprat, Vicky, 'Why The Rise Of "Work Porn" Is Making Us Miserable', *Grazia*, 24 September 2018, graziadaily.co.uk.

Srnicek, Nick, and Alex Williams, *Inventing the Future: Postcapitalism and a World Without Work*, London: Verso, 2015.

Staikov, Zahari, 'Time-Budgets and Technological Progress', in *The Use of Time: Daily Activities of Urban and Suburban Populations in Twelve Countries*, ed. Alexander Szalai, The Hague: Mouton, 1972.

Stark, Agneta, 'Warm Hands in Cold Age – On the Need of a New World Order of Care', in *Warm Hands in Cold Age: Gender and Aging*, eds Nancy Folbre, Lois B. Shaw, and Agneta Stark, Milton Park: Routledge, 2007.

Stavrides, Stavros, *Common Space: The City as Commons*, London: Zed Books, 2016.

Stites, Richard, *Revolutionary Dreams: Utopian Vision and Experimental Life in the Russian Revolution*, Oxford University Press, 1989.

Stoltzfus, Emilie, *Citizen, Mother, Worker: Debating Public Responsibility for Child Care after the Second World War*, Chapel Hill: University of North Carolina Press, 2003.

Strasser, Susan, *Never Done: A History of American Housework*, New York: Pantheon Books, 1984.

———, 'What's in Your Microwave Oven?' *New York Times*, 15 April 2017, nytimes.com.

Strengers, Yolande, and Larissa Nicholls, 'Aesthetic Pleasures and Gendered Tech-Work in the 21st-Century Smart Home', *Media International Australia* 166: 1, 2018.

Stronge, Will, Kyle Lewis, Mat Lawrence, Julian Siravo, and Stavros Oikonomidis, 'The Future of Work and Employment Policies in the Comunitat Valenciana: Research and Proposals for a Transitional Strategy', *Autonomy*, 2020, autonomy.work.

Su, Yichen, 'The Rising Value of Time and the Origin of Urban Gentrification', *American Economic Journal: Economic Policy* 14: 1, 2022.

Suh, Jooyeoun, 'Care Time in the US: Measures, Determinants, and Implications', University of Massachusetts – Amherst, 2014.

Sullivan, Oriel, 'Busyness, Status Distinction and Consumption Strategies of the Income Rich, Time Poor', *Time & Society* 17: 1, 2008.

Sutherland, Zöe, and Marina Vishmidt, 'The Soft Disappointment of Prefiguration', presented at the SSPT Annual Conference, University of Sussex, June 2015.

Sweeney, Pat, 'Wages for Housework: The Strategy for Women's Liberation', *Heresies* 1: 1, 1977.

Syrda, Joanna, 'Gendered Housework: Spousal Relative Income, Parenthood and Traditional Gender Identity Norms', *Work, Employment and Society*, 2022.

Taipale, Sakari, Federico de Luca, Mauro Sarrica, and Leopoldina Fortunati, 'Robot Shift from Industrial Production to Social Reproduction', in *Social Robots from a Human Perspective*, eds Jane Vincent, Sakari Taipale, Bartolomeo Sapio, Giuseppe Lugano, and Leopoldina Fortunati, Springer, 2015.

Tarnoff, Ben, *Internet for the People: The Fight for Our Digital Future*, London: Verso, 2022.

Telegraph, 'NHS Is Fifth Biggest Employer in World', 20 March 2012, telegraph.co.uk.

Thaman, Lauren A., and Lawrence F. Eichenfield, 'Diapering Habits: A Global Perspective', *Pediatric Dermatology* 31: s1, 2014.

Therborn, Göran, *Between Sex and Power: Family in the World 1900–2000*, London: Routledge, 2004.

Thompson, E. P., 'Time, Work-Discipline, and Industrial Capitalism', *Past & Present* 38:1, 1967.

Thompson, Maud, 'The Value of Woman's Work', *International Socialist Review* 10, 1910.

Thomson, Alistair, 'Domestic Drudgery Will Be a Thing of the Past: Co-operative Women and the Reform of Housework', in *New Views of Co-Operation*, ed. S. Yeo, London: Routledge, 1988.

Tierney, William G., and James Dean Ward, 'Coming Out and Leaving Home: A Policy and Research Agenda for LGBT Homeless Students', *Educational Researcher* 46: 9, 2017.

Tilly, Louise A., and Joan W. Scott, *Women, Work, and Family*, New York: Routledge, 1989.

Topping, Alexandra, 'How Do UK Childcare Costs Stack up Against the Best?' *Guardian*, 12 September 2021, theguardian.com.

Tronto, Joan, *Moral Boundaries: A Political Argument for an Ethic of Care*, New York: Routledge, 1993.

UK Parliament, 'Catering Services: Costs to the House of Commons', 2022, parliament.uk/.

UNCTAD, 'Estimates of Global E-Commerce 2019 and Preliminary Assessment of Covid-19 Impact on Online Retail 2020', Geneva, 2021, unctad.org.

United Nations, Department of Economic and Social Affairs, Population Division, 'Database on Household Size and Composition 2022', New York, 2022, un.org.

Usher, Kim, Navjot Bhullar, Joanne Durkin, Naomi Gyamfi, and Debra Jackson, 'Family Violence and Covid-19: Increased Vulnerability and Reduced Options for Support', *International Journal of Mental Health Nursing* 29: 4, 2020.

Vaalavuo, M., 'Women and Unpaid Work: Recognise, Reduce, Redistribute!', European Commission, 7 March 2016, ec.europa. eu.

Vallas, Steven, and Juliet B. Schor, 'What Do Platforms Do? Understanding the Gig Economy', *Annual Review of Sociology* 46: 1, 2020.

Value, Capitalism, and Communism, Red May, 2021, youtube.com.

Vanek, Joann, 'Time Spent in Housework', *Scientific American*, 1974.

Veblen, Thorstein, *The Theory of the Leisure Class*, New York: Dover Publications, Inc., 1994.

Veit, Helen, 'An Economic History of Leftovers', *The Atlantic*, 1 October 2015, theatlantic.com.

Virno, Paolo, 'The Ambivalence of Disenchantment', in *Radical Thought in Italy: A Potential Politics*, eds Paolo Virno and Michael Hardt, Minneapolis: University of Minnesota Press, 1996.

Vishmidt, Marina, 'Permanent Reproductive Crisis: An Interview with Silvia Federici', Mute Publishing Limited, 7 March 2013, metamute.org.

Vishwanath, Mandara, 'The Politics of Housework in Contemporary India', *Blind Field: A Journal of Cultural Inquiry*, 2016, blindfieldjournal.com.

Voce, Antonio, Leyland Cecco, and Chris Michael, '"Cultural Genocide": The Shameful History of Canada's Residential Schools', *Guardian*, 6 September 2021, theguardian.com.

Wajcman, Judy, *Feminism Confronts Technology*, Cambridge: Polity, 1991.

————, *Pressed for Time: The Acceleration of Life in Digital Capitalism*, London: University of Chicago Press, 2015.

Walker, Peter, 'The MPs' Menu: Where a £31 Meal Costs £3.45', *Guardian*, 8 September 2009, theguardian.com.

Warde, Alan, 'Convenience Food: Space and Timing', *British Food Journal* 101: 7, 1999.

Warde, Alan, Shu-Li Cheng, Wendy Olsen, and Dale Southerton, 'Changes in the Practice of Eating: A Comparative Analysis of Time-Use', *Acta Sociologica* 50: 4, 2007.

Waters, Richard, 'Amazon Wants to Be in the Centre of Every Home', *Financial Times*, 26 September 2019, ft.com.

Webb, Alex, 'Amazon's Roomba Deal Is Really About Mapping Your Home', *Bloomberg*, 5 August 2022, bloomberg.com.

Webber, Dominic, and Chris Payne, 'Chapter 3: Home Produced "Adultcare" Services', Office for National Statistics, 7 April 2016, ons.gov.uk.

Weeks, Jeffrey, Catherine Donovan, and Brian Heaphy, 'Everyday Experiments: Narratives of Non-Heterosexual Relationships', in *The New Family?*, eds Elizabeth Silva and Carol Smart, London: Sage Publications Ltd., 1999.

Weeks, Kathi, 'Abolition of the Family: The Most Infamous Feminist Proposal', *Feminist Theory*, 2021.

————, *The Problem with Work: Feminism, Marxism, Antiwork Politics, and Postwork Imaginaries*, Durham: Duke University Press, 2011.

Weikart, Richard, 'Marx, Engels, and the Abolition of the Family', *History of European Ideas* 18: 5, 1994.

Weir, Diarmid, 'Explaining the NHS Crisis: Lies, Damn Lies and

Health Spending', *Future Economics* (blog), 26 January 2017, futureeconomics.org.

Weisman, Leslie, *Discrimination by Design: A Feminist Critique of the Man-Made Environment*, Urbana: University of Illinois Press, 1994.

Whittle, Jane, and Mark Hailwood, 'The Gender Division of Labour in Early Modern England', *Economic History Review* 73: 1, 2020.

Wiener, Anna, 'Our Ghost-Kitchen Future', *New Yorker*, 28 June 2020, newyorker.com.

Williams, Richard J., *Sex and Buildings: Modern Architecture and the Sexual Revolution*, London: Reaktion Books, 2013.

Willimott, Andy, *Living the Revolution: Urban Communes & Soviet Socialism, 1917–1932*, Oxford: Oxford University Press, 2019.

Willis, Ellen, 'The Family: Love It or Leave It', *Village Voice*, 17 September 1979.

Wilson, Rob, Sally-Anne Barnes, Mike May-Gillings, Shyamoli Patel, and Ha Bui, 'Working Futures 2017–2027: Long-Run Labour Market and Skills Projections for the UK', London: Department of Education, February 2020, assets.publishing. service.gov.uk.

Wiltse, Jeff, *Contested Waters: A Social History of Swimming Pools in America*, Chapel Hill: University North Carolina Press, 2007.

Winant, Gabriel, *The Next Shift: The Fall of Industry and the Rise of Health Care in Rust Belt America*, Cambridge: Harvard University Press, 2021.

Woersdorfer, Julia Sophie, *The Evolution of Household Technology and Consumer Behaviour, 1800–2000*, London: Routledge, 2017.

Wolfe, Jan, 'Roomba Vacuum Maker IRobot Betting Big on the "Smart" Home', *Reuters*, 28 July 2017, reuters.com.

World Health Organization, 'Violence Against Women Prevalence Estimates, 2018: Global, Regional and National Prevalence Estimates for Intimate Partner Violence Against Women and

Global and Regional Prevalence Estimates for Non-Partner
  Sexual Violence Against Women'. Geneva, 2021, who.int.
Woyke, Elizabeth, 'The Octogenarians Who Love Amazon's
  Alexa', *MIT Technology Review*, 9 June 2017, technology
  review.com.
Wrigley, Julia, 'Migration, Domestic Work, and Repression', *New
  Politics* 13, 2005, newpol.org.
Yates, Luke, and Alan Warde, 'The Evolving Content of Meals in
  Great Britain: Results of a Survey in 2012 in Comparison with
  the 1950s', *Appetite* 84, 2015.
Yeo, Liyin, 'Which Company Is Winning the Restaurant Food
  Delivery War?' Bloomberg *Second Measure*, 14 May 2021,
  secondmeasure.com.
Yuile, Laura, 'Ungating Community: Opening the Enclosures of
  Financialised Housing', University of Northumbria, 2022.
Zaidi, Sarover, 'The Gift of Food', *e-flux*, August 2021, e-flux.com.
Zhang, Sarah, 'How "Clean" Was Sold to America with Fake
  Science', *Gizmodo*, 12 February 2015, gizmodo.com.
Zuzanek, Jiri, 'Time Use, Time Pressure, Personal Stress, Mental
  Health, and Life Satisfaction from a Life Cycle Perspective',
  Journal of Occupational Science 5: 1, 1998.
———, 'What Happened to the Society of Leisure? Of the Gap
  Between the "Haves" and "Have Nots" (Canadian Time Use
  and Well-Being Trends)', *Social Indicators Research* 130: 1, 2017.

Index

arguments about needless repetition
of domestic work by, 109
demise of male breadwinner
approach as aim of, 103
feminist post-work imaginaries, 45,
87, 113, 131, 151, 181–2
feminist technologies, 174
food standards as important for,
62–3
New York Feminist Alliance, 123
on private sufficiency and public
luxury, 179
second-wave feminists, 10, 144, 157
on single-family home, 119–20
on spatial design of the home, 112,
113–14, 124
temporal inequality as issue for, 86
on twenty-four-hour universal care,
170
on work, 242n66
Finland
Finnish Women's Co-operative
Home, 121–2, 125
free school meal programme, 174
Fisher, Mark, 143
Five-Year Plan (1928–1932), and
housing crisis in Russia, 117
Folbre, Nancy, 8
food delivery services, rapid expansion
of, 37–8
foodie culture, 64–6
food processing, as per cent of US
manufacturing, 21
food production, outsourcing of, 37–8
France, subsidised payments for
housework, 177
Frankfurt Kitchen, 127–9
Fraser, Nancy, 167
Frederick, Christine, 61, 62, 122–3, 127
freedom
having choices as key part of, 163
positive form of, 154–5
realm of. *See* realm of freedom
as requiring absence of domination,
154
free time
as disappearing, 106, 107, 108

fighting for, 11
housework as impinging on, 79
infrastructure for, 161
men as having better quality of than
women, 85
new politics of, 95
as prerequisite for meaningful
conception of freedom, 11
standard of productivity of, 77
Friedan, Betty, 10
Fuller, Buckminster, 139

G7 countries, social reproduction jobs
in, 6
Gabe, Frances, 182–3
gardening, impact of increased interest
in, 26
gender bias, in early technologies, 26
gendered division
of labour in general, 27, 101, 104,
144, 145, 167
of labour in the home, 12, 47, 48, 82,
113, 132, 143
between work of 'digital' and
'traditional' housekeepers, 44
gendered dynamics (around standards),
51
gendered expectations
about arrangement and conduct of
unpaid domestic labour, 166
confronting and challenging
of surrounding caregiving
practices, 87
gendered hierarchies, consolidation
of, 44
gendered imaginary (of how housework
should be done), 48
gendered inequalities
family as vast repository of, 82
growing entrenchment of, 94
on hours spent in waged and
unwaged work, 104–5
partial erosion of regarding labour,
104
in pay, 105
gendered nature (of social
reproduction), 124

Postone, Moishe, 268n46
post-scarcity, 156
post-work feminism. *See* feminists/
   feminism
post-work project
   childcare in post-work world, 170
   children in post-work world, 171–2
   cooking in post-work world, 174–5
   on domestic standards, 49–50
   elder care in post-work world, 172
   gender politics as largely
      unmentioned in, 50
   goal of, 156
   housework in post-work world,
      176–7
   housing in post-work world, 177–9
   ideology of, 2–3
   as needing to take into account
      reproductive labour, 9
   as saying nothing about organisation
      of reproductive labour, 5
   social reproduction in post-work
      world, 167–85
pre-packaged meals, 63
Pret, 176
private rentals, growth in, 151
professional self-presentation, shifts
   around, 57
promiscuous care. *See* communal care
public canteens, 175–6
public luxury, as key principle to guide
   construction of better world, 157,
   161–3

race. *See also* Black families; Black
   women
   and child protective services'
      scrutiny, 74
   domestic ideology as marker of, 91
   impact of on paid work, 257n83
Rawls, John, 158
realm of freedom, 11, 153, 154, 155, 156,
   162, 163, 187
realm of necessity, 155, 156
remote work, rise of, 244n99
reproductive labor. *See also* social
   reproduction

and 'end of work', 4
   as form of autonomously chosen
      activity, 94
   in nineteenth century, 87–9
   perspectives about, 4–5
   and reduction in labour-saving
      potential of early domestic
      technologies, 86
robots, use of, 15, 16
Roombas, 28–9, 46
'rug rat race', 72–3
Russian commune, as architectural
   experiment, 114–19

Salatin, Joel, 66
Sandberg, Sheryl, 10
'sandwich generation', 106
Schor, Juliet, 70
Schütte-Lihotzky, Margarete, 127–9, 130
screen time, for young children (1997 to
   2014), 35
Seccombe, Wally, 104
The Second Shift (Hochschild and
   Machung), 106
self-cleaning house, 182–3
self-serve culture, described, 32–3
separatist communities, as architectural
   experiment, 143–9
service-based economies, shift to, 76
Seymour, Richard, 160
Shakers, communalist ambitions of, 182
shared domestic infrastructure,
   popularity of in early twentieth
   century, 120
shelter against communism, 133–9
shopping
   impact of digital platforms on, 39
   impact of shifts in habits of, 27
side hustles, 77
single-family residence
   alternatives to, 150
   as aspirational norm, 112
   dissenting voices regarding, 119–20
smart home technology, 15, 41–7
social housing, emergence of, 126–7
socialist feminists/feminism, 10, 18,
   126, 130

social reproduction. *See also*
  reproductive labor
  after capitalism/in post-work world,
    167–85
  contemporary challenges of, 103
  digital social reproduction, 35–47
  family as dominant unit of, 108
  government assistance for, 96
  jobs in as percentage of all wage
    labour, 6*f*
  little acknowledgement of spatial
    elements of, 135
  as major source of jobs, 5
  many tasks of as quite difficult to get
    machine to perform, 34
  transformation of during industrial
    revolution in the home, 17–22
  unpaid work of, 8
  work of and 'end of work', 4
  work of as necessary, 155
South Korea, laundering standards in,
  56
space of counter-communism,
  emergence of, 134
spatial design of home, characterization
  of, 112, 113
standards
  around childcare, 66–75
  around cleanliness, personal and
    domestic, 51–7
  around cooking, 60–6
  gendered dynamics around, 51
  guilt about not meeting them, 79
  impact of changes in, 49–51
  limits for individual choices about,
    81
  role of class distinctions in setting
    of, 80
stay-at-home housewife, mythical era
  of, 100
suburban housing
  attractions of, 138
  emergence of, 135
'sustainability work', government as
  imposing of upon households, 33
Sweden
  social reproduction jobs in, 5

subsidised payments for housework,
  177
universal breadwinner model in, 101
Syracuse Washing Machine
  Corporation, 59

tablet computers, as new tool of
  childcare automation, 35
Taiwan, American-supported housing
  aid to, 137, 138
technology
  growing number of devices as being
    used to transfer activities from
    waged to unwaged spheres in
    effort to save costs, 33
  as insufficient to reduce work on its
    own, 27
  medical technologies as having
    brought work back into home,
    32
  new developments in to replace
    servants, 24
  paradox of, 49
  slower pace of change of post-1940s
    (stagnation), 28, 33–5
  as sometimes increasing temporal
    burdens associated with
    healthcare work, 30
  as transferring work from household
    to market, 36
  use of in reducing work of social
    reproduction, 15–48
  washing machines as having brought
    work back into home, 32
temporal sovereignty, as key principle to
  guide construction of better world,
  157, 163–7
Texas, child protection services in, 80–1
Therborn, Göran, 253n1
time, as not free under capitalism, 153
time pressure, feelings of, 107–8
tool libraries, 183–4
transportation work, impact of digital
  platforms on, 39
Tribune Institute Co-operative Club,
  262n35
two-parent households, 102